Marketing
to the New
Majority

Marketing to the New Majority

Strategies for a Diverse World

DAVID BURGOS and
OLA MOBOLADE

palgrave
macmillan

First published in 2011 by
PALGRAVE MACMILLAN®
in the United States—a division of St. Martin's Press LLC,
175 Fifth Avenue, New York, NY 10010.

Where this book is distributed in the UK, Europe and the rest of the
world, this is by Palgrave Macmillan, a division of Macmillan Publishers
Limited, registered in England, company number 785998, of Houndmills,
Basingstoke, Hampshire RG21 6XS.

Palgrave Macmillan is the global academic imprint of the above companies
and has companies and representatives throughout the world.

Palgrave® and Macmillan® are registered trademarks in the United States, the
United Kingdom, Europe and other countries.

ISBN: 978–0–230–11165–3

Library of Congress Cataloging-in-Publication Data

Burgos, David.
    Marketing to the new majority : strategies for a diverse world / David
Burgos and Ola Mobolade.
        p. cm.
    Includes index.
    ISBN 978–0–230–11165–3 (hardback)
        1. Marketing—United States. 2. Multiculturalism—United States.
    3. Minorities—United States. I. Mobolade, Ola. II. Title.

HF5415.1.B847 2011
658.8′02—dc22   2011005271

A catalogue record of the book is available from the British Library.

Design by Newgen Imaging Systems (P) Ltd., Chennai, India.

First edition: August 2011

10 9 8 7 6 5 4 3 2 1

Printed in the United States of America.

Contents

Acknowledgments

First, we want to thank the following people who kindly agreed to an interview for this book and provided valuable insights and ideas on the subject of marketing in multicultural societies:

- Joy Abdullah, Senior Consultant, Daily Baraka
- Bob Barocci, President and Chief Executive Officer, Advertising Research Foundation (ARF)
- Nancy Bates, Senior Researcher, Survey Methodology, US Census Bureau
- Daniel Bloom, Senior Vice President, Consumer Research, Bank of America
- Jeffrey Bowman, OgilvyCULTURE Lead and Marketing Strategy, Ogilvy & Mather
- Peter Francese, Demographic Trends Analyst, Ogilvy & Mather and Founder, *American Demographics Magazine*
- Ron Franklin, ARF Ambassador, GlobalHue and President, NSights Worldwide
- Marcela Garcia, Multicultural Senior Planner, Diageo
- Saul Gitlin, Executive Vice President, Strategic Marketing Services and New Business, Kang & Lee Advertising
- Claude Grunitzky, Founder and Chief Executive Officer, *TRACE Magazine*
- Julia Huang, President and Chief Executive Officer, interTrend Communications
- Bill Imada, Chairman and Chief Executive Officer, IW Group
- Gwen Kelly, Senior Marketing Manager, Walmart
- Felipe Korzenny, Professor, Founder, and Director, Center for Hispanic Marketing Communication, Florida State University

- Martha Kruse, Senior Director, Multicultural Marketing, Rooms to Go
- Byron Lewis, Chairman and Chief Executive Officer, Uni-World Group
- Lisa Mabe, Founder and Principal, Hewar Social Communications
- Luis Miguel Messianu, President and Chief Creative Officer, Alma DDB
- Yvonne Montanino, Senior Manager, Multicultural Consumer and Market Insights, Unilever
- Kathy Mowrey, Senior Manager, Consumer Insights, The Home Depot
- Jessica Pantanini, Chief Operating Officer, Bromley Communications and Board Member, Association of Hispanic Advertising Agencies (AHAA)
- Jacob Perez, Vice President, Strategic Planning Director, Saatchi & Saatchi
- Cynthia Perkins-Roberts, Vice President, Multicultural Marketing and Sales Development, Cable Television Advertising Bureau (CAB)
- Reginald Ponder, Vice President, Senior Account Director, E. Morris Communications Inc. (EMC) and Chief Entertainment Officer, Movie Information Services Company
- Burton Reist, Associate Director, Communications Directorate, US Census Bureau (CAB)
- Rudy Rodriguez, Director, Multicultural Marketing, General Mills
- Loida Rosario, Senior Vice President, Edelman and Director, Partner Relations Multicultural Program, DePaul University
- Mark Rukman, Global Planning Director, Young & Rubicam Brands
- Brad Smallwood, Director, Monetization, Facebook
- Jim Stengel, President and Chief Executive Officer, The Jim Stengel Company and Adjunct Professor, Marketing, UCLA Anderson School of Management (former Global Marketing Officer, Procter & Gamble)
- Christina Vilella, Marketing Director, McDonald's
- Mark Watson, Director, Sklar Wilton + Associates (SW+A)
- McGhee Williams Osse, Co-Chief Executive Officer, Burrell Communications
- Sherman Wright, Founder and Managing Partner, common-ground (CG)

We have talked with and listened to many other practitioners and academics in meetings and conferences across the country. They are far too many to acknowledge by name here, but we thank them nevertheless.

Numerous colleagues have provided us with insights and ideas for the book. In particular, we would like to single out those who helped us understand the status of multicultural marketing in other regions of the world: Valkiria Garre, Millward Brown Brazil; Sabrina Clarke, Paul Gareau, Rahim Premji, and Josh Rosenblum, Millward Brown Canada; Albert Sim, Millward Brown China; Maria de Juana, Reyes Neira, Benoit Tranzer, Juan Ferrer-Vidal, and Tim Wragg, Millward Brown Europe; Masahisa Ogawa, Kantar Japan; Nitesh Lall and Christopher Choong, Millward Brown Malaysia; Isabel Behr and Maribel Pulache, Millward Brown Peru; and Matthew Angus, Charles Foster, Kim Reddy, and Carole Stevenson, Millward Brown South Africa.

Special thanks as well to the team that helped us with the extensive research done for the book: Saba Ahmed, Hortensia Aldana, Sharon Hallock, Brian Harmon, Rill Hodari, Jackie Hughes, Will Jacobus, and Kristen Kowalkowski, Millward Brown; Jesse Caesar, Jackie Raimann, and Brett Zinober, Firefly Millward Brown; Cheryl Pedroza, Kantar Operations; Maria Tazi, Millward Brown Optimor; Lawrence Yeung, 361 Degrees Consulting; and the entire Millward Brown and Kantar teams that handled the field of the quantitative phase. We would also like to thank whY-Q? Inc. for their assistance in recruiting respondents and providing their facility for the qualitative research. Sincere thanks to Lisa Parente, Heather Stern, and Morgan Bullock for their guidance on the book-related marketing initiatives, and to Dede Fitch for helping us proofread the manuscript.

And last, but certainly not least, we would like to thank Nick Findlay and Cheryl Stallworth-Hooper for believing in *Marketing to the New Majority* and providing their unconditional support throughout the process.

CHAPTER 1

Majority Minority

You most likely already knew it, or at least felt it when walking down the street in your neighborhood, but the 2010 census just made it official: The United States is a multicultural nation.

> ## 111,927,986
> The number of racial or ethnic minority persons living in the United States in 2010.[1]

This figure represents 36% of the total population, or roughly 1 in every 3 people, broken down as follows:

- Hispanics or Latinos: 50,477,594, or 16% of the population
- Blacks or African Americans: 37,685,848, or 12% of the population
- Asian Americans: 14,465,124, or 5% of the population
- Other races: 3,332,939, or 1% of the population[2]
- Two or more races: 5,966,481, or 2% of the population

Put another way, there are more Hispanics in the United States than Canadians in Canada, Malaysians in Malaysia, or South Africans in South Africa. If they were a country, Latinos in America would be the second-largest Hispanic nation, right after Mexico and before Spain, Colombia, and Argentina. As a nation,

Blacks or African Americans would be the 35th most populous country in the world, after Poland and before Algeria. More Arabs live in America than in the Gaza Strip in the Middle East.

In addition to the racial and ethnic groups mentioned above, there are close to 8 million White immigrants in the country,[3] many of whom come from Eastern or Southern Europe. While Caucasian in race, these immigrants do have distinct cultural backgrounds that are often overlooked by the business community and society at large. If this group were counted along with the groups previously mentioned, the US ethnic segment would swell to 38% of the total population.

Within the population under 18, the pattern is even more pronounced. Racial and ethnic minorities comprise more than 50% of this group when foreign-born Whites are included (see figure 1.1). Hispanics and Blacks represent 23% and 14% of this population respectively; Asians stay at 4% and this proportion of multiracial children jumps to 4%.

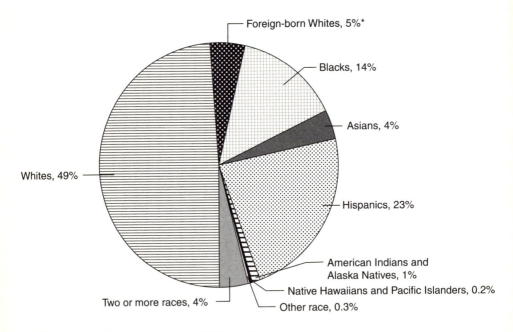

Figure 1.1   Population under 18 Years Old

Source: US Census Bureau, 2010

* Foreign-born Whites based on 2009 estimates

While the influence of ethnic segments is still strongest in the traditionally multicultural markets of the West, South, and East, it's no longer limited to the largest metropolitan areas. Ethnic consumers are gradually expanding to the Central and Northern regions of the country and to smaller urban centers, as the statistics cited below demonstrate.

Key areas in the United States that are already "majority-minority" include:[4]

- The two largest US states: California (60%) and Texas (55%), plus Hawaii (77%) and New Mexico (60%)
- The two largest metropolitan areas: New York–Northern New Jersey–Long Island (51%) and Los Angeles–Long Beach–Santa Ana (68%), plus Houston–Sugar Land–Baytown (60%), Miami–Fort Lauderdale–Pompano Beach (65%), San Francisco–Oakland–Fremont (58%), Las Vegas–Paradise (52%), Memphis (54%), Washington DC–Arlington–Alexandria (51%), San Diego–Carlsbad–San Marcos (52%), and several smaller urban centers
- 28 of the 50 most populous US counties, including the largest three: Los Angeles County in California (total population of 9.8 million, 72% ethnic), Cook County in Illinois (total population of 5.2 million, 56% ethnic), and Harris County in Texas (total population of 4.1 million, 67% ethnic)

Those areas on the verge of becoming majority-minority, with ethnic populations in excess of 40%, include:

- States: Nevada (46%), Maryland (45%), Georgia (44%), Arizona (42%), Mississippi (42%), Florida (42%), New York (42%), New Jersey (41%), and Louisiana (40%)
- Metropolitan areas: Dallas–Fort Worth–Arlington (50%), Atlanta–Sandy Springs–Marietta (49%), New Orleans–Metairie–Kenner (46%), Austin–Round Rock–San Marcos (45%), Chicago–Naperville–Joliet (45%), Orlando–Kissimmee–Sanford (47%), Durham–Chapel Hill (45%), Phoenix–Mesa–Glendale (41%), and Sacramento–Arden–Arcade–Roseville (44%), and several smaller urban centers

- Counties: 7 more of the top 50 US counties: Travis and Tarrant Counties in Texas, Mecklenburg County in North Carolina, Hillsborough County in Florida, Milwaukee County in Wisconsin, Fairfax County in Virginia, and Pima County in Arizona.

Among the areas where ethnic segments grew by 50% or more between 2000 and 2010 are:

- States: Nevada (78%), New Hampshire (68%), Maine (66%), Utah (65%), Idaho (63%), Iowa (60%), Minnesota (54%) and Vermont (52%)
- Metropolitan areas: Sioux Falls, South Dakota (110%); Pocatello, Indiana (76%); Fargo, North Dakota (84%); Saint Joseph, Missouri (94%); Orlando–Kissimmee, Florida (74%); Madison, Wisconsin (72%); Providence–New Bedford–Fall River, Rhode Island–Massachusetts (66%); Columbia, South Carolina (61%); and Duluth–Superior, Minnesota–Wisconsin (69%); and other urban centers
- Counties: 915 counties (almost 30% of all the counties in America), including Martin County, Kentucky with the largest growth (746%); followed by Forest County, Pennsylvania (722%) and Gilmer County, West Virginia (677%)

Even for a country that has long thrived on immigration and prided itself on diversity, these numbers are surprising. And the ethnic mingling of the United States will surely continue, as demonstrated by these snapshot facts:

- Eighty-three percent of people in the United States report at least one foreign ancestry. The top five are German (51 million), Irish (37 million), English (28 million), Italian (18 million), and Polish (10 million).
- Ethnic segments make up 40% of the population in urban America and 18% in rural America. Racial or ethnic minority populations are present in every US county.
- Two Hispanic surnames, Garcia and Rodriguez, are among the top ten surnames in the United States.

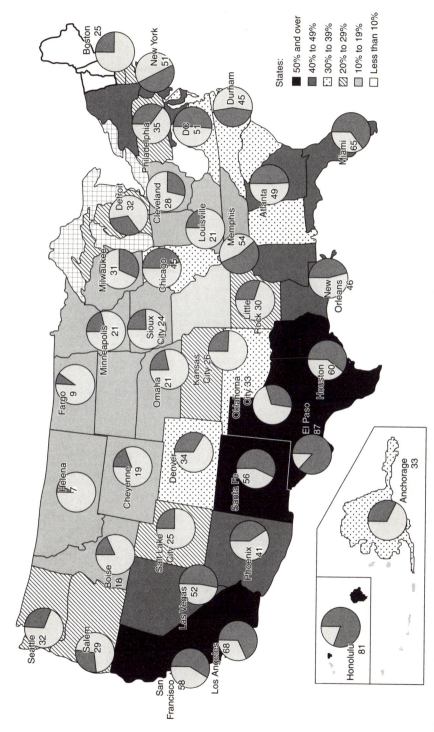

Figure 1.2 Size of Ethnic Segments in Cities across the United States

Source: US Census Bureau, 2010

- Eighty-three of the 435 members of the United States House of Representatives are minorities (44 African Americans, 30 Hispanics, and 9 Asian Americans). Keith Ellison from Minnesota is the first Muslim American elected to the House.
- The multiracial population grew 19% between 2000 and 2010 and is expected to grow by 194% between 2010 and 2050.
- Every hour, 114 Hispanic babies are born in the United States. During the same hour, 253 non-Hispanic White babies, 70 Black babies, and 29 Asian babies are also born.
- By 2025, more than half of the families with children in the United States are expected to be multicultural.
- By 2042, the United States is expected to become a majority-minority country. By 2050, ethnic segments (defined by the census as everyone except non-Hispanic, single-race Whites), will make up 54 percent of the US population.
- Minorities owned 21% of all non-farm businesses in 2007, a 46% increase from 2002.

The population and macro-economic figures and trends discussed before are indisputable. The United States *is* already a multicultural nation, and its future growth will primarily come from ethnic segments, especially Hispanics or Latinos. The business implications of this "new normal" are enormous. To stay relevant to consumers now and in the future, brands need to rethink the way they do business in America. Catering to minority segments is no longer just a matter of developing nice niche markets. Ethnic consumers have become an integral part of the so-called general market or mainstream, and are truly reshaping it. Brands must make ethnic segments an integral part of their overall business strategies if they want to remain viable and grow.

HOW DID WE GET HERE?

The United States has always been a nation of immigrants. The growth of ethnic segments did not happen overnight, and it's certainly not slowing down. While marketers usually focus on the most recent immigrant segments—Hispanics, Asians, Middle-Eastern Muslims or Blacks coming from Africa or the Caribbean—let's not forget the many others that came before them. According to the US Census Bureau's historic records, there were close to 12 million European immigrants living in the country in the years before America's entry into World War II. They represented more than 80% of the country's foreign-born population at that time (see figure 1.3).

Today, of the approximately 83% of the population that reports at least one foreign ancestry, the vast majority cite a European origin. The top three European ancestries reported are German (51 million), Irish (37 million), and English (28 million). Migration from these countries took place mainly during the last decades of the nineteenth century. The fourth- and fifth-largest European ancestries are Italian (18 million) and Polish (10 million); the largest immigrant waves from these countries occurred during the first half of the twentieth century.

These are substantial figures. However, businesses in the United States tend to be indifferent toward the potential these segments represent. They feel that because European immigrants

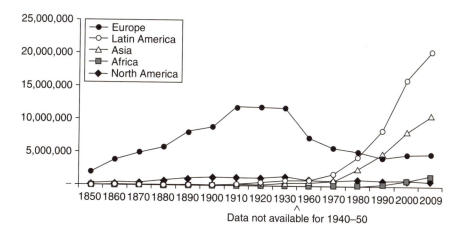

Figure 1.3   Foreign-Born Population in the United States, by Region of Origin
Source: US Census Bureau, 2009

and their descendents are White or Caucasian, their experience is the same as the general population. Although this assumption probably holds true for the generations born in the United States, it does not always apply to the foreign-born groups or their children.

During the Italian immigration boom, companies seemed to understand this well. They developed many initiatives targeted to this segment, especially on the media front. As Jeff Topping wrote in *The Italian Tribune*:

> By the 1920s, several major cities had Italian-language newspapers: Philadelphia, *Il Popolo Italiano* and *L'Opinione*; Boston, *La Gazzetta del Massachusetts*; and San Francisco, *Il Corriere del Popolo*. However, the best known by far was New York's *Il Progresso Italo-Americano*, then America's largest circulated Italian-language daily...Italians anywhere who read [*Il Progresso*] were greatly influenced by national issues as well cultural and social issues of concern to millions of Italians who had made America their new home.[6]

Rarely do we see any European immigrant group catered to in this way today. That's because more recently, as figure 1.3 shows, the most dramatic growth in immigration has come from Latin America and Asian countries. In the past four decades, the number of foreign-born persons from those regions has increased 368% and 320%, respectively! While the size of this population alone is a clarion call to action for businesses, the speed at which the ethnic makeup of America is changing heightens the urgency of their response. In the twentieth century, it took more than one generation of business leaders to witness and fully assimilate the cultural shifts that occurred as a result of European immigration. But thanks to the rapid pace of change today, businesspeople who began their careers as late as the 1990s have already witnessed the transformation of the Hispanic market from a small national minority to an actual majority in many parts of the nation. Business professionals who started their careers in the 2000s will likely experience a similar phenomenon with the Asian segment.

SOURCES OF ETHNIC GROWTH

Immigrants are not the sole source of ethnic growth in the United States. The American-born minority population plays a huge part as well. In fact, the consensus among demographers is that most of the ethnic growth in the coming years will come from the children and grandchildren of immigrants. We analyze this in the following section, but first, let's look at the impact that the Great Recession of the late 2000s had on immigration rates.

Immigration in Times of Recession

In the late 2000s, multicultural marketing pundits responsible for the ethnic business in their companies became unsettled by reports of a slowdown in Hispanic immigration as a result of the economic downturn. Their concern was exacerbated when the debate over illegal immigration took center stage in the political sphere. Many feared that Hispanics would start leaving the country in the wake of the controversy. As researchers, we felt the concern firsthand when marketers started asking us whether we would continue interviewing Latino consumers face-to-face in the malls of Phoenix, the city that was at the epicenter of the illegal immigration controversy. "Can you still find Hispanics there?" they asked.

As it turns out, there is no shortage of Hispanics in the malls of Phoenix. But the economic downturn that began in late 2007 did have a real impact on immigration, especially within the undocumented segment, whose members are likely to be more mobile than their legal counterparts. Figure 1.4 shows estimates of the number of undocumented Hispanic immigrants who entered the country between 2000 and 2009. There is a clear turning point in the years 2007 and 2008, when the worst of the recession hit. Hispanic unauthorized immigration has continued to decline since then.

Although there are many macro- and microeconomic factors at work, the trend shown in figure 1.4 is fairly straightforward: People go where opportunities are. Opportunities during the recession years were scarce in the United States, even for the local population. Logically, undocumented immigrants also felt the impact of the downturn, and since the situation was not as dire in some Latin American countries, many may have decided to stay put, or go back—at least for now.

Given that the Great Recession has differed qualitatively from other economic downturns that the United States has witnessed, it is hard to predict what will happen with immigration in the future. Some are saying that things have changed forever, while others predict that immigration levels will bounce back once the waters are calmed. We're not economists, but based on our knowledge of Hispanic consumers, we believe they will return.

Additional data from the Pew Hispanic Center supports our position. Figure 1.5 tracks the flow of immigrants from Mexico to the United States versus the US employment rate. As you can see, both lines track very closely to each other, demonstrating that

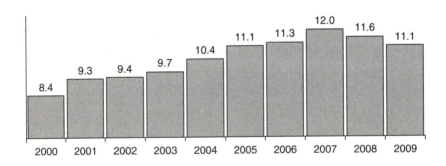

Figure 1.4 Estimates of the Unauthorized Hispanic Immigrant Population (in Millions)

Source: Pew Hispanic Center, September 2010.

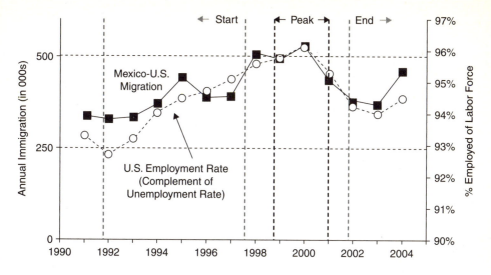

Figure 1.5 Mexican Migration to the United States and US Employment Rate, 1991–2004

Source: Pew Hispanic Center, September 2005

immigration goes up when employment in the United States is up and declines when employment is in short supply. Obviously, this trend may be affected by conditions in Latin America in the coming years. Countries like Brazil, Mexico, Chile, and Peru have been doing particularly well lately. This might discourage people from emigrating, at least in the near future.

The Bicultural Revolution

Sixty-three percent of the US Hispanic population and 33% of Asian Americans were born in the United States. That is more than 30 million and 5 million people, respectively. Not surprisingly, the vast majority of African Americans were born in the United States as well: 92%. These figures clearly indicate that most of the growth that the ethnic segments will experience in the coming years will indeed come from their US-born members.

Figure 1.6. shows the US-versus-foreign-born ratio among Latinos and Asians, grouped by those under 18 years and those 18 years and over. As expected, the vast majority of kids are

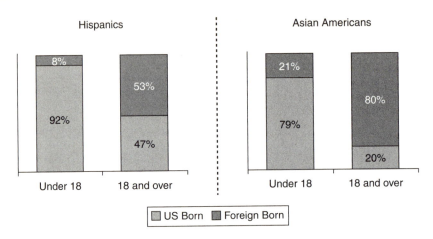

Figure 1.6   United States vs. Foreign-Born Hispanic Population by Age
Source: US Census Bureau, 2009

American-born in both cases. The numbers confirm that these young people will lead the growth of the ethnic population in the decades to come—they are the consumers of the future.

As we will discuss in more detail in a later chapter, ethnic young people who were born in the United States are more likely to be bicultural, or even multicultural, in terms of taste and life-style. They grow up surrounded by the American culture, but are still very much influenced by their parents' heritage and that of the many other races or ethnicities they interact with on a daily basis. The children of nineteenth- and twentieth-century European immigrants tended to let their immigrant identities fade over time; the young people in today's ethnic segments are less likely to do that. Two factors contribute to this dynamic: (1) the actual size of the ethnic segments, which are no longer tiny minorities; and (2) the fact that the general population itself has become more receptive to the idea of multiculturalism. Instead of ethnic segments assimilating into American culture as they historically have, they are reshaping it. Because of multicultur-alism, both ethnic segments and the general population are changing; that is one of our primary reasons for writing this book.

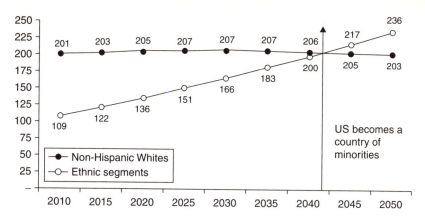

Figure 1.7 United States Population Growth Projections, 2010–2050 (in Millions)
Source: US Census Bureau, based on 2000 Census figures

WHAT THE FUTURE HOLDS

Now that we know how we got here, let's take a look at where we are going as a nation. The demographic shift underway in the United States is unstoppable. The country will become a nation of minorities at some point during the first half of the 2040s, as seen in figure 1.7.

At this time, non-Hispanic Whites will take the place Hispanics currently hold as the largest minority of the country. By the year 2050, it is expected that there will be 203 million non-Hispanic Whites, 133 million Hispanics, 52 million Blacks or African Americans, and roughly 33 million Asians (see figure 1.8). Chinese and Indian segments will remain the majority within this group.

A group that will likely have a strong say in the future of the country is the multiracial segment—the group that the US Census Bureau describes as people of two or more races. According to the 2010 census, there are close to 6 million persons in this category, and the group is expected to grow by 194% between now and 2050, to roughly 11 million. The most common racial combinations are White with Black or African American, White with Asian, and White with American Indian or Alaska Native. These groups represent 27%, 25%, and 20% of the multiracial population respectively.

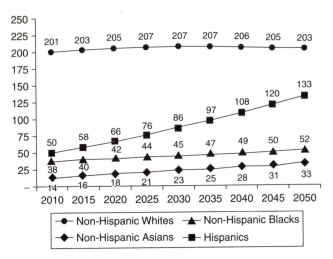

Figure 1.8 United States Population Growth Projections by Ethnic Segments, 2010–2050 (in Millions)

Source: US Census Bureau, based on 2000 Census figures

It is noteworthy that these figures are based on race-specific combinations only. They do not account for the mixture that also happens between people of the same race, but different ethnicities, such as White Hispanics and non-Hispanic Whites, or Asian Hispanics and non-Hispanic Asians. Unfortunately, the census does not keep track of these numbers.

The multiracial segment poses a new and different set of challenges and opportunities to businesses. How do you approach a teenage boy who has a Chinese American father and a Black Jamaican immigrant mother? What takes priority—his Asian ancestry, his Caribbean roots, or the fact that he is half Black? How do you classify the household in which he lives? Is there a hierarchy in prioritizing the different cultural backgrounds, or does the combination create a new and different sort of culture?

Racial and ethnic dynamics can be quite complex within multiracial people and households, and we have a long way to go until we really understand them. As we saw before that, according to projections of the Nielsen Company, more than half of the families with children in the country will be multicultural by

2025; so there is indeed a sense of urgency in learning more about this segment.

THE MULTICULTURAL ECONOMY... AND WHAT IT MEANS TO YOU

Businesses are all about numbers. Before venturing to a new endeavor, businesspeople want to clearly understand what the return on their investment will be. While the population figures discussed so far should be sufficient indicators of the potential represented by ethnic segments, both on their own and as an integral part of the new mainstream, it is worth looking at the macroeconomic data associated with them as well.

According to projections from the Selig Center for Economic Growth, the United States' total buying power—defined as "the total personal income of residents that is available, after taxes, for spending on virtually anything that they buy, but it does not include dollars that are borrowed or that were saved in previous years"[5]—was $11.1 trillion in 2010, up 52% from 2000. As they are still the majority and one of the wealthiest segments in the country, Whites control 85% of that buying power, at $9.4 trillion—up 49% from 2000.

However, the contribution of ethnic segments is growing at a much faster pace, as indicated in figure 1.9. In 2010, the buying power of the three largest racial or ethnic minorities was:

- Hispanics: $1.0 trillion, up 106% from 2000
- Blacks: $957 billion, up 60% from 2000
- Asians: $544 billion, up 98% from 2000

To put these numbers in context, let's consider how the buying power of these US minorities ranks in comparison with the economies of some entire countries. If they constituted their own nation, US Hispanics would have the fifteenth-largest economy in the world, right after Canada and before Indonesia, which had GDPs of $1.3 and $1.0 trillion respectively in 2010, according to the CIA's World Factbook. Within the context of Spanish-speaking

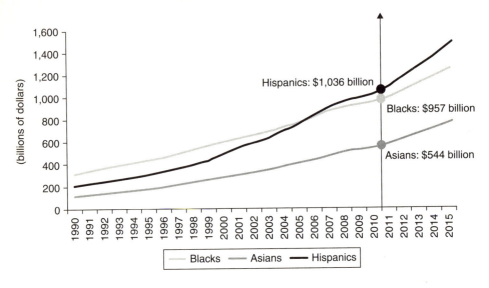

Figure 1.9 Buying Power by Race or Ethnicity

Source: The Multicultural Economy 2010, by Jeffrey Humphreys

Selig Center for Economic Growth, Terry College of Business, University of Georgia

countries, US Hispanics represent the third-largest economy, after Mexico ($1.6 trillion) and Spain ($1.4 trillion), and are almost twice the size of Argentina's economy, which had a GDP of $596 billion in 2010. Demographics are without a doubt a driving force of Hispanics' growing buying power, but an increase in entrepreneurial activity and a rising level of educational attainment are important contributing factors as well.

In a similar analysis, if African Americans were a nation, they would be the 17th largest economy in the world, between Turkey ($958 billion) and Australia ($890 billion). It is worth mentioning that, according to the Selig Center, the increased buying power observed among African Americans is not just the result of population growth either. The increasing number of Blacks who are starting and expanding their own businesses has been a major contributor as well. The US Census Bureau's 2007 Survey of Business Owners showed that the number of black-owned firms increased by 61 percent from 2002 to 2007.[7]

Finally, with a comparatively smaller population of 15 million, Asian Americans' total buying power is larger than the entire GDP of countries like Egypt (population: 82 million), South Africa (population: 49 million), or Colombia (population: 45 million). In fact, Asians in America have the highest average income among all racial or ethnic groups, including non-Hispanic Whites. According to the Selig Center, "Despite the severity of the 2007–09 recession, employment gains can still be cited as one of the forces supporting the growth of Asian buying power. From January 2000 through July 2010, the number of jobs held by Asians increased by 1,013,000. That cumulative gain is impressive when compared to the minuscule 298,000 jobs realized by whites and the job losses suffered by African Americans."[8] Asians' higher levels of education play a key role on this.

Earlier, we highlighted the importance of the growing multiracial segment. Well, they are also attractive from an economic perspective. Their buying power in 2010 was $116 billion, a 94% increase since 2000. The Selig Center predicts that their buying power will continue to grow, and will reach $165 billion by 2015.

	Hispanics	Blacks	Asians
Where they spend more	Groceries Phone services Apparel Footwear	Phone services Utilities Children's clothing Footwear	Food Housing Clothing Education Personal insurance
Where they spend less	Alcohol and tobacco Healthcare Entertainment Education Personal insurance	Restaurants Alcohol Healthcare Entertainment Pensions	Utilities Vehicles Alcohol and tobacco Healthcare Entertainment

Figure 1.10   The Multicultural Economy

Source: Jeffrey Humphreys, *The Multicultural Economy 2010*

Selig Center for Economic Growth, Terry College of Business, University of Georgia

Figure 1.10 lists the product and service categories where Hispanic, Black, and Asian consumers spend more and less money, all according to the Selig Center's projections. Despite the lower income when compared to the general population, Latinos spend more on groceries, telephone services, apparel, and footwear. They also spend a higher proportion of their money on dining out, housing, utilities, and transportation. Compared to non-Hispanics, they spend less on healthcare, entertainment, education, cash contributions, personal insurance, and pensions.

African Americans, on the other hand, spend more on telephone services, utilities, children's clothing, and footwear. They also spend a significantly higher proportion of their money on housing. Compared to non-Blacks, Black consumers spend less on eating out, alcoholic beverages, healthcare, entertainment, education, and pensions. Thanks to their higher median income levels, Asian households spend more than the average US household on homes, transportation, education, pets, toys, pensions, and Social Security. They also spend more on food (groceries and dining out) and clothing. They spend less on alcoholic beverages, utilities, household operations, healthcare, vehicle purchases, personal care products and services, housekeeping supplies, and entertainment.

These figures represent serious business for most industries in America. Experts estimate that a large part of the growth that businesses in several product and service categories will experience will in fact come from ethnic segments, especially from the Latino market. According to projections presented by the Nielsen Company at the ARF's 2010 Annual Convention in New York, for example, 49% of the growth within the children's cologne category between 2010 and 2020 will come from Hispanic consumers, while 25% will be generated by the Asian segment.[9] The contribution of Hispanics and Asians to the growth of the refrigerated juice and drinks category will be 40% and 11%, respectively. The African American share of growth in the feminine hygiene and fresheners and deodorizers categories will be 15% and 14%, all within the same 2010–2020 period. Smart businesses in these and other categories that will witness the same type of growth are already tapping into these segments with different approaches. Those that are not must hurry if they want to stay viable in the future.

MARKETING TO THE NEW MAJORITY

We have dedicated this first chapter of the book to talking about what multicultural means today in America, both in terms of the size and presence of ethnic populations across the country as well as the purchasing power of these groups and what it represents for the American economy—and for your brand. Most of our attention during this analysis has been focused on the ethnic segments themselves. However, to succeed in the New Majority, we must not forget about one of its most important players: the non-Hispanic White consumer.

Non-Hispanic Whites have been, and will continue to be for many years, the largest ethnic segment in America. Ignoring them, or treating them as a monolith, is a grave and common mistake. As we'll discuss later, they have become an active part of the New Majority. On a daily basis, they influence and are influenced by ethnic segments. You can't fully understand the ethnic segments without the backdrop of the non-Hispanic White group, nor can you grasp the so-called general market of today if you don't understand the ethnic segments.

Most people in the industry downplay the role of non-Hispanic Whites when it comes to multicultural marketing. It is true that since they are still the majority, race is less relevant to them. But as the non-Hispanic White group continues to shrink in proportion to the total population, its members are likely to become more race- or culture-conscious.

"The very definition of being an American is going through a profound change," says Tim Wise, author of the book *White Like Me*, in an article published on CNN.com.[10] "We can no longer take it for granted that we (whites) are the dictionary definition of an American." We have already seen some evidence of this White consciousness in politics, especially on the right and among older people who grew up in a "Whiter" America.

It is hard to measure quantitatively how "multicultural" non-Hispanic Whites are. But to be honest, this is hard to measure in any segment. The designation involves many variables, both objective and subjective. However, for the purposes of this book, we present a lifestyles segmentation we just conducted among non-Hispanic Whites and the two major ethnic segments, which is illuminating in many respects.

We present the full cross-cultural segmentation in chapter 2, but for now let's focus on the non-Hispanic White segment. We divided it into six lifestyles. Since some of the variables that we used in the analysis were subtly culture- or race-related, we tried to identify which of the six segments were more multiculturally inclined than the average—more open to interethnic relations, high scoring in the search of equality for all, and so on. We also included some attitudinal questions around ethnic advertising.

Figure 1.11 shows the results of our analysis. Of the six non-Hispanic White segments we defined, three were more multiculturally inclined than the average. Combined, these segments

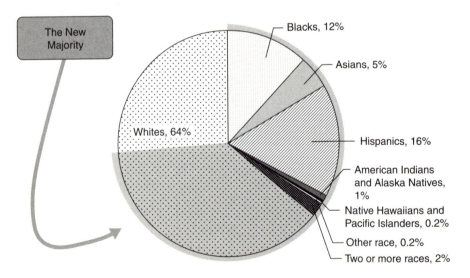

Figure 1.11   The New Majority Is Multicultural
Source: US Census Bureau, 2010 and Millward Brown

represented 55% of the non-Hispanic White majority. The transparent gray section of the pie in figure 1.11 represents what we call the New Majority, composed of the ethnic segments as well as this more-multicultural-than-average, non-Hispanic White group.

This book will help you identify and target this New Majority. First, we look at its diversity in chapter 2, and at how ethnic segments are influencing each other and the so-called general population in chapter 3. In chapter 4 we take a quick trip through the history of ethnic marketing, to then talk about what companies are doing today in the multicultural space in chapter 5. In chapter 6 and 7 we share with you several best practices when marketing to the New Majority, focusing on three main areas of marketing: product development, communications, and media. In chapter 8 we take a closer look at the role of the non-Hispanic White segment. Finally, because we know that the multicultural experience is not exclusive to the United States, in chapter 9, we explore the ways in which companies in other regions of the world are coping with their own multicultural realities.

CHAPTER 2

Diversity within Diversity

"What's the Hispanic, African American, or Asian American insight?" This simple question, posed to and by multicultural marketers attempting to uncover actionable consumer learnings, inadvertently reveals a more problematic subtext. It assumes that each ethnic segment is a monolithic group, with more or less similar characteristics, beliefs, and experiences. Once the so-called ethnic insight is established, marketers develop a strategy and campaign with the goal of striking a resonant chord across the entire segment. And often, when the communication is not broadly effective within the target ethnic bloc, the execution is blamed. In fact, there may be a far more fundamental flaw in this premise: Multicultural marketers view ethnic diversity strictly as a function of ethnic groups being distinct from each other and from the non-Hispanic White mainstream. Rarely do they take into account the diversity *within* these segments.

Of course, marketing must generalize target audiences to some degree in order to present a focused brand message. For example, not all seniors are alike, but it's perfectly viable for a brand like AARP to gear its advertising to this generational segment, because the trait that these consumers share—their stage in life—is immediately relevant to the brand's offering. But this same thinking doesn't quite work with ethnic audiences, because the common trait shared by Hispanics, Blacks, and Asian Americans—their respective ethnicities—represents an incredibly varied set of experiences, which often don't apply directly to the product offering. Failing to acknowledge the nonuniformity of ethnic audiences results in the following negative consequences:

Ethnic Stereotypes Are Reinforced
Relying on a single trait or set of traits to characterize an ethnic group leads to one-dimensional depictions of these groups, which reinforce and perpetuate stereotypes.

Undifferentiated Advertising Is Produced
Relying on the same few ethnic themes (e.g., music and dancing for African Americans, family and celebration for Hispanics, education and discipline for Asian Americans) leads multiple brands to use similar imagery and limits the opportunity to produce unique and memorable ads.

Opportunities to Connect with Ethnic Consumers Are Missed
Although many ethnic consumers have grown accustomed to being portrayed in clichéd scenarios and don't necessarily penalize the brands that use these scenarios, brands that acknowledge the variation in a given ethnic group are given extra attention, which may lead to increased purchase consideration.

The good news about resolving this industry-wide problem is that there is an established precedent for addressing the diversity of an ethnic group in marketing. Marketers have done this effectively with non-Hispanic White consumers throughout history. There are no campaigns that rely on a broad-stroke depiction of White consumer behavior; instead, marketers have always targeted various subsegments of this group to convey a focused and relevant message. Why, then, has this same approach not been applied to ethnic minority groups? To answer that question, we look to social psychology.

In broad terms, social psychology is the study of intergroup relations. One of the most basic tenets of social interaction is an individual's sense of belonging to some groups, referred to as "in-groups," and not belonging to others, known as "out-groups." The "out-group homogeneity" theory states that people tend to view members of an out-group as largely similar to one another, while they view members of their in-group as much more diverse and varied. This pattern is fairly universal and, interestingly, doesn't seem to be affected by how familiar the individual is with people in the out-group. Applied to race relations, this means that there is a natural tendency for people outside of a given ethnic group to perceive the members of that group as more homogenous and less unique than they actually are. Add the impact of advertising and other media that reinforce these ideas, and it's not surprising that mainstream marketers often default to flat, repetitive depictions of consumers in ethnic groups different from their own. Using ethnic agencies helps bridge the gap, leading to more nuanced and diverse portrayals of ethnic consumers.

FACTORS DRIVING DIVERSITY WITHIN ETHNIC SEGMENTS

While the portrayal of non-Hispanic Whites' diversity is a useful precedent for an improved ethnic marketing model, there are several unique factors driving diversity within ethnic segments. It is rare that a brand's offering appeals to traits shared by an entire ethnicity (unless these traits are physiological, as in hair or skin characteristics, or propensity to a medical condition). Therefore, marketers who target Hispanics, African Americans, or Asian Americans should determine the impact of the following factors when developing their consumer profile:

Drivers of Diversity within Ethnic Segments: Generational Differences

Some aspects of generational diversity transcend race. Consumer categories like Millennials, Young Adults, Baby Boomers, and Seniors are applicable regardless of ethnicity. However, there's another crucial level to generational segmentation where ethnic consumers are concerned. Take African Americans, for example. Studies have shown considerable differences in attitudes toward race and society at large depending on whether African American consumers were alive during the civil rights movement or born after it. Pre–civil rights era Blacks tend to be more race-oriented in their interpretation of world and national events. This distinction was apparent during the 2008 US presidential elections. While for pre–civil rights era Blacks, Barack Obama's victory represented a watershed moment in African American achievement and a landmark in the quest for racial equality, many post–civil rights era Blacks interpreted it as a victory of the ideals and hopes that Obama's campaign stood for and viewed race as secondary. One can imagine that the generation of African American consumers born during and after the first Black presidency will have an even more matter-of-fact relationship with this historic moment. As for media depictions, pre–civil rights era Blacks often have a greater affinity toward ads and TV programming with an all-Black cast, whereas post–civil rights era Blacks may reject this imagery as segregated and unrealistic.

Other ethnic groups have had similarly pivotal historical occurrences shape their outlooks. For example, the internment of roughly 120,000 Japanese Americans into US government camps during the 1940s and the emigration of hundreds of thousands of Cuban nationals to the United States during the 1950s in the wake of the Cuban Revolution have contributed to significant distinctions within these ethnic groups' values and attitudes. Well-rounded campaigns should take these generational influences into account when targeting ethnic consumers.

Driver of Diversity within Ethnic Segments: Household Composition

The composition of the average American household is evolving before our very eyes. According to the 2010 US census, the response "married with children," long the reigning standard household composition, is now the third-most-likely answer, surpassed by "married with no kids" and "living alone."

There are also cultural nuances to household composition that contribute to the diversity within ethnic groups. It is common for ethnic households, particularly those that are Hispanic and Asian American, to be multigenerational, with grandparents, parents, and children all residing under one roof. So while marketers may be directing their message toward one generation of primary purchasers within the household—generally parents—in ethnic homes, they might want to consider the role that other influencers, especially bicultural youth, play in purchase behavior.

The unique household compositions within ethnic homes also affect the imagery and storylines of targeted advertising. The comedic trope of poking fun at the twentysomething "loser" who still lives with his parents may resonate among mainstream audiences, but is likely to fall flat in multigenerational ethnic households. Likewise, it is not uncommon in African American

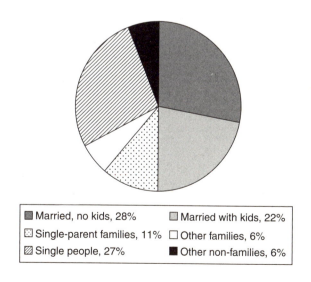

Married, no kids, 28%   Married with kids, 22%
Single-parent families, 11%   Other families, 6%
Single people, 27%   Other non-families, 6%

Figure 2.1   American Households in 2010

Source: Peter Francese projections from 2009 Census Bureau survey data

households for grandparents to be the primary caretakers for young children. To depict Mom as a busy, on-the-go young adult is to fail to recognize the variations in household composition for these audiences. In shaping their ethnic target profile, savvy marketers should identify the various household types represented by the group and take care to reflect a representative experience in their advertising.

Drivers of Diversity within Ethnic Segments: Different Immigrant Experiences

There are as many different immigrant stories as there are immigrants. Why they came, how they came, and where they came from are factors that will shape their lives in this country. We analyze some of these dynamics in this section, but let's take a quick look at the numbers first.

As noted in chapter 1, 13% of the United States population is foreign born. That's more than 38 million people, a figure larger than most countries' total population. Figure 2.2 shows that while 63% of Hispanics are US-born, roughly two-thirds of Asians living in the United States are immigrants. Further, although the Black foreign-born population is the smallest among the three major non-White ethnic groups, the number of Black immigrants has increased in the past decade, from nearly 2 million in 2000 (6% of the total Black

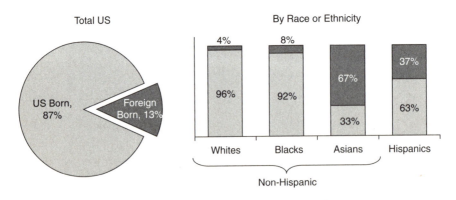

Figure 2.2   Foreign-Born Population in the United States
Source: US Census Bureau, 2009

population) to more than 3 million in 2009 (8% of the total Black population). Most of these immigrants come from the Caribbean or Africa. Finally, there are also close to 8 million non-Hispanic White immigrants in the country. To understand the role of the immigration experience in driving diversity within ethnic segments, let's look at some of the common situations faced by people moving to the United States.

The Why

According to Everett S. Lee's seminal article "A Theory of Migration," published in the journal *Demography* in 1966, the reasons why people migrate can be divided into two groups: push factors and pull factors.[1] Push factors are the problems in the country where you live that make you want to leave. Pull factors are positive things in other countries that attract you, encouraging you to move there. Examples of push factors are: a lack of opportunities or jobs, fear of political persecution, natural disasters, discrimination, and wars. Pull factors can include: better jobs or economic opportunities, better living conditions, political and religious freedom, security, and a more agreeable climate.

While most recent migration to the United States has been driven by pull factors—especially better job and economic opportunities—new arrivals report a range of motivations. Some recent cases involving push factors are the migration of Haitian nationals after the 7.0-magnitude earthquake that struck their country in 2010, or the admittance of refugees from Middle Eastern countries like Iraq or Afghanistan due to the war on terror. The exodus of Cubans following the ascent of dictator Fidel Castro, mentioned earlier, is an older example.

Immigrants' attitudes toward their new lives in the United States can vary significantly depending on whether they came under a push or a pull situation. For instance, while a person who came in search of better opportunities is likely to embrace his or her new life here, people who were forced to leave their home may be inclined to see their situation in the United States as temporary and never really put down roots—at least not emotionally. From a marketing perspective, dynamics like these make a huge difference in how consumers adapt to the local culture and interact with brands.

The How

How immigrants get to the United States also influences how they live their lives here, at least during the first few years. The most obvious differentiation is whether they come to the country legally or not. Obviously, undocumented immigrants face more limitations than people entering the country legally. This situation impacts not only their overall living conditions, but also their behavior as consumers. For instance, illegal immigrants have less access to financial services, healthcare, and other products and services that usually require some form of identification. The resulting insecurity is also likely to prevent them from embarking on large projects like buying a house. Companies are aware of this situation and have found ways to overcome some of the challenges of marketing to a transient population, as we explain in chapter 6.

Another differentiating factor among immigrants is whether they are alone in their adventure or they already have family or friends living in the country. While the process of adapting to the new reality can be long and painful for those in the former situation, it's slightly easier for those in the latter. From basic things like how to pay for fuel in a gas station or how to order a prescription in a pharmacy to more complex transactions like buying insurance or opening a bank account, having the guidance of an experienced resident can make a huge difference, especially if language barriers are a problem.

Knowledge of the English language is certainly another discriminating factor among immigrants in the United States. While it may not be politically correct to point it out, it is a fact that the more fluent immigrants are in the local language, the better positioned they are to succeed. A 2006 research and development project conducted by the global agency Millward Brown found that while the average household income among Hispanic immigrants that spoke English "very well" (top quintile) was $46,400, the average annual income for Latinos that did not speak English well (bottom quintile) was $17,300. Further, the same research found that while 49% of Hispanics in the former group felt that they "fit in the American way of life," only 29% of their peers with limited knowledge of English agreed with the same statement. Although the relationship between English fluency and these variables might not be pure and exclusive, the numbers certainly illustrate the importance of learning the language.

The Where

Where immigrants come from is a strong driver of diversity within ethnic segments as well. According to 2009 census data, immigrants coming from Mexico are likely to have lower income and lower levels of education than immigrants coming from other Latin American countries. Does this mean that people in South America are smarter than people in Mexico? Absolutely not. It's just that the proximity factor makes coming to the United States much easier for Mexicans. Hispanics from South America have to invest more time and money to be able to migrate, legally or otherwise. This works as a natural filter. Those who clear the hurdles of immigration are likely to have had a better education and economic situation in their home country, and therefore a better overall situation once they are in the United States as well. We can draw a similar analogy when comparing immigrants from Latin America overall and people coming from Asian countries like China or India, who have much higher income and levels of education than Latinos and the US general population at large. The "filter factor" is obviously greater for people coming from more-remote regions. Just imagine how different the history of immigration to the United States would be if we shared borders with China or India.

Where immigrants settle is another factor that will shape their lives in the United States. Climate can play a key role in this regard. Most immigrants come from warmer countries located in the tropic zone or in the Southern Hemisphere. Settling down in a cold northern state versus a warmer southern city impacts not only the immigrant's behavior, but also his or her attitudes and feelings, especially during the first few years. Similarly, a place with high ethnic density—such as San Francisco for Asian Americans or Los Angeles for Hispanics—will feel completely different from a place like Missoula, Montana.

Drivers of Diversity within Ethnic Segments: Countries of Origin

Marketers often refer to Hispanic consumers as if they were a homogeneous group, regardless of whether they are of Mexican, Nicaraguan, Chilean, or other descent. Needless to say, this is not how Hispanics think. One focus group participant in a study we conducted captured this sentiment perfectly: "I didn't know that I was Hispanic until I came to the United States. Before that, I was just a guy from Ecuador." It is true that Latinos share many values and have several characteristics that are unique to their culture. But when it comes to their ethnic group, Hispanics identify first and foremost with their respective countries of origin. You don't hear many Latinos proclaiming, "I am from Latin America." Instead, they'll say, "I am Colombian," or "My family is from Guatemala." Why? Because despite the common language and history, there are tangible differences among Latin American peoples, and these differences usually hold true within the US Latino population.

Some marketers argue that these distinctions are irrelevant because, in the end, two-thirds of the Hispanic population in the United States is of Mexican origin. While the number is true— see figure 2.3—several factors challenge this position. Although Hispanics of Mexican origin represent 66% of the Latino population on a national level, proportions vary significantly across the states, from 84% in California to 50% in Ohio to 13% in New York. If you are a marketer doing a national campaign, you had better take these nuances into consideration to increase your chances of success.

Another challenge to the above premise is the fact that Hispanics of different countries of origin, including Mexicans, interact among and influence each other at different levels. These cultural influences are most evident in music, food, holiday celebrations, and enthusiasm for celebrities. Finally, even if in spite of the above arguments, you still wanted to focus on the Mexican segment, you would have to take the diversity of Mexico into account. The north and south of Mexico have several cultural differences, and Mexico City, the capital, has another flavor altogether. While people in the north feel some American influence because of proximity, people from the poorer southern states tend to lead midest, quieter lives. And because Mexico City has so much international influence, immigrants from the capital city are likely to be more cosmopolitan in general.

Non-Mexican Hispanics are more likely to be conscious of the heterogeneity of the group because they are a minority within

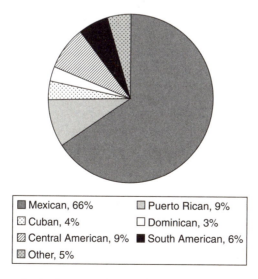

Legend	
■ Mexican, 66%	☐ Puerto Rican, 9%
⊡ Cuban, 4%	☐ Dominican, 3%
▨ Central American, 9%	■ South American, 6%
▩ Other, 5%	

Figure 2.3 Hispanics in the United States by Country of Origin
Source: US Census Bureau, 2009

the Latino segment, and they are especially annoyed when they are lumped in with Mexicans by well-meaning but clueless marketers. A Bud Light commercial captured this concept with a hilarious twist. In the ad, an American guy approaches four good looking Latinas in a bar, and in rudimentary Spanish asks them where they are from. The ladies respond: Buenos Aires, Caracas, Montevideo, and Rio de Janeiro. The man then turns to the bartender and asks him for four Bud Lights for his *"amigas Mexicanos!"* The women look confused for a couple of seconds, but as they are handed their drinks, they immediately launch into a chorus of Mexican colloquialisms: *"Orale!," "Si!," "Buena onda," "Que padre!"* A voice-over ends the spot with a knowing wink: "There are people who would do anything for a Bud Light."

There are many variables you could use to chart the diversity within Latin American countries. Two that we think are especially relevant to the case of US Hispanics are differences in ethnic backgrounds and differences in standard of living, not only among countries, but also within each nation.

There are three major ethnic backgrounds in Latin America: (1) Indigenous or Amerindian, predominant in Mexico, parts of Central America, and in the Andean countries of South America, such as Peru, Ecuador, and Bolivia; (2) European, largest in the southern cone of South America, especially Argentina, parts of Chile, and southern Brazil; and (3) African, especially in Caribbean countries, including Venezuela and other coastal areas of the continent, as well as in Brazil. The region also has traces of other, more specific cultures, such as Japanese and Chinese in Peru (the country even had a native-born president of Japanese descent, Alberto Fujimori, in the 1990s), German in Brazil, or French in parts of Mexico.

In terms of living conditions, while many Latin American countries have seen serious progress in the past couple of decades, there are still many inequalities among nations—and, more importantly, within each country. According to the 2009 United Nations Human Development Report, the average ratio between the richest 20% and the poorest 20% of the populations in Latin American countries is 19 to 1.[2] This means that the richest 20% of the population in Latin American nations is, on average, 19 times richer than the poorest 20% of the population. This ratio is 8 to 1 in the United States, but the cultural and socioeconomic differences the higher ratio engenders are internalized and carried on by Hispanics when they immigrate to the United States.

Among Asian Americans, diversity by country of origin is much more pronounced. In fact, one could argue that there is no such thing as an "Asian American market" in the United States. Rather, there is a Chinese American segment, or an Indian American market, or a Vietnamese community. Cultural differences across these consumer segments can be so sharp that generalizations will almost certainly do more harm than good. When talking about Asian Americans, you are talking about different races, different languages, different religions, different values, and so on; not only between countries of origin, but also among segments within the same nationalities. Figure 2.4 shows the size of the largest Asian segments in the United States. Chinese Americans lead with 23%, followed by Asian Indian and Filipinos at 19% and 18%, respectively.

There are several key demographic differentiators among Asian immigrants that further contribute to the diversity of this

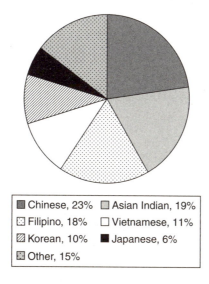

Chinese, 23% Asian Indian, 19%
Filipino, 18% Vietnamese, 11%
Korean, 10% Japanese, 6%
Other, 15%

Figure 2.4 Asians Americans in the United States by Country of Origin
Source: US Census Bureau, 2009

market in the United States. To name a few: According to the US Census Bureau's 2009 American Community Survey (see figure 2.5), Indian immigrants are on average younger than those from China or Vietnam, and they are also more likely to have come to the country after 1990. Indian immigrants are also significantly more likely than their Chinese and Vietnamese counterparts to have achieved higher levels of education and have higher income. While female Vietnamese immigrants are more likely to work in service occupations, Indian and, to a lesser extent, Chinese immigrant women usually hold management or professional positions.

Finally, diversity by country of origin also applies to the country's Black minority—not the American-born segment, but the growing number of Black immigrants coming to the United States. They have two major regions of origin: Africa and the Caribbean. Both places contain a huge range of cultures, socioeconomic strata, and languages.

Drivers of Diversity within Ethnic Segments: Language Differences

Hispanics speak Spanish, right? Not so fast. While yes, Spanish is the language of Latinos, you'll find there are several versions

Profile of immigrant populations from …	India	China	Vietnam
Median age	38	45	43
Average family size	3.41	3.42	3.91
Entered to the US before 1990 (%)	25	39	45
Are US Citizens (%)	45	59	75
Speak English "very well" (%) Base: do not speak English at home	69	34	28
Attained Bachelor's degree or more (%)	75	50	23
Female in labor force (%)	57	59	64
Female employed in management, professional occupations (%)	65	52	27
Female employed in service occupations (%)	8	20	39
Median household income ($)	95,830	64,430	53,431
No health insurance (%)	13	16	21
Own their home (%)	56	62	66

Figure 2.5   Profile of Asian Immigrants
Source: US Census Bureau, 2009

of the Spanish language depending on who you ask. A Heineken commercial aired in Spanish media markets highlighted this well. The ad takes place in a bar. One at a time, four Latino men approach the bartender:

FIRST: *"Hey tigre, dame dos* frías...*y las que estén más full."*

SECOND: *"Compa, dame tres* chelas *bien chidas."*

THIRD: *"Manito, ponme cuatro* bravas *ahí, compadre."*

FOURTH: *"Dame cuatro* birras, *pero de prima, eh."*

What were they asking for? Just beer (*frías, chelas, bravas,* or *birras*). But each requested it in his own Spanish slang. While the bartender gives the beer to his customers, text saying "The language teacher" flashes on-screen.

This diversity in the slang or local flavor within the Spanish language is quite important for marketers. For one thing, it can generate interesting creative concepts, like the one described above. But more important, it's helpful when working on packaging translations or similar initiatives.

In most cases, language nuances are subtle, and Hispanics of different origins can usually understand each other with little problem, especially here in the United States, where they interact with other Latinos. Take the word for "car," for instance. While Hondurans call it *carro,* Uruguayans and Venezuelans call it *coche* and *nave,* respectively—though each would probably get the other's gist from context. The real problem comes when the *same* word has completely different meanings across countries. A controversial example of this is the word *cajeta.* In Mexico, *cajeta* means "dulce de leche," a caramel syrup. Some companies in the food category have used the word *cajeta* in their packaging translations, which is good for consumers of Mexican origin. However, this translation might not work that well among Latinos of Argentinean descent: In that country, *cajeta* is used to refer to the female private parts! In situations like this, the safest option is to stick with the most neutral version, usually the formal one.

Language is much more complex in the case of Asian Americans, as well as within communities of African or Arab descent, as the 2010 census advertising campaign clearly illustrated. According to Nancy Bates, senior researcher for survey methodology for the US Census Bureau, although the census forms were available in only six languages (English, Spanish, Chinese, Korean, Vietnamese, and Russian), the campaign was advertised in 28 languages across the country! "All of those language decisions were based on the hard-to-count population in the country, but then also the existence of media vehicles that were consumed by those populations," Bates told us of the effort to reach out to every ethnic segment.

A final layer of language-based diversity among ethnic consumers is their use of the English language versus their native language.

Language other than English spoken at home

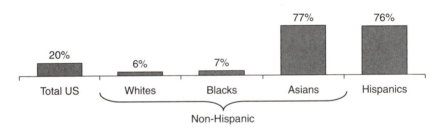

Ability to speak English among those who speak another language at home

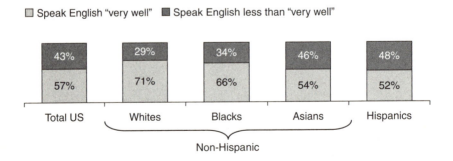

Figure 2.6   Language at Home

Source: US Census Bureau, 2009

Immigrant consumers are usually more likely to speak their mother tongue across the board. And while their American-born descendants go back and forth from English with ease depending on who they are with, they are usually encouraged to learn and speak their parents' language as well, especially Hispanics.

Figure 2.6 shows that, in the majority of Asian and Hispanic homes, a language other than English is spoken. As we saw before (see figure 2.2), only 37% of Hispanics in the United States are foreign born. Yet 76% of Latinos speak Spanish at home. The math confirms that a large part of the American Latino population maintains their parents' native language. We analyze this in more detail in the following section.

Drivers of Diversity within Ethnic Segments: The Process of Acculturation

How immigrants and their descendants adapt to American culture is another key driver of diversity within ethnic segments. For lack of a better word, this process is typically known as *acculturation*.

To be clear, acculturation is not the same as assimilation, another common term in the multicultural marketing lexicon. Acculturation occurs when immigrants integrate their native culture with the culture of their host country. Assimilation, on the other hand, occurs when immigrants adopt the culture of the host country and leave their native culture behind in the process. We believe that true assimilation rarely occurs. Immigrants almost never leave their past completely behind, even if they have adopted most of the cultural cues of their new country. This is true today with Hispanics and Asians, and was true in the past with immigrant populations such as the Italians or the Irish. These European segments are now very much integrated into American society, but talk to anyone with Italian or Irish ancestry, and you'll find some native cultural cues that endure.

Hispanic Acculturation

The notion of acculturation is applicable to virtually any immigrant population. However, in the United States, Latinos provide the most apt case study. Although there is no industry standard on how to measure Hispanic acculturation, companies typically segment the market into three groups: unacculturated, bicultural, and acculturated Latinos (see figure 2.7).

Some companies divide the market into four or five segments, or use fancier names, but in the end, most approaches measure the same thing. Useful variables focus on such factors as where a Hispanic consumer was born and educated (in the United States or abroad), the number of years foreign-born Hispanics have lived here, languages spoken at home and elsewhere, and orientation toward foreign-language media. Some models also include attitudinal variables in order to understand how various aspects of a consumer's life—family, food, interests, etc.—are influenced by each culture (US and Hispanic). Because of these variations in approach, it is hard to find consensus around the size of each of the segments. While some models talk about each group representing roughly one-third of the Hispanic population, others report a larger unacculturated segment. All agree on one thing, though: Bicultural Latinos are the fastest-growing group.

Of course, the process of acculturation is not necessarily a linear one. While most new immigrants would be classified as

Acculturated	Bicultural	Unacculturated
• Typically US born • English-language dominant in most situations • Highest consumption of English media • Strong self-identification with the American culture, while still keeping ties to their Hispanic background • Likely to be older adults • Highest income and level of education overall	• US born, or foreign born but has lived in the country for several years • Bilingual, switches between languages depending on situation • Consumes both English and Spanish media • Identifies with both American and Hispanic cultures • Can be of any age, but skews to younger segments • Middle ground in terms of income and education	• Mainly foreign born • Spanish-language-dominant in most situations • Higher consumption of Spanish media • Strong self-identification with Hispanic culture • Likely to be younger adults • Lowest income and level of education, on average

Figure 2.7   Hispanic Acculturation
Source: Millward Brown, 2011

unacculturated, not all of them will follow the path toward becoming fully acculturated. Given the size and presence of the Hispanic segment across the nation, many Latinos see less of a need to become fully acculturated, even if they've been in the country for many years already. Los Angeles and Miami are two examples of areas saturated with Latino culture. If you are Hispanic and live in one of those cities, you can live your life in a very Latin way. You can speak Spanish almost one hundred percent of the time, you can find almost any Latin-specific food product in any major supermarket, and so on.

In fact, there's an emerging trend that's come to be called "retro-acculturation." Just a few decades ago, when Hispanics were still a tiny and often stereotyped minority, many Latinos felt forced to hide their Latin heritage. Parents took pains to ensure that their children spoke only English, and with no accent. Now that it is "cool" to be Hispanic, many of these acculturated people are gravitating back to their roots, not only by learning and speaking Spanish, but also in their overall customs and traditions.

The business implications of these consumer dynamics are huge. Marketing strategies vary significantly depending on whether you are after the unacculturated consumers or the bicultural segment. However, while segmentation by acculturation can help you make better decisions in many circumstances, it doesn't cover everything. Simply put, do not assume that all unacculturated or Spanish-language consumers are the same.

Drivers of Diversity within Ethnic Segments: Demographic Nuances

Just as in the general population, demographic differences within minority segments can significantly impact the thoughts, feelings, and actions of consumers. As marketers, we must be aware of the diversity driven by these factors.

A few examples:

- While many ethnic segments skew younger, there are, of course, also elderly Hispanic, Black, and Asian people in the

United States. So, if your target segment is the Boomer population, ethnic consumers can represent an attractive group as well. According to the 2009 US census, the proportion of consumers age 55 or older within the Hispanic, Black and Asian segments are 12%, 18%, and 20%, respectively.

- The situation is similar with income. On average, Hispanic and Black consumers have lower income than the general population. However, according to the 2009 US census, roughly 1 in 5 Latinos and African Americans make more than $75,000 per year (compared to approximately 1 in 3 among non-Hispanic Whites). Luxury brands can certainly find a nice niche within ethnic segments, especially among Asians, almost half of whom have incomes over $75,000.
- While the proportion of minority segments is usually larger in metropolitan areas, ethnic consumers are gradually moving to lower-density areas such Omaha, Nebraska; Boise, Idaho; or Louisville, Kentucky. Their experiences in these places is likely to differ markedly from those of their urban counterparts.

DISTINCTIONS AMONG ETHNIC CONSUMER GROUPS

Although there is great diversity within ethnic groups, there are also unifying factors that can be leveraged in marketing and communications campaigns geared to those audiences. The trick is balance. The difference between an ethnic insight—which is by nature a generalization—and an ethnic stereotype can be difficult to discern. At its most basic, the former is distilled through research and observation, ideally among a predetermined subsegment of

	Total US	Non-Hispanic			Hispanics
		Whites	Blacks	Asians	
Median age	37	41	32	36	27
Attained Bachelor's degree or more (%)	28	31	18	50	13
Median annual income ($)	50,221	54,671	33,449	68,930	39,923
Average household size	2.63	2.45	2.66	3.09	3.56

Figure 2.8 Key Demographic Indicators by Race and Ethnicity

Source: US Census Bureau, 2009

an ethnic group. The latter is often based on limited interaction with individuals within that group. In plain terms, stereotypes are more poorly informed and more widely applied. To address defining characteristics of a given ethnic group is to acknowledge their members' shared experiences, shaped by various aspects of their culture (food, values, language, etc.), as well as their history in the United States, which has contributed to their current socioeconomic status. Figure 2.8 illustrates the most prominent differentiating factors from a demographic perspective.

We see that ethnic consumers, and especially Latinos, are much younger than the non-Hispanic White population. While the median age among non-Hispanic Whites is 41, the median age among Hispanics is 27. An understanding of these age differences is helpful in interpreting many of the generalizations you may hear about Latinos.

Take technology. Chances are that you have heard many times that Hispanics over-index in the adoption and use of technology. While Hispanics are more likely to use the Internet and mobile products in spite of their lower average income, this behavior is more a function of age than ethnicity. The Hispanic population is relatively young, and young people adopt digital technology at a much faster rate. We see a similar pattern in the use of social media tools like Facebook, Twitter, or MySpace. However, in this case, the more social nature of Hispanic culture does play an important role. Looking at data broken by age, you would see that older Latinos with Internet access also over-index in the use of these gadgets when compared to their non-Hispanic White counterparts.

Education and income are also important differentiating factors between ethnic consumers and non-Hispanic Whites. On average, both Blacks and Hispanics exhibit lower levels of formal education and lower levels of income. These facts have several implications for marketers. But when analyzing the income variable, especially among Hispanics, it is important to remember that Latinos do not necessarily spend their money the same way that non-Hispanic Whites do.

Let's take home improvement as an example. If you only looked at the income numbers shown in figure 2.8, you might conclude that Latinos are less likely to spend on home improvement projects—that they would have to put their smaller incomes toward more essential categories, like health or transportation. But that is not necessarily true. Homes are very important for Latinos in general. For many of them, the condition of their home is an indicator of how well they are doing in America. So, within limits, they may be willing to spend a larger than "normal" (by non-Hispanic White standards) portion of their income on home-improvement projects.

A similar dynamic occurs in the personal care and beauty industry among both Latinos and African Americans. Personal appearance is hugely important for both segments, and many reports show these groups outspending their non-Hispanic White counterparts when it comes to beauty-related products. Interestingly, this is not just because these populations skew younger than non-Hispanic Whites. The emphasis on personal appearance is deeply rooted in the culture of both Latinos and Blacks, and beauty brands have finally embraced it, to handsome profits.

A final demographic differentiator is household size. On average, ethnic households are larger than their non-Hispanic White counterparts, especially those of Hispanic and Asian origin. Although this has important implications for marketers, and certainly represents unique opportunities for specific industries, trends show that household sizes among all ethnic segments are gradually coming down, just as they are in Latin America and Asia.

In addition to these basic demographic differences, there are several unique cultural nuances that make ethnic segments different from each other and from the general population. These factors are more difficult to measure quantitatively, but in some cases, they're even more important than the demographic data discussed above.

Let's take a look at some of these cultural traits.

Among Hispanics

In our qualitative research, we have found that if there is one aspect of their culture that Hispanics miss or value the most, it is the *flexibility of the Latin way of life*. This is hard to explain because it is all about feelings, a state of mind that applies to almost everything Latinos do. For example, we talked about the importance of houses in the previous paragraphs. In this case, the concept of flexibility would translate into opening the door to any friend or family member who wanted to visit unannounced. Hispanics enjoy those kinds of surprises.

Flexibility is also about time. Carl Kravetz, chairman and CEO of the Latino marketing firm Cruz/Kravetz: Ideas and former chair of the Association of Hispanic Advertising Agencies (AHAA), says that for Latinos, "Time is a goal." A focus-group participant once told us how shocked she was the first time her son was invited to a birthday party in the United States. The invitation read "From 2 P.M. to 4 P.M." "In my country," she said, "we send invitations saying that the party starts at 3 P.M., everybody shows up at 4 P.M., and the party lasts until 8 or 9 P.M.!" Finally, flexibility is also about interpersonal relations— being free with gestures of affection, such as giving hugs or kissing hello. A 2010 Corona beer campaign captured these concepts nicely. One of the commercials showed a Hispanic couple arriving at a barbecue party. When they get to where the other guests are, they keep their distance and merely wave hello. After hearing a voice calling them from behind, the couple turns around to see a large chorus of people standing on a platform. Using a very engaging tone, the group starts singing to the couple, playfully chiding them about their "waving hello," saying things like, "Don't be cold as penguins, we hug even people we don't know!" Hearing that, the couple adopts a more relaxed posture and starts kissing and hugging everybody in the party—the Latin way. The song goes on, linking the brand to the situation by saying that "Corona refreshes who we [Latinos] are."

Family is undeniably another crucial Hispanic value. Yes, family is the most important aspect of life to almost every consumer, regardless of race or ethnicity. But the concept of family seems to have a special meaning for Latinos, not only in terms of what it signifies, but also in terms of what they are willing to do for their families. One differentiating factor between Hispanics and non-Hispanic Whites is the concept of extended family. For Latinos, family is not just the nuclear group; it expands to grandparents, uncles, aunts, cousins, and even people who are not actually related. Interestingly, African Americans and some Asian groups also share this cultural trait, which obviously can be a base for some cross-cultural initiatives.

Another common Hispanic trait is the idea of *helping and providing support* to each other. Unlike non-Hispanic Whites, who are more likely to value self-reliance, Latino families are more open and willing to support their members, both emotionally and materially, even beyond the nuclear group if needed. In a 2010 Millward Brown study, we found that while 42% of Hispanics provided their parents with some sort of financial help or support on a regular basis, only 29% of Blacks and 9% of non-Hispanic Whites did.

Among African Americans

By and large, *religion and spirituality* play a heightened role in the day-to-day life of many African Americans, particularly in comparison to their non-Hispanic White counterparts. While the pervasiveness of this cultural cue may be diminishing with each passing generation, the role of the church in African American life traces its roots back to slavery. Not surprisingly, themes of comfort, escape, and freedom resonated strongly with the first African Americans, given their dire circumstances. Religion provided a means of endurance and a glimmer of hope to an otherwise bleak existence. These ideas were passed on from generation to generation, and have carried Blacks through various hardships across the centuries. And while this segment, like most of American society, is more secular now than at any other point in American history, spirituality still finds its way into mainstream behavior. Watch any awards show featuring Black stars, whether they are churchgoers or not, and you are bound to hear acceptance speeches that thank God first. There is a degree of permissibility and latitude built into African American worship that may seem strange and contradictory to outsiders. But religiosity and worldliness are often simultaneously expressed in African American life. Brands frequently use churches as a way to approach their African American target consumers, either using word-of-mouth strategies or direct marketing, and religious themes have been incorporated in advertising targeted to this segment as well.

While *music and dance* are among the most universal forms of expression across all ethnic groups, they play a unique role in African American culture. Dating back, once again, to the dark beginnings of Black life in America, music and dance provided a linkage to the national and tribal affiliations that had been cut off through the slave trade. Music provided solace and a means of veiled communication among slaves in America, and later became a cathartic form of emotional release and expression within Black churches. Countless contemporary Black musical artists point to the music of the church as having influenced their style and passion for singing or playing instruments. Throughout the first half of the twentieth century, the ability to entertain through music and dance was, sadly, one of the only means of societal advancement for many African Americans. So while an appreciation of music is universal, the history of song and dance for African Americans holds a special cultural significance. Unfortunately, due to this insight, music and dance are among the most overused themes in communications geared toward this group. Marketers should avoid relying upon music as a cultural passion point, and use it instead as part of the context for a more profound insight.

Among Asian Americans

It is hard to talk about Asian cultural traits because, as we discussed before, there is no actual "Asian" market in the United States. So let's focus on the two largest segments, Chinese and Indian Americans.

Embedded in Chinese American culture is a fascination with *luck, chance, and fate*, which comes from a combination of philosophical and religious origins. Symbols of and references to these concepts are pervasive. Several casinos have tapped into this cultural predilection for themes and symbols of good fortune by targeting Chinese American consumers in their marketing communications.

Indian Americans place great emphasis on *education* in their culture. According to the 2000 US census, 64% of Indian Americans have attained a bachelor's degree or higher, compared to the 28% national average, and 44% for all Asian Americans. The number of medical degrees is also considerably higher among Indian Americans than the national average.

IMPLICATIONS FOR MARKETERS

On its face, such demographic distinctions may seem like a marketer's catch-22. On one hand, gearing a message to a broadly painted picture based on ethnic stereotypes will alienate the subsegments of that group that don't relate to the singular depiction. On the other hand, focusing on a specific subsegment with messaging based on a targeted insight leaves out the many other subsegments within that ethnic group. The solution is not necessarily to become more granular *within* ethnic target definition. Instead, by targeting a specific behavioral, attitudinal, or lifestyle segment, and identifying consumers who fit this profile *across all* ethnic groups, marketers can acknowledge the diversity within each ethnic group, and still reach a large enough audience to justify their expenditures.

The Millward Brown Lifestyle Segmentation Study

In late 2010, Millward Brown conducted a national lifestyle segmentation among Hispanic, African American, and non-Hispanic White consumers. The analysis used attitudinal variables related to various topics, including family, work, human relationships,

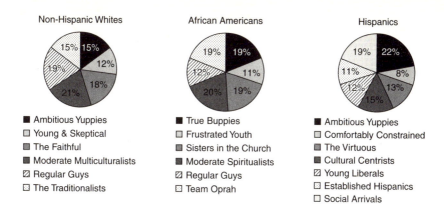

Figure 2.9 Millward Brown's Lifestyles Segmentation
Source: Millward Brown, 2011

religion, traditions, race, sex, and others. Six lifestyle segments were identified for both African Americans and non-Hispanic Whites, while the Hispanic market was divided into seven groups. The resulting segments are shown in figure 2.9 (group size) and figure 2.10 (summary description of the segments).

While this analysis provides valuable insights in many areas, there are two key findings that apply specifically to our discussion here.

Diversity within Ethnic Segments Goes beyond Traditional Demographic or Acculturation Aspects

Earlier in this chapter, we analyzed several ways in which you can look at the diversity within ethnic segments, most of them related to the condition of immigrants or descendants of immigrants. The results of the lifestyles segmentation prove that their diversity goes far beyond that. As with non-Hispanic Whites, there are also liberal and conservative people among Hispanics and Blacks. There are Latinos and African Americans for whom religion plays an important role, and those for whom material things like money and sex are more top-of-mind. While family is important to consumers

Non-Hispanic Whites	African Americans	Hispanics
Ambitious Yuppies (15%) This group of young people is concerned with appearances and the trappings of success. They are likely to seek positions of leadership at work, and their personal interests include the latest trends, going out, and the opposite sex. They also tend to have a religious side.	**True Buppies (19%)** This group of young men and women is more hedonistic and socially outgoing than the norm. Feeling the invincibility of youth, they are more ambitious and open to taking risks, and are less religious or spiritual than other groups.	**Ambitious Yuppies (22%)** This group of young single go-getters is very concerned with success in their careers. Independent and open to risk, the members of this group pursue very adventurous, multicultural lives.
Young and Skeptical (12%) This group of young men and women tends to have lower incomes and ambitions than the norm. Religious, tradition bound, and race conscious, the members of this group are more likely than others to feel that they are discriminated against.	**Frustrated Youth (11%)** This group of young people feels constrained by their circumstances, and as a result they are much less ambitious than the norm. Less spiritual and much more race conscious than average, they are less likely than others to feel empowered.	**Comfortably Constrained (8%)** This mostly male group is conscious of race and sensitive to discrimination, but its members do not feel empowered to improve their status. Though they are less professionally ambitious than others, they are still concerned about looking attractive, keeping up with fashion, and acquiring material things.
The Faithful (18%) This group, which skews older in age and slightly female, is more attached to religious beliefs than the norm. Less focused on living in the moment, the members of this group are driven by a sense of duty rather than enjoyment.	**Sisters in the Church (19%)** This group tends to be older, female, and less concerned about appearance than other groups. Well established in their churches and communities, the members of this group enjoy investing their energy into family and community service.	**The Virtuous (13%)** This group skews older in age and slightly female. Religious, conservative, and home centered, the members of this group are risk averse and race conscious. Although they value work, they are not extremely ambitious. Rather than seeking leadership roles, they focus on fulfilling their duties.
Moderate Multiculturalists (21%) This group skews middle-aged and is much less religious than the norm. The creative and multicultural members of this group make family a priority and value equality.	**Moderate Spiritualists (20%)** This group is spiritual, family oriented, and relatively unconcerned with status and material goods. The members of this laid-back group tend to hold views that are "middle of the road."	**Cultural Centrists (15%)** This group consists of men and women who value their appearance more than average, but don't necessarily want to steal the spotlight. They are risk averse and prefer same-race marriages. Though they are career focused, they don't want work to interfere with family time.
Regular Guys (19%) This mostly male group is much less religious than others. Less traditional and more multicultural as well, they are more open to interracial marriage than average.	**Regular Guys (12%)** This group skews male; has a pragmatic, materialistic view; and is far less religious than the norm. The members of this group tend to value self-reliance.	**Young Liberals (12%)** This group of young single people skews slightly male and is less religious than average. Focused on equality and less conscious of racial differences, the members of this group are adventurous and seek to have control over their professional lives.
The Traditionalists (15%) This group skews older in age and appreciates religion and family. More risk averse and less vain than others, the members of this group tend to embrace conservative social values.	**Team Oprah (19%)** This group of professionals skews female but includes a range of ages. Ambitious and spiritually centered, the typical member of this group believes it is as important to give as it is to take or achieve.	**Established Hispanics (11%)** This group is less traditional, less race conscious, and more multicultural than average. The members of this group feel self-empowered and tend to prioritize family over work and time over money.
		Social Arrivals (19%) This group values looking young and attractive, balancing work and family, and living in the moment. Less inclined to plan ahead or to take on leadership roles, members of this group are also less likely than others to marry outside of their race or move out of their parents' homes.

Figure 2.10   Millward Brown's Lifestyles Segmentation

Source: Millward Brown, 2011

in general, there are Hispanic and Black consumers for whom work and career are equally relevant, just as is true among the general population. Finally, contradicting some common stereotypes about minority segments, the study shows that while there are ethnic consumers for whom race is an important factor in their lives, there are also consumers for whom it is completely or mostly irrelevant.

When discussing acculturation, we mentioned that it is important not to rely on it exclusively when trying to understand the Hispanic market. While acculturation does provide valuable insights to understand the immigrant experience and overall cultural differences between immigrants and US-born Latinos, acculturation alone does not explain Hispanic consumption habits. Indeed, a blind spot of the acculturation theory is that it assumes that Hispanics who are close to their native culture will think and behave alike as consumers, just because of their ethnic affinity. It also makes similar assumptions regarding the bicultural and acculturated segments, which the results of the lifestyle segmentation prove wrong.

Figure 2.11 shows the Hispanic lifestyle segmentation by acculturation levels. Although there are some interesting skews across levels of acculturation that indicate a correlation between the two approaches, you can clearly see that there are people of all lifestyles within each level of acculturation. Look at the unacculturated group, for instance. Defenders of the acculturation theory usually argue that Spanish-language-dominant or unacculturated

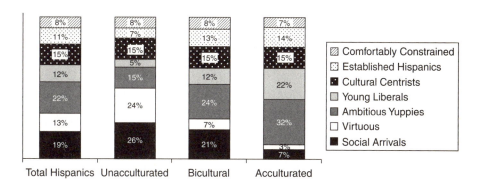

Figure 2.11   Lifestyles among Hispanics, by Level of Acculturation
Source: Millward Brown, 2011

Hispanics are all very similar. Based on the segmentation analysis, however, we know that this group comprises many different types: You have yuppies who care little about race, religious people for whom home is a cornerstone, risk takers, those who are risk averse, and so on.

Cross-Cultural Marketing Is Possible When You Understand Consumers Holistically

When marketers put race or ethnicity front and center, they find few synergies between ethnic segments and the general population. These populations are so different, they conclude, that there can be little crossover in messaging directed to non-Hispanic Whites, Latinos, and African or Asian Americans. But consider the source: For obvious reasons, this viewpoint is most often championed by multicultural marketing firms that specialize in race-based targeting.

However, when you approach a marketing challenge with an open mind, without factoring in race and ethnicity up front, chances are that you will find a way to develop truly multicultural initiatives that include both ethnic segments and the non-Hispanic White population. The Millward Brown lifestyle segmentation reinforces this idea decisively. At least five of the consumer groups it denotes have enough in common across ethnicities that efficiencies might be gained when targeting them:

- The *young adult professional* segment within all three ethnic groups tends to actively engage in the classic hedonistic American pastimes of dating and grooming to attract the opposite sex, seeking adventure, and aggressively pursuing career goals. The members of this group are ambitious and image conscious. Messaging to this target can be consistent across groups, but the execution will probably need to represent all groups—i.e., show actors or models of various races interacting—since this is a reflection of their world. Since they are more likely to be gainfully employed, members of this group respond to brands more than prices, and because they are sensitive to style and appearance packaging needs to reflect a high design standard. Digital marketing is a must for reaching this group.

- There also exists a segment of *frustrated youth* who report a diminished sense of empowerment and opportunity. The members of this group are more race conscious and apt to feel discriminated against and less active in changing their circumstances. Marketing to members of this group should be local and tailored to them, since they are less likely to relate to mainstream advertising. It also needs to offer some positive affirmation of their experience in order to cultivate their confidence to respond.

- In all three groups, there are religious women who work actively in their churches and families. Targeting "the Church Ladies" means appealing to their sense of morality, family, and community. Similar messaging can be used across the groups, but visual execution will probably need to be tailored to each group, since both the Black and Hispanic subsegments are race conscious and may look for cultural affirmation. The archetype of this group, is also altruistic, in that she volunteers for causes she believes in, so cause marketing will work with her. However, messaging should not make her the star or flatter her vanity about her efforts—she works for the glory of God. In an interesting potential for crossover, the frustrated youth highlighted before might be high on the Church Ladies' list of benefactors. Providing solutions to their life problems or sponsoring causes for their benefit, such as educational or community-building resources, might appeal to both groups.

- Conversely, there is a group of men, dubbed the *"Regular Guys,"* who are self-reliant and pragmatic rather than religiously inclined. They look for practical solutions. They are not vain, so advertising doesn't need to make them feel heroic; it simply needs to make them feel effective. They are also risk averse, so messaging needs to steer clear of controversy. They are open to multiculturalism and are less race conscious than the norm, so they can relate to any ethnicity represented in an ad. Thus the message and execution can be the same across media vehicles.

- Lastly, there is also a gender-balanced group of *liberal moderates* across ethnicities who are work- and family-focused and a little less risk averse than the Regular Guys detailed above. Well-crafted messaging might appeal to both groups.

While the Millward Brown Lifestyle Segmentation presents a theoretical model for cross-cultural targeting, this approach is far more than a hypothetical construct. Brands that regularly target kids, tweens, and teens, such as Kraft, Nickelodeon, and McDonald's, know well that the shared life stage, generation, and media landscape play a much more significant role than ethnicity in defining these audiences. But for the majority of brands, creating effective and culturally sensitive programs geared to a cross-cultural adult audience seems a bit more nebulous. There is, however, one well-defined cross-cultural group that marketers are starting to find some success with: the Gay, Lesbian, Bisexual, and Transgender (GLBT) segment. While the adoption of GLBT-focused initiatives into multicultural and niche marketing strategies is not yet standard practice, mainstream marketers in travel- and tourism-related industries are leading the pack with their targeting of this well-heeled segment. In July 2010, Amtrak generated quite a bit of buzz for a $250,000 campaign targeting this multiethnic, lifestyle-driven group. Such an approach flies in the face of today's marketing practice, which typically involves divvying up a brand's marketing budget by ethnic groups, often leaving insufficient resources for further lifestyle subtargets. The future of ethnic marketing may call for a model more like the GLBT approach, where cross-cultural lifestyle segments are identified and budgets allocated accordingly. Identifying lateral similarities across ethnic segments, as in the Millward Brown study, is a crucial first step to moving the multicultural marketing paradigm into the future.

CHAPTER 3

Beware the Ethnic Silo Trap

The annual Association of National Advertisers' Multicultural Marketing and Diversity conference in 2010 felt markedly different than the typical ethnic advertising gathering. Like longstanding residents of gentrifying urban neighborhoods, the African American and Hispanic agency executives, consultants, and researchers in attendance were abuzz about the "new neighbors." Much of the chatter over coffee breaks and sponsored luncheons centered on how impressively "diverse" the crowd was this year. To put it bluntly, ethnic marketers were shocked at how many White folks were interested in the multicultural discourse that was about to occur.

The reason for this interest became crystal clear when Gilbert Dávila, chair of the ANA Multicultural Marketing and Diversity Committee and former vice president of global diversity and multicultural market development at the Walt Disney Company, made the opening presentation, entitled "Multicultural—The New Mainstream." Over the next two days, subsequent presenters riffed on this theme, which was magnified repeatedly in deck after deck of PowerPoint presentations on two gigantic screens in the Glimmer Ballroom at Miami's Fontainebleau resort. The substance of this chorus? Multicultural is the new mainstream, and ethnic segments are driving mainstream business growth. Throughout the conference, these ideas were approached from a variety of angles, suggesting that while there was consensus on the facts, many were still uncertain about their implications for the marketing industry. One thing, however, was very clear: Major brands felt there was a rich new vein to be tapped, and everyone wanted a piece of the multicultural action. The only question was how best to mine for share of ethnic dollars.

Advertisers have traditionally sought ethnic hearts and wallets by communicating through the lens of cultural identity. But with new terms like "cross-cultural" and "total market approach" floating through the lavish, high-ceilinged meeting rooms at the Fontainebleau, there was a sense that traditional ethnic segmentation and targeting may be outdated approaches in a rapidly evolving marketplace. To understand the most fundamental problems with "old-school" target marketing with an ethnic focus, one must return to Marketing 101.

The idea of market segmentation is built upon a simple premise: A marketing message designed to take into account the unique preferences, attitudes, and behaviors of a specific population will resonate more strongly with that group than will a more broadly geared message. The wider your target audience, the more diverse the rational and emotional needs of the group, and the harder it is to choose messaging that effectively speaks to everyone. The more precisely an audience is defined, however, the more homogenous its members' rational and emotional needs will be, which makes it much easier and more efficient to prompt a certain type of behavior from that group with a single set of stimuli.

For example, if Automotive Insurance Brand X tries to appeal to Connie Consumer simply as a person living on Earth, it has far less chance of striking a personally relevant chord with her than if it speaks to her as a busy suburban mother of three. Both group designations ring true for Connie (she is after all, both an Earthling and a busy suburban mom), but the latter, more detailed focus offers a closer point of connection to insights about her day-to-day life—which, if well-executed, could convince her that Brand X's insurance offering meets her specific needs. Makes sense, right?

But what happens when the target consumer belongs to several different segments, all of which are specific and relevant? What if Connie, in addition to being a busy suburban mom, is also a business owner whose company owns a small fleet of vehicles used on the job? Well, if the brand has identified both families and business owners as high-opportunity targets and has the luxury of creating multiple executions to reach them, they can conceivably create two separate pitches with equal potential to convey the campaign's message. Connie might respond to either or both ads, given that each one appeals to a different facet of her identity. Let's see how that scenario plays out in real consumer life:

> Connie is at home preparing a quick dinner for her family before driving her oldest son to his football game. She's thinking about how much easier things will be next year when he starts driving and is considering purchasing a used car for him. She has concerns about how much his monthly insurance payments will run, and she wonders whether there are any special offers available for families with new teen drivers. Connie has CNN on in the background, as she often does, to try to keep up on news that may affect her business's industry. Brand X's auto insurance ad comes on. Connie's ears prick up, but the problem is that the particular commercial that runs is the one aimed at small business owners. Although it's a relevant message for a certain facet of her life, it doesn't leave her with the sense that the brand understands her needs as a mother. Also, because the majority of the business-owning audience is male, the ad has a heavily masculine sensibility that she finds off-putting and slightly insulting.

In this hypothetical scenario, there are two main issues contributing to an unfavorable consumer response:

1. The ad spoke to an aspect of the consumer's identity that wasn't salient at the time and place that she encountered it.
2. The ad did not acknowledge the possibility that the consumer could belong to two segments. In speaking to one dimension of her identity, it alienated the other.

THE TROUBLE WITH TRADITIONAL MULTICULTURAL MARKETING

These same two problems form the crux of a major flaw in traditional multicultural marketing theory. So much ethnically targeted marketing places cultural cues at the front and center when, in many cases, ethnicity is not the most salient or relevant dimension of the consumer's identity.

In addition, many targeted ads treat ethnic consumers as if they live within cultural silos—as though African America, Hispanic America, and Asian America were separate nations within the United States comprised exclusively of those groups. And while the existence of distinct Black, Hispanic, and Asian cultures is undeniable, clearly no such subnations exist. Ethnic groups in America interact with and influence one another, as well as the so-called mainstream population. Advertising in the age of American multiculturalism must evolve to match this reality if it hopes to remain relevant to this quickly emerging majority.

Melting Pots versus Salad Bowls

We use metaphors to frame and describe the world around us. Chains and links suggest connection, light implies innovation, and so on. Savvy advertisers invoke these familiar and often universally understood symbols to stir emotions they hope will become the bedrock for meaningful and sustained brand relationships. In offices and boardrooms around the world, such metaphors are employed to convey complex ideas about business dynamics, brand architecture, or consumer behavior. American multiculturalism is one such complex idea, and it has spawned a number of metaphors with varying degrees of utility for marketing applications. Most have been problematic. So in order to elevate the marketing dialogue surrounding today's multicultural America, we must replace our broken framework for discussing it.

For years, the discussion surrounding American multiculturalism has been dominated by two camps with very different models for understanding the relationship between ethnic minorities and the predominant culture. For the purposes of this discussion, we will refer to these two groups as the "Melting Pots" and the "Salad Bowls."

The Melting Pots view American cultural identity as an amalgamation of ethnicities, blended into a uniform elixir. *E pluribus unum*, Latin for "out of many, one," is this camp's credo. The problem with the Melting Pot metaphor is that it tends to reflect more of a historic ideal than the reality of our modern, heterogeneous national identity. The truth is, while many minorities do become part of mainstream American culture, it often isn't at the expense of their ethnic identities.

The Salad Bowls have a nuanced but decidedly different take on American multiculturalism. They see our society as a mix of distinct but complementary cultures, which together produce a final product that is flavorful and vibrant. But in this metaphor, the individual taste and appearance of each ingredient remains intact after being folded into a larger whole—the lettuce, for instance, while coexisting with the other ingredients, will always be lettuce. This aspect of the Salad Bowl model does hold water: The ethnic consumer who identifies with his native culture, in many cases, does not give it up in exchange for an exclusively American identity. But—and this nuance is important—his or her ethnic identity is often *influenced by* American culture and, conversely, his or her ethnic identity also *influences* the very makeup of American culture. The Salad Bowls generally do not acknowledge this mutual influence. Like the folksier "patchwork quilt" and "mosaic" metaphors, the Salad Bowl framework conveys only the "part of a whole" dimension of an ethnic minority's relationship with American culture and, at best, suggest that the whole may be better off for having such diverse elements within it.

There may be a more suitable representation for the current state of American multiculturalism within food symbology. What if we thought of America's multicultural society as a chicken soup? The broth would represent the predominant American ethos, seasoned with distinct cultural influences over the years, and now representative of those things we have come to associate with classic Americana—like baseball, hot dogs, and apple pie. The other ingredients, which make the soup substantial and textured, would represent America's ethnic populations. On the one hand, these elements—chicken, noodles, and vegetables—each have their own distinct appearance, texture, and taste. However, immersed in the broth of the predominant American culture, they have absorbed some of its properties, while at the same time adding their respective flavor notes to the broth. In this framework, we can envision how the natural by-product of America's increasing cultural diversity is the influence of these cultures on one another and on the predominant national culture.

Spheres of Influence

"What's the number-one sauce in America?" From his tone, it's clear that Daniel Bloom has asked this question before, and most likely heard the incorrect answer more than once. Bloom is senior vice president of consumer research at Bank of America and a champion for the mainstreaming of multicultural consumer insights at the financial services brand. He has turned the tables on his interviewers, barely allowing time for them to utter the correct, but tentative-sounding response (*Salsa?*), before shooting out two more rapid-fire questions. "Yeah, and what's the number-one chip?" (*Tortilla?*) "Yeah. What is the number one type of food that people go out to eat?" (*Mexican, right?*)[1] Bloom's point couldn't be clearer: Ethnic consumers in America have certainly influenced American food culture. Ethnic restaurants of various origins line the main streets of our city centers and the strip malls of our suburbs. We barely think twice about ordering up an *arroz con pollo* or stopping by the neighborhood Korean restaurant for some *bibimbap*. But the trend is bigger than this. From fast food to fine dining, even traditional American restaurants have been incorporating ethnic-influenced menu items into their mass-market offerings. In a presentation entitled "Multicultural America: Redefining the Mainstream," New American Dimensions CEO David Morse explained that while the introduction of ethnic foods in America may have been originally driven by ethnic consumers, their popularity with the mainstream has led to a majority-driven demand for these flavors. The point is illustrated in figure 3.1.

Logic suggests that *any* trend in America with an ethnic origin would have to catch on among the White majority in order to gain broad popularity—at least until minorities become the New Majority, at which point pop-culture trends may be able to sustain themselves based on appeal among ethnic consumers alone. And while food is probably the most obvious example of ethnic influence on American society, it's just the tip of the iceberg. The influence of ethnic populations in America is on

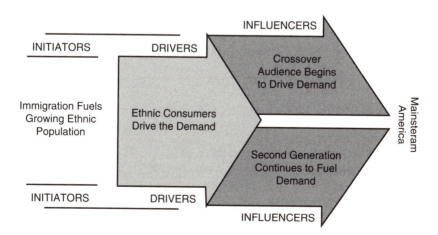

Figure 3.1   The Mainstreaming of Ethnic Foods: Push and Pull Factors
Source: David Morse, New American Dimensions

the upswing and will continue to accelerate as minorities comprise an ever-larger percentage of the population.

However, it is important to distinguish between the proliferation of ethnic minorities in historically White arenas from the phenomenon of these ethnicities' preferences influencing mainstream culture. It is one thing to say that ethnic minorities are more integrated within mainstream society than ever before. It is another to say that mainstream American society's interests and preferences have changed as a result. The two ideas are interrelated; however, this particular discussion focuses on the second one. Part of the reason people of diverse ethnicities have been able to influence the American mainstream is that their collective size has increased steadily over the years, along with their access to previously restricted channels of society. The idea of minority influence on the mainstream may seem like a matter-of-fact concept to Americans. However, it is not the case in all multicultural societies. In fact, in many countries, especially in Europe, the expectation of recent immigrants is that they will either enter the country already speaking the national language or quickly learn it, and that their new citizenship will replace their ethnic identity.

German chancellor Angela Merkel raised international eyebrows in 2010 when she claimed that multiculturalism in Germany, which has a large population of Turkish immigrants, had not succeeded. The Associated Press covered the story in an October 17 article, excerpted here:

> *"Multikulti,"* the concept that "we are now living side-by-side and are happy about it," does not work, Merkel told a meeting of younger members of her conservative Christian Democratic Union (CDU) party at Potsdam, near Berlin.
>
> "This approach has failed, totally," she said, adding that immigrants should integrate and adopt Germany's culture and values.
>
> Turkish president Abdullah Gül, in a weekend interview, also urged the Turkish community living in Germany to master the language of their adopted country.

"When one doesn't speak the language of the country in which one lives, that doesn't serve anyone, neither the person concerned, [nor] the country, nor the society," the Turkish president told the *Suedeutsche Zeitung*.

"That is why I tell them at every opportunity that they should learn German, and speak it fluently and without an accent. That should start at nurseries."[2]

In stark contrast, American political and social policy, at least in theory, encourages ethnic minorities to retain their distinct cultural identities, rather than pressuring them to fully absorb the majority culture at the expense of their roots. The United States has no official national language and is the second-largest Spanish-speaking country in the world, behind only Mexico. ESL classes are offered in the majority of public schools, and ethnic holidays are observed and celebrated around the country. The American premium on cultural retention and expression has opened the door for mainstream culture to absorb aspects of its various ethnic groups.

Since ethnic influence on America is a function of cultural intermingling, it's no surprise that minority cultures have had the greatest influence on the mainstream spheres they have had access to the longest—namely, food, music, and sports.

Before they were allowed to join their peers in White-only dining rooms, African Americans and Hispanics were relegated to kitchens, where they prepared food for the exclusively Caucasian mainstream. So it's no wonder that over the years, Americans developed a palate for the indigenous flavors of those cultures, which eventually led to the proliferation of national and global restaurant chains providing those flavors. Their success speaks volumes: KFC (formerly Kentucky Fried Chicken), with a menu based on Black soul food from the South, has over 5,100 stores across the United States, and Taco Bell, the number-one Mexican fast-food chain in the country, has over 5,600.

Similarly, before the Civil Rights Act of 1964, there were very few opportunities for Blacks and Hispanics to achieve the

American Dream of meritocratic financial success. In this bleak era of twentieth-century American race policy, many non-White Americans' only hope for affluence was in entertainment-related fields, such as music and sports. The legacy of their relatively early access to these select fields is reflected in the overrepresentation of ethnic minorities in them today. As an example, out of the ten musical artists and groups achieving number-one rankings in the Billboard Top 100 year-end lists from 2000 through 2009, six were non-White. In Major League Baseball, Latinos make up about 30% of players and according to the league's own statistics "comprise many of the game's highest-paid and most-celebrated stars."[3] And today, the *NBA Encyclopedia* reports that the "overwhelming majority of players in the NBA are African American," and the game has changed considerably as a result of their unique style of play.[4]

But there are plenty of other examples of ethnic culture's influence on the mainstream. To see the impact of immigration on language, for instance, one needs simply to crack a dictionary. On Ellis Island in New York City stands a tree-shaped sculpture memorializing the impact of foreign cultures on American English. Words like "barbecue," "nosh," "cabana," and "boondocks," are printed on its faux leaves, representing their foreign-language origins. This phenomenon is even more pronounced in American slang and pop culture, which has absorbed phrases from Black and Latino culture: "You go, girl," "hasta la vista," "the bomb," "la vida loca." In a November 2010 interview with *Today* show host Matt Lauer, former president George W. Bush responded to rapper Kanye West's televised apology for implying that his actions in the wake of Hurricane Katrina were motivated by racism. To the surprise of many, Bush's comments took the form of a popular African American youth idiom: "I'm not a hater," he claimed.[5]

In addition to the African American and Hispanic influence on American slang, Asian Americans are influencing a number of youth subcultures today. As anyone well-versed in automotive culture will tell you, the import tuner scene (the subculture of modifying imported vehicle makes for street racing) is heavily driven by this diverse segment, as are the Japanese anime and manga styles of cartoon art. And for those paying attention to the trends in new forms of fashion, music, and art, the heavy influence of African American, Hispanic, and Asian cultures is hard to ignore.

Of course, many of these examples are youth-specific. It would be an overstatement to claim that ethnic cultures are *driving* trends among the over-40 set outside of food, music, and sports, although they are certainly *influencing* them. Today's adult and senior populations display more trend-seeking behavior than previous generations, and are influenced by the multiculturalism of their children's social spheres and affinities. But youth culture is the true frontier of minority influence. Nowhere is this more apparent than in the global phenomenon that is hip-hop culture. Hip-hop's many dimensions have had a lasting impact on popular language, fashion, dance, visual art, and media. While reliable figures on the demographics of hip-hop consumers are hard to find, most sources agree that the majority of spending in this multibillion dollar industry comes from White youth. David Morse of New American Dimensions writes, "Hip-hop has numerous manifestations, yet encompasses all aspects of life from music to style, sports, and world outlook. Its inclusiveness and adaptability allow it a staying power like no other trend before it."[6]

THE URBAN MINDSET CONSUMER

As trends such as social networking and word-of-mouth continue to gain importance in consumers' purchasing patterns, the "urban" concept is becoming a little less ethnic and a little more of a mindset every day.

—Advertising Age, August 2008

While the influence of ethnic minorities in American pop culture is more visible all the time, the real story lies beneath the surface, in the microtrends just now on the verge of breaking through on a larger scale. Today, trend-conscious marketers are tapping into a savvy segment of innovative, cutting-edge, and transcultural consumers (i.e. those that identify with multiple and often shifting ethnic cultures) to forecast these movements. This group is called the Urban Mindset Consumers (UMCs). Their value to marketers lies not only in their trendsetting behavior, but also in their unique approach to cultural self-identification. Ask Urban Mindset Consumers about the role of race in their personal identities, and they will tell you that it is but one of several pieces in the complex jigsaws that define them. Consider the following quotes from young adults asked about the role of race in their self-definition:

- NINETEEN-YEAR-OLD HISPANIC MALE: "I feel like nowadays in this generation, in this cultural setting, just America, period, there's more definition of a person in ways other than race."
- TWENTY-ONE-YEAR-OLD NON-HISPANIC WHITE MALE: "Youth in America today, it's like, not about African American, Asian American, Hispanic American; we're all part of a whole American culture."
- TWENTY-THREE-YEAR-OLD BIRACIAL FEMALE: "I don't see myself as different than anybody, just because I don't want to see anybody different from anyone else. You know, I see everyone the same, regardless of what color you are, or what language you speak, or what dialect you're using. Everybody's the same; we're all God's children."

Some believe this segment represents the future of American society. Today's young adults live in a world where the walls between African, Asian, and Hispanic identity have become permeable, so much so that individuals can construct and live out a multicultural personal identity made up of the culture(s) they are born into, marry into, socialize with, or with which they simply have a strong affinity.

For marketers, Urban Mindset Consumers present a complex opportunity, because they are extremely influential, but at the same time difficult to understand. They pose three challenges in particular:

1. The term "urban" has been co-opted and misappropriated to the point where it almost always requires an explanation.
2. The downscale connotations of some of the older definitions of "urban" are unattractive to many marketers.
3. UMCs defy traditional demographic definition, making them difficult for market researchers to capture and study.

There are solutions to each of these challenges, but first, a profile of the Urban Mindset Consumer is in order.

WHO IS THE URBAN MINDSET CONSUMER?

Before explaining who the Urban Mindset Consumer is, it may be a helpful exercise to look at what he is not. Unlike the Urban Consumer (note the missing "Mindset"), the UMC is not simply—or even necessarily—a big-city dweller. And, contrary to the misappropriation of the term "urban" as a euphemism for "racial minority" in news media, the UMC is not exclusively Black or Hispanic.

The Urban Mindset Consumer belongs to a multidimensional segment that spans many traditional demographic and psychographic dimensions. ("Psychographic" refers to the lifestyle, attitudes, and values that predispose people to certain behaviors.) In marketing terms, the UMC is the love child of the "Metropolitan Mindset" and "Ethnic Youth Culture" segments. Both groups are defined by a combination of demographic and psychographic characteristics.

Those in the Metropolitan Mindset segment share four distinct traits:

1. They are concentrated in the largest cities.

2. They are fast-paced multitaskers—they process multiple information feeds simultaneously.
3. Their lifestyle and passions are heavily influenced by the city environment.
4. They place high value on independence and "street smarts."

Similarly, the members of the Ethnic Youth Culture segment also share four defining traits:

1. They are predominantly African American and Hispanic Millennials.
2. They are aspirational.
3. Their creativity is bred by economic hardship and lack of access to mainstream resources.
4. They make unique music, fashion, and language central to their identity.

Put more simply: The Carrie Bradshaw character from *Sex and the City* exemplifies the Metropolitan Mindset, while the rapper Lil Wayne exemplifies Ethnic Youth Culture. Imagine, if you will, the peculiar mix of traits that the offspring of two such figures would represent, and you begin to grasp just how interesting and multidimensional the UMCs really are.

In fact, to extend the earlier chicken-soup metaphor, the UMC segment represents a gumbo of cultural elements, including but not limited to the following characteristics:

- Racial and socioeconomic diversity
- Fusion of ethnic cultures in the formation of personal identity
- Street-smart
- High value placed on authenticity
- Grassroots sensibilities
- On-the-go lifestyle
- Self-expression via aesthetics of music, art and design, and fashion subcultures

Unfortunately, another defining characteristic of Urban Mindset Consumers is that they are quite small in number. While it's difficult to accurately size the segment because of its complex and largely psychographic definition, it's certainly not large enough to be the primary, secondary, or even tertiary target for any brand's national campaign supported by traditional media. Further complicating matters, UMCs tend to be highly skeptical of mass marketing, making them an elusive group for advertisers to engage directly.

Given these challenges, you might be wondering why marketers should care about the UMC at all. The answer is simple: They are important influencers of mainstream behavior among both ethnic and nonethnic consumers. Urban Mindset Consumers are an added-value group, which means that although they are small in number they drive significant sales volume, not only from within their own segment—they are prolific spenders in categories that facilitate their passions and self-expression—but also by influencing members of the mainstream market. UMCs are thus powerful ambassadors for any brand that can capture their interest.

Think of the Urban Mindset Consumer as the bull's-eye at the center of a series of concentric circles. Moving outward, each subsequent ring represents a subsegment closer and closer to the mainstream. And each subsegment plays a role in the migration of trends from the UMC out to the mainstream, as you can see from figure 3.2.

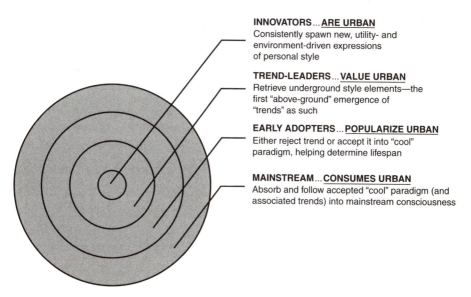

INNOVATORS...**ARE URBAN**
Consistently spawn new, utility- and environment-driven expressions of personal style

TREND-LEADERS...**VALUE URBAN**
Retrieve underground style elements—the first "above-ground" emergence of "trends" as such

EARLY ADOPTERS...**POPULARIZE URBAN**
Either reject trend or accept it into "cool" paradigm, helping determine lifespan

MAINSTREAM...**CONSUMES URBAN**
Absorb and follow accepted "cool" paradigm (and associated trends) into mainstream consciousness

Figure 3.2   UMC Trend Dispersion Model
Source: Firefly Millward Brown, 2011

To summarize, many trends originate at the center of UMC culture and move outward, creating a ripple effect of consumer activity. So for brands that seek to gain a hold in the youth, young adult, or trend-conscious older-adult markets, the Urban Mindset Consumer is a key segment to understand.

Savvy brands respond to this phenomenon with urban-flavored campaigns. Their goal is rarely to convert the small segment of UMC innovators into their primary audience; rather, the objective is to associate the product or brand with a trend that the mainstream will find authentically appealing. In order to achieve that authenticity, smart brands mine insights and creative fodder from as close to the center as possible, aiming for (if only rarely hitting) the bull's-eye. If the communication is effective enough to get picked up by the Trend Leaders or Early Adopters close to the center, these subsegments can then help build the critical mass of credible, peer-driven buzz that later reaches the mainstream with powerful momentum behind it.

Connecting with the Urban Mindset Consumer

Before outlining success principles for effectively leveraging the power of Urban Mindset Consumers, let's look at the primary challenges we laid out earlier—the unfavorable linguistic connotations and the hazy demographic definition.

In a marketing context, the term "urban" has carried with it considerable baggage. Over the last 30 years, its meaning has morphed from a literal geographical definition to a euphemistic term used to refer to inner-city and low-income African Americans, later on expanding to include poor Hispanics. Since then, its implications have softened somewhat, at least within a marketing context, as it became associated with trend leadership and innovative youth culture. Still, the popular usage within a number of industries carries with it the residue of its association with the minority underclass. Journalist, magazine publisher, and marketer Claude Grunitzky experienced the loaded term's damaging effects on prospective advertisers' perceptions of his magazine, *TRACE*. He recounted these challenges in a 2010 interview:

> The magazine was initially called *TRACE Urban Magazine,* and I was very much focused on going after rappers and MCs and R&B singers and fashion that had more of an urban feel to it. Now that was 14 years ago. I moved to New York in 1998 and started trying to grow and expand the magazine, launching a U.S. edition in addition to the U.K. edition, . . . I realized [because I used to go on all the sales calls] that the term "urban" had been kind of ghettoized, for lack of a better word, in that "urban" meant "Black and poor," and "Hispanic and poor," and "inner-city," and so on. [S]o that was a difficult sell, because I was going after advertisers like Absolut Vodka, but also Gucci. I met with Donna Karan and I met with Calvin Klein. I literally was knocking at everyone's door, and I finally found that the term "urban" was inappropriate.[7]

Grunitzky landed on "Transculturalists" as a more appropriate term for the group of young people he saw moving fluidly from one culture to the next, constructing mosaic identities from a range of diverse ethnicities. The lesson gained here is that through creative rebranding, the baggage was shed. Likewise, shifting the label from "Urban" to "Urban Mindset" regrounds the discussion in psychographics, rather than demographics alone.

The other major challenge UMCs present stems from these defining psychographic parameters. While agencies and marketing departments pay considerable lip service to the complex personal characteristics of their target consumer profiles, when it comes to traditional media planning, the discussion turns almost exclusively to demographics and their associated media markets. By only focusing on factors like income, age, and ethnicity in choosing the appropriate media channel and environment, advertising can fail to reach consumers whose media choices are driven by less tangible aspects of their identity.

By contrast, psychographic and behavioral audience definition is much more evolved in digital media, since these outlets offer content according to interests and affinities rather than strictly demographics. In the long term, traditional media forms will shift in this direction as well, with the advent of Google TV and other old-new media hybrids. In the meantime, progressive marketers should demand that their research providers develop quantitative surveys that capture the defining traits of these consumers more comprehensively. Partnering with qualitative research agencies to help identify these psychographic traits before conducting larger-scale quantitative studies is a crucial starting point.

Now that the challenges have been addressed, here are a few principles for successfully engaging the Urban Mindset Consumer segment:

- Executions depicting groups of urban consumers should avoid all-Black or all-Hispanic casting. Advertising that accurately reflects the diversity of the Urban Mindset Consumers' culture will stand out as more authentic.
- Go beyond imagery and genres traditionally associated with Black and Hispanic consumers. This will attract a truly Urban Mindset audience and not just ethnic mainstream consumers. It also boosts a brand's cool among trendsetters, fanning out to the high-volume mainstream audience.
- Instead of trying to give a mainstream brand an Urban Mindset image, consider co-branding with entities that have established Urban Mindset credibility, particularly in the areas of music, fashion, art, and design.
- Favor below-the-line (i.e., viral and other nontraditional media) and event-based marketing. When traditional media is used, prioritize the digital, print, and out-of-home (especially placement along mass transit pathways) categories over TV.
- Mine insights from Innovators and Trend Leaders, but use them to focus on moving the needle among early adopters and mainstream consumers.

TRANSCULTURALS AND BICULTURALS

To be fair, not everyone believes that society is moving toward a more transcultural reality. Multicultural marketing professionals in particular stick steadfastly to the idea that ethnic consumers see the world through a definitively cultural lens, and always will.

Listening to marketing professionals who operate in the ethnic space, it becomes abundantly clear why they may be dragging their feet in the march toward more cross-cultural communications. The livelihood of some agencies, their raison d'être, is built upon the premise that non-White consumers need culturally targeted advertising to motivate them to respond or take action. And to a certain extent they are right. While the various cultures that make up America's ethnic populations may be coming together, ethnic distinctions themselves aren't going to disappear in the foreseeable future. Instead, individual consumers *will* become increasingly multiethnic and multicultural.

If there is any question about this impending "micro-multiculturalism," we need only look to the statistics. According to the US census, in the past ten years the multiracial population in the United States has grown by 32%. This does not include the 57% of Hispanics who also consider themselves White, Black, Native American, Asian, or Pacific Islander. Because Hispanic origin and race are classified by the census as separate concepts, these people would not be considered multi-racial or multi-ethnic in technical terms, despite the fact that American society may view them as such.

Further blurring the neat lines between racial and ethnic groups is the rapid growth and increasing acknowledgment by marketers of the bicultural population. In a marketing context, "bicultural" most commonly refers to Hispanic consumers who embrace both the Hispanic and American dimensions of their cultural identities. Biculturalism has become the new buzzword, replacing the old acculturation model. Recall that acculturation is the degree to which ethnic minorities (usually immigrants) have taken on traits of mainstream American culture. Targeting unacculturated (or low-acculturation) consumers generally involves messaging in their native language with heavy cultural cues, while the approach for acculturated consumers is much more like mainstream marketing, and often doesn't call for a separate ethnic campaign at all. The accepted wisdom was that acculturation was essentially a function of how long the immigrant consumer had been living in America. Segmenting ethnic consumers by acculturation has been problematic because it is based on the zero-sum assumption that all immigrants are on a steady path toward becoming fully American in their lifestyle, behavior, and preferences, thereby becoming less and less ethnic with time. Marketers rarely target the so-called fully acculturated Hispanic, because the accepted belief is that generations of removal from one's country of origin lead to complete absorption of White mainstream identity.

Given the history of African American targeted marketing, it's surprising that the old Hispanic assimilation model went unchallenged for as long as it did. After all, African Americans have been in the country for a number of generations, yet some race-based distinctions still exist. It stands to reason that the same thing will happen with the Hispanic population.

The impetus to reframe the Hispanic acculturation model has caught on like wildfire, largely because of the dual phenomenon of expected flat growth in the number of Hispanic immigrants compounded by the continued rise in numbers of US-born, English-language-dominant Latinos. According to most experts in the area, bicultural Hispanics now comprise the majority of the Hispanic population in the United States.

So just who are these Bicultural Hispanic consumers, and what makes them different from their Hispanic counterparts? According to Daniel Bloom, senior vice president of Consumer Research at Bank of America, marketers should prepare for the oncoming wave of biculturalism. Bloom led the research behind Bank of America's 2009 Hispanic campaign, "Hacia Adelante," ("Moving Forward") which was the "Gold" winner in its category (Financial Services) in the 2009 ARF David Ogilvy Awards. Addressing biculturals and the unique middle space that they occupy, Bloom says, "You are proud of your Latin American roots and your Latin American heritage. You are proud to be a US Hispanic. You are proud to be a US citizen. You think in both cultures. You behave in both cultures. You move back and forth from Spanish to English. And that's a growing segment in the population."[8]

At the Advertising Research Foundation's Multicultural Super Council presentations, which took place during Advertising Week 2010 in New York, Marta Insua, vice president of strategic insights for the Hispanic agency Alma DDB, introduced attendees to the concepts of "Fusionistas," otherwise known as bicultural consumers, and "Preservers," who cling to a more traditional and singular Hispanic identity. According to Insua, these two segments represent a better construct for thinking about higher- versus lower-acculturation Hispanics, since they don't begin with the premise that all Hispanic immigrants are headed toward full acculturation. In one of Alma DDB's signature "Yellow Papers," entitled *A Brave New World of Consumidores...Introducing Young Fusionistas,* Insua and her strategists go on to describe this bicultural audience:

> As a segment, [Fusionistas] are naturally multicultural, serving as the linchpins of cultural influence for their peers of all ethnicities. American culture is an essential part of their identity.
> The term "bicultural" means different things to different people. Often people mean the degree to which a person speaks two languages. Yet language is just one aspect of culture.... Fusionistas self-define as 100% Latino plus 100% American.[9]

It is interesting to note that the term "bicultural" is rarely used to refer to any group other than Hispanics. Surprisingly, there has been very little discussion of Asian-American biculturalism within the multicultural marketing community. This may very well be a function of this segment's relatively low (but steadily growing) population, and the fact that they are at an earlier point in the immigration and cultural embedment cycle than their Hispanic and African American counterparts.

And what about African Americans? Can they also be considered bicultural? The question is not a new one. In one of the earliest writings on American biculturalism, the Black intellectual leader and Harvard academic W. E. B. DuBois wrote about the challenge of "double consciousness" for Blacks in America in the August 1897 issue of *The Atlantic Monthly*:

> The history of the American Negro is the history of this strife,—this longing to attain self-conscious manhood, to merge his double self into a better and truer self. In this merging he wishes neither of the older selves to be lost. He would not Africanize America, for America has too much to teach the world and Africa. He would not bleach his Negro soul in a flood of white Americanism, for he knows that Negro blood has a message for the world. He simply wishes to make it possible for a man to be both a Negro and an American, without being cursed and spit upon by his fellows, without having the doors of Opportunity closed roughly in his face.[10]

The idea of simultaneously inhabiting two worlds is very familiar to African Americans. Sociologists and educational experts refer to the linguistic changes they make from American English and Black vernacular depending on social context as "code-switching." One could argue that many Black professionals have had to become bicultural by necessity in order to successfully rise in various predominantly White business sectors. Yet a majority of marketing geared to this audience ignores their experience within mainstream American culture.

There is also an important distinction between African American biculturalism and that of modern-day immigrant populations. A key driver of immigration to America is an affinity for its ideals. Since the nation's very earliest days, people have uprooted their lives and abandoned the familiarity of their native lands in pursuit of the freedoms and opportunities that America affords its residents. African Americans represent a very different story because of the historical context of their migration to America, and the legacy of slavery and institutionalized racism that followed. As recently as the 1960s, African Americans were categorically barred from participation in many facets of mainstream American society. African American culture, while originally made up of traditions and values of the various root cultures, was bolstered by a shared experience of subjugation, exclusion, and ultimately a fight for equal rights. So although it works to describe Hispanic biculturals as both fully Hispanic and fully American, it seems somehow inappropriate to describe African Americans as both fully African and fully American. Each of the two identities that flank the symbolic hyphen for Blacks in America has contributed to a distinct identity unique to their experience in this country. For now, biculturalism may be best applied to groups that have immigrated to the United States more recently, and under circumstances over which they had a reasonable degree of control.

CHAPTER 4

The Past: A Brief History

Se wo were fi na wosankofa a yenkyi: "We must go back and reclaim our past so we can move forward; so we understand why and how we came to be who we are today."
—*Loose translation of*
Ghanaian Akan proverb

Throughout American history, each new wave of immigrants has made use of media to deliver content geared to their own cultural community, usually in their own language. The capitalist ideal of free enterprise and the collectivist mindset of many immigrant cultures have made for strange bedfellows, spawning the earliest forms of culturally targeted advertising. And as ethnic minorities have grown in size and power, adopting American lifestyles and values, their depictions in mainstream media have also evolved.

This evolution continues in today's advertising. On the brink of a new cultural frontier in the twenty-first century, the old African proverb about taking from the past to help illuminate the future could not be more relevant, particularly since America's history of adapting commerce to immigrant cultures is as old as the country itself. Marketing professionals can learn important lessons by studying the sociohistoric conditions during each era in ethnic advertising and the innovators who blazed the trail to modern multicultural marketing.

It is important to distinguish between advertising created by minority businesses to appeal to that same group's consumers and advertising created by national or global mainstream brands for ethnic consumers. While the former provides important historical context for understanding the unique role of targeted media in America today, the latter helps chart the movement of ethnic minorities into the mainstream marketing audience. In this chapter we will explore both.

THE BIRTH OF ETHNIC MEDIA IN AMERICA

The history of culturally targeted marketing in America is rooted in its first forms of ethnic media. Let's revisit the early days of the country's first mass medium: the newspaper.

The first American multipage broadsheet, *Publick Occurrences both Forreign and Domestick,* was founded in Boston in 1690, and by 1783, on the heels of the Revolutionary War, there were 43 newspapers in operation throughout the country.[1] This number grew to 346 by 1814, and exploded to 2,526 titles in 1850, according to that year's census. Over roughly the same time period these shores were experiencing massive waves of immigration, primarily Europeans fleeing tyrannical rulers to pursue freedom and opportunity in the New World. During this first onslaught of immigration, which lasted from about 1640 to 1820, America's cultural diversity was at its height, even by today's standards. Germans were nearly a majority in Pennsylvania, much to the dismay of Benjamin Franklin, as reflected in his 1751 essay: "Why should the boors be suffered to swarm into our settlements and by herding together establish their language and manners to the exclusion of ours? Why should Pennsylvania, founded by the English, be becoming a colony of aliens, who will shortly be so numerous as to Germanize us instead of our Anglifying them?"[2] As we can see, the influence of ethnic cultures on mainstream life is hardly a new concept, nor is the perception of them as a threat to the mainstream status quo.

Given the tumultuous events surrounding the country's formation, including four wars fought between 1775 and 1865, it's no wonder that the earliest American newspapers were highly political and partisan. Add the fact that three of those four wars (the Mexican-American War, the American Civil War, and the Spanish-American War) were arguably directly triggered by widespread dissent over the role that Hispanics and Blacks should play in the new nation, and it becomes obvious that the mainstream view of these events couldn't possibly have aligned with that of the growing immigrant fringe.

The early mainstream publications that sprang up around national affairs delivered content relevant to and from the perspective of the English-speaking White population—understandably so, since they comprised the overwhelming majority and were exclusive holders of political and economic power at the time. In addition to the language barriers that these newspapers presented to some eighteenth-century immigrants, their editorials failed to reflect the distinct outlook of ethnic constituents.

These factors in combination laid the groundwork for the first ethnic newspapers in the 1700s. Nearly every group arriving on American shores eventually created and disseminated publications in its native language. In the early- to mid-eighteenth century, cultural relevance in print media was an issue of language, not sociological nuance, and the immigrant population comprised far more Whites than Hispanics and Blacks. For this reason, the ethnic press looked quite different in its early years than the way we think of it today.

By the 1800s, newspapers founded by, published by, and geared to immigrant populations had become common. Some were even wildly successful. The German-language newspaper *New Yorker Staats-Zeitung* had more than 60,000 readers at one point in the 1800s, and some historians estimate that there were 800 German-language newspapers by the 1880s.[3] But even as ethnic European publications thrived, there was no real journalistic representation for Hispanic immigrants or Black Freedmen (as emancipated slaves and freeborn African Americans were then called). All this changed in the early nineteenth century with the emergence of the first Hispanic newspaper in America. According to Nicolás Kanellos, a professor at the University of Houston and director of the Recovering the Hispanic Literary Heritage of the United States project, "The first Spanish-language newspaper published in the United States was *El Misisipí,* founded in New Orleans in 1808 to advocate the independence of the Spanish colonies in the New World."[4] Not long after, the first African American newspaper, *Freedom's Journal,* was published in New York in 1827 by Samuel E. Cornish and John B. Russwurm. According to the Wisconsin Historical Society, "*Freedom's Journal* provided international, national, and regional information on current events and contained editorials declaiming slavery, lynching, and other injustices."[5] Less than 30 years later, in 1854, the first Chinese American newspaper, *Golden Hills News,* was published in San Francisco by Howard & Hudson. The publisher's note on the front cover of the inaugural issue read (in English):

> Merchants, Manufacturers, Miners, and Agriculturists, come forward as friends, not scorners of the Chinese, so that they may mingle in the march of the world, and help to open America an endless vista of future commerce.

This message of Chinese integration and contribution to the building of America was remarkably inviting in its tone, particularly in light of the persistent and institutional anti-Asian sentiments that would continue for decades to follow.

Although the geneses of the three publications spanned almost 50 years, they shared an important subtext that remains a key differentiator of targeted media even today. Namely, they aimed to not only present a fair and honest account of relevant news, but also to convey the political and social ideals that benefited their own interests. These early ethnic newspapers, like many of their successors, were also committed to uplifting and motivating their constituents, who lived against a backdrop of pervasive marginalization and disenfranchisement. The ideals of these three historic publications spoke to a shared desire for acknowledgment, respect, resistance against oppression, and a fight toward equality.

Not surprisingly, the readers of these early publications were almost exclusively Hispanic, Black, and Asian, respectively—a fact that remains true for ethnic newspapers today. But of the members of these already small factions, even fewer were literate. This meant few paying readers and financial struggle for most upstart ethnic publications. Nonetheless, their value was undeniable. They cultivated strong, trusting relationships with their ethnic readers, and helped foster a sense of ownership of experience and freedom of expression that persists in targeted media today. It's important to note, however, that both *El Misisipí* and *Golden Hills News* were bilingual publications. The pioneers running them were determined to get their views on racial politics out to the mainstream English-speaking public. Interestingly, their approach to bilingualism was not to simply translate the same in-language stories their primary audience read, but to provide separate English-language content geared to the mainstream audience. In fact, in their book, *Racism, Sexism, and the Media,* authors Clint C. Wilson, Félix Gutiérrez, and Lena M. Chao explain that *Golden Hills News* was founded "to reach the Chinese in San Francisco and foster a better understanding of them among Whites"—a dual purpose for a dual audience.[6]

As long as there has been media content geared specifically toward ethnic groups in America, there have been advertisers using those platforms to market goods and services to those consumers. Due to segregation and minority exclusion from many aspects of mainstream society, the earliest forms of targeted advertising were produced by ethnic business owners looking to connect with consumers within their own racial or cultural groups. In his book *Madison Avenue and the Color Line,* Jason Chambers, an associate professor in the Department of Advertising at the University of Illinois at Urbana-Champaign explains the origins of the "for us, by us" approach employed by Black-owned businesses:

> Throughout the late nineteenth and early twentieth centuries, racism and segregation drove most Black businesses to operate in an "economic detour" where they served an almost exclusively Black clientele.... Black business owners faced a two-edged sword: Segregation allowed them to set up profitable companies serving Black consumers, but it also prevented most from having access to larger markets serving white consumers.[7]

Even today, vestiges of this segregation continue to be the foundation of African American businesses that thrive within Black communities but have yet to experience success outside of it.

The second issue of *Freedom's Journal,* published on March 23, 1827, included what may be considered the first occurrence of advertising in Black press:

SOMETHING TO BE SAVED

CHARLES MORTIMER,

> Respectfully informs his customers, and the publick in general, that he has opened, and expects to continue, his shop, at 93 Church-street; where he will make and repair Shoes and Boots, in the best manner, at the following reduced prices:

New Boots	$6.00
Soling & Heeling Boots	1.00
Soling Boots	.75
Footing Boots	3.50

Although this ad was not "targeted" in the sense of appealing to specific cultural cues, the de facto nature of its audience was all Black, presaging the model supported by ethnic media platforms today. The phenomenon of using ethnic publications to reach an ethnic market was just as common among Hispanic and Asian businesses as among Blacks. Reaching out to one's fellow immigrants was, and still is, the default approach to navigating the foreign landscape of a new country. The media channels ethnic businesses used to sell to their own communities formed an important foundation for what would eventually become ethnic marketing. According to Félix Gutiérrez, a professor at the University of Southern California's Annenberg School for Communication, *El Misisipí* "set the stage for thousands of publications, broadcast, and Internet news outlets currently serving Latinos."[8]

Ethnic advertising evolved and grew with the market from there. As the nation rolled into the twentieth century and pushed through the hardship of World War I, ethnic printing presses flourished and spread throughout the country. While there are not reliable statistics on the number of ethnic publications at this point in history, scholars believe that the ethnic press was at its height in 1917 with an estimated 1,323 non-English titles.[9] This surge has been partially attributed to World War I, which caused a spike in interest in overseas news. While this figure does not take into account the figures for the English-language Black press, it too grew tremendously in the early 1900s.

In 1913, Claude Albert Barnett, a graduate of historically Black Tuskegee University, started a business. Inspired by the many magazine and newspaper ads he encountered at his job as a postal worker, he began to sell reproductions of photographs of notable Black figures by advertising them in African American newspapers. By 1917, this concept had flourished into a thriving mail-order enterprise. Following this success, Barnett started a cosmetics company called Kashmir Chemical and took on the role of advertising manager. As part of his due diligence in placing advertisements, Barnett conducted a comprehensive audit of the unmet needs within the Black newspaper industry. This process led him to found, in 1919, the Associated Negro Press (ANP), a news service providing Black newspapers with articles and other content relevant to their readers. In doing so, Barnett set one of the earliest examples of an end-to-end African American marketing strategy consisting of a target needs assessment, targeted product development, targeted advertising, and targeted media placement, which then led him to develop targeted content—all this, before even radio existed as a form of mass media.

In 1920 the first broadcast radio airwaves were licensed, breaking print's virtual monopoly over mass media. By 1928, there were three nationally syndicated radio stations, two owned by the National Broadcasting Corporation (NBC) and one by the Columbia Broadcasting System (CBS). Despite considerable barriers, ethnic media continued to develop in lockstep with the mainstream, albeit on a smaller scale. Pedro Gonzalez, a Mexican railroad worker, telegrapher, and gifted singer, immigrated to Texas in 1917 and then to California with his family in the 1920s and found himself in the heart of the technological revolution sparked by the burgeoning radio industry. Gonzalez began recording commercials in Spanish for small businesses throughout the West and Southwest. This led him to seek out his own commercial accounts, which ultimately supported a radio slot purchased on brokered time from mainstream radio stations. Gonzalez's show flourished through the early 1930s, featuring a number of top Hispanic musical acts, including his own group, the Madrugadores (the Early Risers). Like the ethnic newspapers that preceded them, the first Hispanic radio stations' existence relied heavily on local and regional advertising, which almost always came from Hispanic businesses. The fact that Hispanic stations were able to sustain themselves through the early years of broadcast radio underscores the power and tenacity of the market even then.

In 1934, the total number of radio stations in America grew to four with the founding of the Mutual Broadcasting System. At this time, radio existed mainly for entertainment purposes but was also used throughout the Great Depression and World War II to impart breaking news. During the war, restrictive radio licensing regulations that began to be enforced on non-English broadcasts presented a significant barrier to the progress of Hispanic radio. In the midst of this period, in 1944, Raoul A. Cortez, a Mexican radio show host and former reporter for the

Spanish-language newspaper *La Prensa,* applied for a license to broadcast his own radio station; he obtained his license two years later by positioning the station as a vehicle to mobilize Mexican Americans in support of the war effort, thereby skirting the government restrictions.

Although Hispanic radio was the first to break the color barrier in this new form of advertising-supported mass media, African American radio was not far behind, with the first Black station, WDIA, launching in Memphis, Tennessee, in 1949. These early advances in ethnic media paved the way for the present-day minority presence in television programming and advertising.

Against the backdrop of broadcast radio's growth, print media, which had been culturally segmented for at least a century, continued to evolve. In 1942, John H. Johnson, an office assistant at a Black-owned insurance company called Supreme Life, got the idea to create a Black publication modeled after *Reader's Digest.* He founded the successful *Negro Digest,* which reached a circulation of 50,000 in its first six months. Johnson went on to launch a number of other Black-targeted publications under the corporate umbrella of Johnson Publishing Company. He capitalized on the success of *Negro Digest* with *Ebony* magazine (which he modeled after *Life* magazine) and *Jet,* which took an entertainment-and-celebrity angle. Johnson later went on to found *Tan, Hue, Ebony Man,* and *Ebony Jr.,* giving him a lock on advertisers looking to reach the growing Black market. *Ebony* was his most successful publication by far, but he struggled to find advertisers in the first few years, a challenge he eventually overcame by starting a beauty product line that he sold through the magazine. It wasn't until 1947 that Johnson landed his first major advertiser, Zenith Radio Company. Legend has it he then sent a salesperson to Detroit every week for ten years until he landed the Chrysler account. While earning mainstream businesses' advertising dollars was difficult, Johnson's eventual success is attributed to his focus on the distinct needs and desires of Black consumers and his ability to position the African American market as a unique—and heretofore untapped—market opportunity for national corporations. In doing so, Johnson paved the way for mainstream brands to engage ethnic consumers.

EARLY MAINSTREAM USES OF ETHNIC IMAGES IN ADVERTISING

The history of ethnic imagery in mainstream advertising follows a quite different path than that of ethnic media. With the rapid proliferation of mainstream print media throughout the eighteenth and nineteenth centuries came an accompanying rise in cartoons featuring distorted and demeaning depictions of Hispanics, African Americans, and Asian Americans. As ethnic populations grew in major cities, public fear and outcry against these groups was reflected in editorialized caricatures. Since slavery did not officially end until 1865 with the passage of the Thirteenth Amendment, the White mainstream in the last decades of the nineteenth century shared a peculiar relationship with Blacks—a relationship steeped in institutional oppression, objectification, and abuse, but also complicated by the intimacy of domestic servitude. For this reason, it is not surprising that in the late 1800s, African American images began to be co-opted in the branding, packaging, and advertising of products of that era. Advertising scholar Marilyn Kern-Foxworth describes the White mainstream's attraction to the stereotypical Black image during the antebellum years in her book *Aunt Jemima, Uncle Ben, and Rastus*:

> Subsequently, manufacturers, advertisers, companies, and entrepreneurs who had to relinquish their rights to their "black mammies" and "black Sambos" declined to eradicate such images of blacks completely and very subtly had these caricatures resurface on advertising trade cards, bottles, tins, dolls, and the like—thus reinforcing the stereotypes that had been forged during slavery and offering comfort to those whites who had exonerated slavery as a necessary trade.[10]

In the 1880s and 1890s, tobacco brands like Nigger Head and Nigger Hair co-opted Black imagery in the most derogatory and offensive ways, featuring characters with exaggerated African hair and lips on their packaging. Throughout the last decade of the nineteenth century, household brands like Alden Fruit Vinegar, Rising Sun Stove Polish, and Durkee's Salad Dressing ran ads in such publications as *Harper's Magazine* that featured demeaning lifestyle snapshots of Blacks, with the accompanying captions written in crudely caricatured slave vernacular.

The use of Black caricatures was common, even among companies that are today household names. In the 1880s, Charles Rutt, one of the founders of Aunt Jemima pancake batter, decided to trademark the image of a portly, servile "Black mammy" character for his brand after watching a minstrel show that featured the then popular song "Old Aunt Jemima."[11] Although the company was acquired by Quaker Oats in 1926 and the image of Aunt Jemima has evolved throughout the decades, she remains on the product's packaging and in its advertising to this day.

In 1890, a year after the Aunt Jemima logo was trademarked, Emery Mapes, an owner of the Diamond Milling Company of North Dakota, introduced the character of Rastus (a derogatory name for older Blacks at the time) on his Cream of Wheat boxes in the form of a smiling chef posing with a bowl of the product, which he appeared eager to dish up. Throughout the following decades, the brand's ads depicted Rastus in a number of ignoble roles, including several scenarios where he is subservient to young white children. Incredibly, like Aunt Jemima, Rastus too remains on the brand's contemporary packaging.

Similar scenarios of mainstream brands co-opting stereotypical African American characters and vernacular continued through the first half of the twentieth century, with dozens of now-familiar brands like Uncle Ben's, General Electric, Listerine, Pillsbury, Pabst Blue Ribbon, Bass Ale, and others featuring unsavory depictions of Blacks in their ads directed toward a White audience.

Hispanics and Asian Americans faced an altogether different problem in that they were largely unrepresented in the advertising of the early 1900s. Their relatively lower proportions in mainstream society—driven by a number of factors related to geographic immigration patterns, endemic racism, and the natural formation of concentrated ethnic communities—rendered them virtually invisible. In the case of Asians, the government labored to keep them that way. As Marye C. Tharpe notes, "Waves of immigration from China and Japan in the nineteenth century were reduced to a trickle by strict quotas set forth early in the twentieth century that gave priority to European immigrants."[12] While fewer numbers may have resulted in fewer racist depictions of these two groups in American media, the lack of representation in mainstream media wouldn't be reversed until 1980 for Hispanics and 2000 for Asian Americans.

THE FIRST ETHNIC MARKETING COMMUNICATION AGENCIES

In the tense years leading up to America's civil rights movement of the 1950s and '60s, the earliest ethnic marketers were preparing to breach their own barriers—first by entering the advertising industry, a groundbreaking move in its own right, given the *Mad Men* milieu of White male dominance that permeated the industry—and then by rising within its ranks. Representation of minorities in advertising had grown significantly, yet there remained a stark contrast between two types of ethnic imagery—the mostly demeaning minority images in mainstream marketing, versus the far more positive ethnic advertising placed by ethnic business owners, hoping to appeal to their own communities. It was not until African American, Hispanic and, later, Asian American marketers formed the first ad agencies dedicated to reaching their respective ethnic audiences that the wheels of change were truly set in motion.

The African American Pioneers

While the media vehicles for reaching African American consumers existed (albeit to a very limited degree) by the mid-1950s, the legacy of segregation meant there was virtually no Black representation in American advertising agencies. As a result, when it came to reaching this market, cultural competency was non-existent. Some well-meaning advertisers chose the route of basic inclusion, which led to token casting choices—a Black character awkwardly inserted into an otherwise all-White cast. A few left their African American efforts in the hands of individual consultants and newly hired specialists.

Edward F. Boyd was one such specialist. Boyd was hired by Pepsi in 1947 to help the company better connect to the African American audience. According to his 2007 *New York Times* obituary, "Mr. Boyd hired some of the first Black advertising models, flooded Black papers with ads and added new sophistication and prominence to the ads already being published in magazines like *Ebony.* He created the first point-of-purchase displays aimed at minorities. His program also included having celebrities like Duke Ellington and Lionel Hampton give 'shout-outs' for Pepsi from the stage."[13]

Boyd wasn't the only Black marketer to advise a cola brand on how to reach Black consumers in the 1950s. Moss Kendrix was a pioneer of African American market analysis and one of the first experts in pitching the ethnic opportunity to mainstream businesses. Shortly after he graduated from Morehouse College in 1939, Kendrix joined the media industry and created a newspaper entitled *National Negro Newspaper Week.* After serving in the US Army in 1941, he worked in the War Finance Office of the Treasury Department, where he, along with a number of Black celebrities, promoted war bonds to African Americans on the radio. In 1944, after a stint as the PR director for the Republic of Liberia's Centennial Celebration, he started his own public relations firm, the Moss Kendrix Organization. In 1946 he wrote to

Coca-Cola and eventually landed a meeting where he presented a comprehensive proposal outlining how the beverage giant could go about converting the Black audience, which was far more loyal to the flavored sodas offered by a competitive brand called Nehi. Kendrix's proposal outlined a three-pronged strategy including (1) advertisements in the Negro press and at retail channels frequented by Blacks, (2) PR-supported sponsorships with leading Black celebrities like Jackie Robinson, and (3) sales promotions driven at ground level by an expanded force of Black salespeople. It took a few years, but Coca-Cola hired Kendrix in 1951, making him the first African American agency principal with a major mainstream account. While Kendrix's achievements were remarkable, it is even more amazing that his ethnic marketing strategy for Coke bears such a striking resemblance to the targeted strategies of today, despite significant changes in the social circumstances of Black consumers.

Kendrix and Boyd sparked remarkable changes; however, they were the exception, rather than the rule. The vast majority of brands were either not acknowledging Black consumers at all or still employing stereotypical images of Blacks in ads intended for their White mainstream audiences. And those mainstream advertisers who did seek to connect with African Americans had few models for how to do so in a sensitive and effective way. Then as today, there was a clear need for expert guidance in navigating the evolving role of Blacks in American society.

Two years after Johnson founded *Ebony* magazine, during the difficult days he spent soliciting advertisers to little avail, a Black graduate of the Art Institute of Chicago named Vincent T. Cullers was struggling to break his way into the advertising industry. "He made the rounds of the ad agencies in Chicago, and what he ran into was that they did not hire blacks," his wife, Marian Cullers, told *Essence*.[14] Cullers was eventually hired by Johnson Publishing Company in 1953 as a promotional art director for *Ebony*. In 1956, spurred by the events that sparked the civil rights movement, he left the magazine to start his own company, which he called Vince Cullers Advertising, Inc.

Although the agency struggled initially, reporting only $10,000 in billings in its first year, its impact on the industry was significant. For one thing, Cullers introduced the idea that ethnic marketing should consist of more than just a Black face in an ad. In an interview with *Black Enterprise* magazine, *Target Market News* president Ken Smikle explained, "What was fantastic about what Vince did was that he approached corporate America with the idea that rather than integrating Black people into a white concept of advertising, advertisers needed to buy into the idea of creating messages that resonated only with Black people."[15] Tom Burrell, CEO of Burrell Communications Group, told the *Chicago Tribune*, "[Cullers] established the template for targeted marketing in this country."[16]

By the 1960s, the Black Power movement was in full swing, and in 1968, Cullers's agency managed to land its first major mainstream client in Lorillard, makers of Newport, Kent, and True cigarettes. Rather than featuring Blacks in the same scenarios as Whites in mainstream tobacco ads, Cullers's ads for Lorillard featured a proud Black male wearing a dashiki. His next client was Johnson Products' Afro Sheen, a hair care line launched by George Ellis Johnson in 1954 to meet the unique needs of African Americans. Cullers continued to shape the new approach for reaching Black consumers by launching an Afrocentric campaign for the brand aligned with the Black Is Beautiful ethos of African American pride and empowerment the '60s had ushered in. The campaign's tagline, *Watu Wazuri* (Swahili for "beautiful people"), showed that Johnson Products had a finger on the pulse of contemporary Black identity, while also making a political statement with its brazen disregard of the White mainstream.

Cullers's agency also played a key role in the development of Black executives who would go on to start their own agencies. "For years, our agency actually functioned as a training ground for many young students seeking their first exposure to the ad industry," said Cullers in an interview with *The Black Collegian*.[17]

Cullers did indeed lay the groundwork for many African American agencies to come. Luminaries like Burrell, Byron

Lewis, and Frank Mingo were among the wave of enterprising Black marketers who founded agencies in the 1960s and '70s that stayed economically viable for decades. But many others didn't survive. According to a 1976 *Black Enterprise* article, the three top-billing Black agencies of 1973—John Small, Junius Edwards, and Zebra Associates—had all dissolved by 1976. However, all of these pioneering firms left behind a profound legacy. From their ranks came a second wave of African American advertising entrepreneurs in the 1980s who, boosted slightly by new government mandates incentivizing businesses to work with minority-owned vendors, continued the vision of the pioneers who came before them.

Although African Americans were the first group of color to establish dedicated agencies and national print media vehicles utilized by mainstream brands, their efforts in TV advertising were not as successful. In 1950, the Black actress Hattie McDaniel (the first to win an Academy Award, in 1939, for her role as a maid in *Gone with the Wind*) debuted the controversial role of Beulah in the eponymously titled show, which was sponsored by Procter & Gamble. Beulah was a maid in the "Black mammy" tradition, a stereotype that eventually prompted a condemnation of the show by the National Association for the Advancement of Colored People (NAACP). In 1956, Nat King Cole launched a 15-minute musical variety show. Its reign proved short-lived, though, because it could not secure sponsors—companies feared that White audiences would be turned off by their brands' association with Black programming. It was not until 1965 that the nation saw another African American leading character on TV, when Bill Cosby costarred in *I Spy*. This victory opened the door for a handful of other TV programs with Black leads in the '60s and '70s, such as *Julia* and *The Flip Wilson Show*. However, it was not until the 1980s that Black programming began to gain some momentum, and the first African American network, Black Entertainment Television (BET), was launched by Robert L. Johnson.

The Hispanic Trailblazers

In 1959, following Fidel Castro's overthrow of the Batista government in Cuba, a flood of exiled media professionals arrived in New York and Miami. Some were seasoned advertising executives leaving behind positions at the Cuban offices of blue-chip agencies. Luis Díaz-Albertini was one, having worked at McCann-Erickson and J. Walter Thompson's Cuban affiliate in Havana, and then at the Cuban agency Godoy & Godoy, where he had several international accounts, including Del Monte, Kellogg's, and Scott Paper Company (now Scott Brand). When he arrived in New York in 1959, he moved to the client side, working first for Carter Products, Remington Rand, and Standard Brands before taking a position at Vicks Chemical, where he headed up Latin American advertising.

In 1962, Díaz-Albertini founded Spanish Advertising and Marketing Services (SAMS), the first Hispanic advertising agency in the United States. Although this was six years after the first Black agency was created, the executives at SAMS entered the marketplace with already-established relationships with mainstream brand executives. And like their African American contemporaries, Díaz-Albertini and the other Hispanic marketing pioneers of the 1960s and '70s, including Rafael and Alicia Conill (Conill Advertising), Castor Fernández (Castor Advertising), José M. Cubas (Siboney USA), and Pedro Font (Font & Vaamonde Advertising) had a tremendous impact on how advertisers address Hispanic American consumers.

By the time these advertising pioneers arrived on the scene, New York City was experiencing an influx of immigrants fleeing Puerto Rico's widespread unemployment. At the time, marketing to Hispanics in the United States remained a regional effort, with two centers of activity in New York (Puerto Rican and, later, Cuban markets), and the South/Southwest (Mexican market). In other words, there was no singular US Hispanic market to speak of. To further complicate matters, because many of the agencies had historically handled the Latin American accounts for US brands, some struggled to win work intended for the US Hispanic market. Arlene M. Dávila describes this unique challenge in her book, *Latinos, Inc.:*

> Indeed, SAMS's early accounts, such as Lorillard cigarettes (makers of Kent and Newport), were initially commissioned for the Latin American, not the US Latina market, and key leaders of the industry such as Alicia Conill herself worked for Latin American accounts during their early years in the United States prior to working exclusively for the US Hispanic market. Thus, although Hispanic advertising agencies had been operating since the 1960s, the idea of a US Hispanic market would only become important in the late 1970s and early 1980s. Prior to that, Hispanic agencies advertised mostly for the local New York market or else represented clients in Latin America. Alicia Conill, for instance, recalled turning down Latin American accounts in order to convince clients to focus on the US Hispanic market as an exclusive and profitable market totally independent of Latin America.[18]

At the same time that the first Hispanic agencies were launching, Spanish media was also evolving. While African American advances were concentrated in print in the late 1950s and early '60s, the Hispanic market was on the brink of a historic entré into broadcast television. Spanish radio pioneer Raoul Cortez launched KCOR-TV, the first television network targeted to Hispanics in America, in Texas in 1955. A handful of other small networks followed in his footsteps, running strictly Spanish-language programs sourced from Latin America. Despite the bilingual roots of Hispanic media with *El Misisipí,* it was not until Desi Arnaz's historic role as the Cuban bandleader Ricky Ricardo on *I Love Lucy* (1951–1957) that an English-speaking Hispanic character was seen in mainstream television.

Cortez struggled, however, to find success with his network because it ran on UHF (ultra high frequency) receivers, which were relatively uncommon in Spanish-speaking households. In 1961, the same year that Diaz-Albertini started his agency, Cortez sold KCOR to a group of investors that included his son-in-law Emilio Nicolas, Sr. and Mexican entertainment mogul Emilio Azcárraga Vidaurreta. Azcárraga also acquired a Spanish-language TV station in California and went on to form Spanish International Networks (SIN), which acquired a number of additional Spanish-language stations over the years. In 1986, Nicolas sold his share of SIN to Hallmark and the Mexican network Televisa (headed by Azcárraga). The name of the network was changed to Univision, which eventually became the leading Spanish-language television channel in America.

Meanwhile, the first wave of Hispanic agencies had produced a new class of advertising executives focused on the US Latin market. As they slogged through the 1980s trying to convince mainstream marketers to engage with Hispanic consumers, the national TV networks played an invaluable role in the unification of a Hispanic market connected by a common language and similar cultures.

The Asian American Vanguard

The history of Asian Americans in advertising is much more recent than that of their African American and Hispanic counterparts; a number of factors related to a series of anti-Asian policies hampered the development of Asian American media throughout the nineteenth and twentieth centuries.

Following the launch of the first Asian American newspaper, the Asian press, fueled by the wave of Chinese immigrants coming to California for the gold rush, showed some promise into the late 1800s. By the end of the century, at least 26 Chinese newspapers (including bilingual publications like *Golden Hills*) existed in more than eight US cities. But the government dealt a severe blow to the burgeoning Chinese press when it enacted the Chinese Exclusion Act of 1882, severely limiting the flow of that country's immigrants to America.

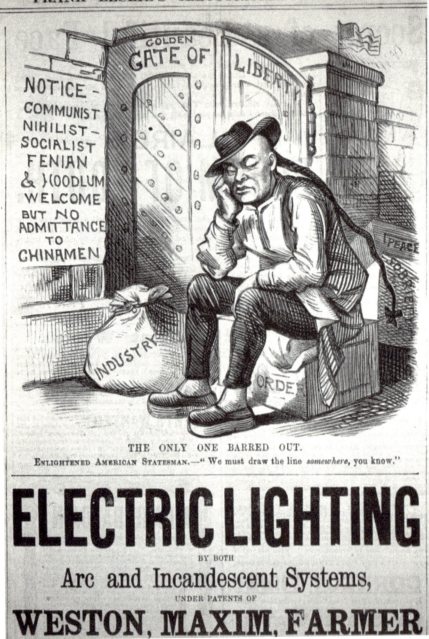

Figure 4.1   Caricature of a Chinese Man Outside the Golden Gate of Liberty, 1882

Source: United States Library of Congress

Despite this setback, the Chinese American press nevertheless continued to expand its foothold. The US newspapers provided an outlet for Chinese in America to freely express their views, unlike the censored press in their home country, and garnered the support of political patrons from China who traveled to the United States to promote their agendas back home. During World War II, progress slowed again as Chinese returned in droves to a homeland that was experiencing a period of peace.

A number of Japanese-language newspapers were also founded and flourished in the late 1800s. However, because their employees were mostly student day laborers, and literacy rates were low among the mostly uneducated farmers who emigrated to escape famine, the circulation of these papers was usually under 300. Also, the growing numbers of US-born Japanese who were English-dominant had little interest in the Japanese-language media of their parents' generation. The industry adapted by transitioning to bilingual content, some even changing to English-only formats.

This seemingly stabilizing move for the industry was once again hindered by a form of anti-Asian legislation. Following the Japanese attack on Pearl Harbor in 1941, Japanese Americans were considered a threat to US security, so the government began an internment program in which 110,000 Japanese Americans were moved to Relocation Camps between 1942 and 1946. Japanese newspapers were a casualty of this dark period in the history of American race relations.

Nevertheless, in the 1950s and '60s the Asian press rebuilt itself, and with the economic boom in Asia came a new group of newspapers in China, Japan, and Korea that were later introduced in the United States. The 1970s marked a period of increased immigration from various Asian countries, which provided these publications a much-needed readership, and they thrived from that point on.

This stabilization of the Asian press occurred at roughly the same time African American and Hispanic agencies were experiencing their second wave of start-ups and succeeding at placing ethnic advertising in their well-established print and radio vehicles. As Black and Hispanic media and entertainment professionals were fighting for fair and dignified representation in broadcasts, Asian American TV and radio were about to emerge simultaneously.

In the 1960s, Arthur Liu, a Chinese-born and Taiwan-educated disc jockey, was enjoying the success of his radio show in Asia focused on Western pop and rock and roll. He managed to find local celebrity in Taiwan through his music shows, which graced the airwaves of three different radio stations over the course of eight years. When Liu turned 30, he left to obtain a master's degree in communication at Syracuse University, and in 1972, after a stint at ABC—one of America's "big three" radio-and-TV networks at the time—Liu felt that he had enough communications experience to start his own company. That year he established Sino TV Incorporated, a Chinese-language TV service. Four years later, in 1976, he founded Sino Radio Broadcasting Company, which produced original Chinese-language radio programming, as well as the *Sino Daily Express* newspaper. In 1982, he created Multicultural Radio Broadcasting Incorporated, which established the first 24-hour Chinese-language radio station (KAZN), and ultimately, according to their website, became the "largest Asian American–owned radio group as well as the largest Asian American–owned television group in the United States."[19]

The expansion of Liu's empire in the early 1980s was not an isolated event in Asian America's progress in media and advertising. In 1981, a Korean man named Young M. Kim founded an agency called Pan-Com, a creative shop that also produced commercials. Kim eventually expanded the agency to a full-service marketing and communications firm, making it one of the earliest of its kind. It is still in existence after 30 years. Three years after Pan-Com, in 1984, Joe Lam, Lawrence Lee, and Wing Lee created their own agency, L3, which became the first US firm to develop and execute an Asian American–targeted campaign for a Fortune 500 company. The second half of the '80s welcomed a new wave of advertising pioneers like Eliot Kang and Kevin Lee, who founded Kang & Lee (now K&L) in 1985. David Chen—who, in 1986 joined Jo Muse's upstart agency as a managing partner—was instrumental in making Muse Cordero Chen one of the first agencies to serve Asian consumer segments as well as other ethnic groups.

Another watershed moment for Asian American marketers was the 1990 US census. Having addressed major shortcomings in its method for counting Asian households in America, the census was finally able to provide marketers with accurate information regarding this target audience. The statistics were promising regarding the growth and value of the grossly overlooked segment. In a document entitled *We the Americans: Asians*, which described the group's gains, the Census Bureau wrote: "We, the American Asians, number 6.9 million, a 99 percent increase since the 1980 census.... The percentage of Asians and Pacific Islanders in the total population also nearly doubled during the 1980s, from 1.5 percent to 2.9 percent."[20] The document went on to present the Asian market in America as a group with higher-than-average spending power, brand loyalty, and household size. This pivotal report painted the largely untapped market as a wide-open frontier, and from 1990 to 1991, three more Asian American agencies were founded: Imada Wong (later called the IW Group), DAE, and interTrend. In a 2010 interview, interTrend CEO Julia Huang described the impact of the 1990 census on her decision to found her Asian American–targeted ad agency:

Truly, the 1990 census was really the first time segmentation was done properly, in that Asian American/Pacific Islander was highlighted in the sense that it was looked at more carefully. Before then it was probably the best-kept secret, but then after the 1990 census, Asian American became, on paper at least, a very attractive market. All of these variables coupled together made it very simple to say, "Hey, people are paying attention to this segment. We think we could do better when it comes to communication." That's how we started.[21]

MOVING AHEAD

While the ethnic media and advertising pioneers of the nineteenth and twentieth centuries laid the foundation for the growth and increased sophistication of marketing to Asian Americans, Hispanics, and African Americans, the evolution of this industry did not stop there. The three largest US ethnic segments all have continued to make great progress in the past 30 years; however, their respective growth cycles have occurred at different rates. As a result, there is an intrinsic challenge to approaching "multicultural marketing" with one sweeping strategy. And the varied histories of each of these sectors help explain the sometimes strained and competitive relationships between African American, Hispanic, and Asian agencies today.

Despite significant variations among these groups' journeys thus far, they will find commonality in the next frontier, which, broadly speaking, involves the following seven phases:

1. Local/regional in-culture advertising within ethnic media platforms
2. Translated mainstream advertising within ethnic media
3. Tokenistic inclusion in mainstream campaigns
4. Originally produced, culturally infused messaging during ethnic holidays and events
5. Dedicated ethnic campaigns with heavy-handed ethnic cues (for categories with high ethnic penetration)
6. Ethnic inclusion in mainstream marketing at levels representative of their category penetration
7. Intelligent targeting, which acknowledges identity dimensions beyond ethnicity and race, employing well-informed cultural cues only when contextually appropriate

To be sure, each group is at a slightly different stage in this process. For example, by early 2011, African American marketing appeared perched between phases 5 and 6. Hispanic marketing seemed more firmly entrenched at phase 5. And Asian American marketing appeared to be somewhere between phases 4 and 5. In the following chapter, we will explore how advertisers and agencies are operating at various points along this continuum. Later, in chapter 7, we will share success principles for marketers at these points, and in chapter 8, we will paint a vision for the future of ethnic marketing, based on insights from industry thought leaders who are already beginning to map out a framework for more-intelligent targeting.

CHAPTER 5

What Companies Are Doing Now

While 84% of the marketers believe multicultural market-ing is "critical to my business," almost 40% said they don't know the financial value of multicultural groups to their companies.

—Advertising Age[1]

ETHNIC MARKETING IN TODAY'S BLUE-CHIP COMPANIES

Just as African American, Hispanic, and Asian American consumer markets have evolved at different rates, so too has the acknowledgment of and engagement with these segments by mainstream advertisers. Looking at a cross section of strategies employed by Fortune 500 brands reveals diverse approaches corresponding to distinct stages in the evolution of multicultural marketing. And sometimes even those at the same stage employ vastly different methods for connecting with ethnic consumers. In this chapter, we will examine the current ethnic marketing strategies of leading brands, hopefully learning something from their experiences navigating this often complex terrain.

Of course, it's important to remember that when we talk about advertisers *progressing* or *evolving* their multicultural approach, it assumes a fixed point in the future toward which most companies are moving, presumably a set of best practices designed for a time when ethnic minorities collectively comprise the majority. In this not-so-distant future, marketing communications strategies that fail to adapt will fall behind. The New Majority will select brands that reflect their transcultural realities while still acknowledging their ethnic nuances, leaving less culturally competent brands to history. The most effective players in this space will be nimble enough to use what we might call "intelligent targeting," wherein the relevance and expression of ethnicity is determined on a campaign-by-campaign basis.

There are certainly innovators in the current arena—companies and brands that have already embraced the fact that America is on the brink of a multicultural majority. But as we'll see in the following chapters, ethnic targeting is not necessarily the most relevant market-segmentation approach for every category or campaign. Ethnic efforts have proven most effective in the food and beverage, automotive, insurance, health and beauty, packaged goods, and financial-service sectors than in other categories. This is not to suggest that other categories should ignore these efforts; on the contrary, the relative success of these six sectors is partially due to their longer track record of connecting to ethnic audiences, and the course corrections they've made in response. The key for new players and old hands alike is to engage with ethnic consumers to the degree that makes the most sense for their particular business objectives. We'll lay out a road map for determining this in chapter 7.

To analyze today's marketing landscape, let's look at companies' behavior in the context of their respective degrees of engaging the New Majority. The methodology for arriving at these segments is qualitative, and should therefore be viewed as a general guide rather than a set of hard-and-fast rules. Our analysis had three main sources: (1) compiled secondary data on the ethnic marketing efforts and performance of several major brands; (2) interviews with chief marketing officers (CMOs), multicultural marketing directors (MMDs), principals of ethnic agencies, and other marketing professionals; and (3) firsthand experience providing research-driven consultation on multicultural strategies and executions to leading brands over a number of years.

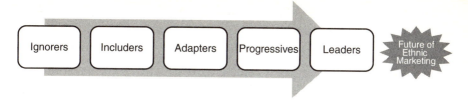

Figure 5.1   Evolutionary Segmentation of Brands Engaged in Ethnic Marketing
Source: Millward Brown, 2011

We propose that there are five categories that brands fall into (see figure 5.1), ranging from those that have completely ignored America's cultural revolution to those that have completely updated their approach to meet this new reality. Given the rapidly shifting nature of interactions with ethnic consumers—particularly in 2010, a census year—identifying where today's brands fall within these categories would probably lead to designations that would be outdated by the time this book is read. Instead, the model we will describe below may be more useful for determining which segments the brand(s) you work with align with generally, and then considering the corresponding marketing recommendations.

The future represented in this model is one where all brands are *intelligent targeters* that have fully updated their ethnic marketing approach. Companies that have already achieved this are few and far between but tend to be overrepresented in categories like technology and entertainment. In chapter 8, we will explore examples of brands that are well positioned for the future of ethnic marketing. For now, the focus will be on the vast majority of companies that have not yet reached this point.

Segment 1: Ignorers

The brands least engaged with ethnic consumers are the Ignorers, who do not acknowledge the existence of ethnic consumers within their current or potential customer base. For example, luxury brands sometimes fall into this group because of the myth that there aren't enough high-income minority households to address with an inclusive or targeted strategy. They point to sales figures and category indices that show that ethnic consumers are a negligible percentage of their customer base. Of course, in the case of luxury goods, the sensible target is customer with significant disposable income. Of course, in the case of luxury goods, the sensible target is consumers with significant disposable income. This market has traditionally skewed White due to long-standing economic disparities, and even though the affluent ethnic audience has grown considerably in recent years, companies have continued to overlook them. (Incidentally, Asian Americans are one of the most affluent yet least-often engaged ethnic segments in America due to their small population.) Recently, however, a handful of former Ignorer luxury brands such as Gucci, Hermès, and Jaguar have all recently engaged affluent ethnic consumers via targeted event marketing programs, allowing them to develop meaningful relationships (and valuable early leads) among these small but growing segments. But luxury brands aren't the only Ignorers. Many pharmaceutical companies have not begun to engage ethnic consumers, despite being one of the heaviest-spending sectors in the advertising space. In September 2010, former global CMO of Procter & Gamble Jim Stengel told a *Financial Times* reporter: "The consumers that are important to you today and into the future are Hispanic, African American and Asian American. How are you preparing for that?"[2]

Marketing Recommendation

Initiate a dialogue with ethnic consumers. An important starting point is foundational research that explores the relationship that African American, Hispanic, and Asian consumers have with your category and brand. Assess the effectiveness of existing marketing efforts in engaging these consumers as part of that exploratory research to gain a benchmark. Based on the insight gained, develop short- and long-term goals for improving the brand's engagement with ethnic consumers who fall within your target. It's not necessary to wait until the organization has achieved full cultural competency to start the dialogue. Dipping a toe in the water with small-scale ethnic marketing efforts is an important first step to developing a road map to a comprehensive ethnic strategy.

Segment 2: Includers

Includers only engage with ethnic consumers through general-market communications that are cast for some racial diversity. The omission of deeper cultural nuance in Includer campaigns reflects their arrival at this approach without a research-driven assessment of the role of ethnicity in category, brand, or media behavior. It is very difficult for Includer brands to perform optimally among ethnic audiences, because their product offering, their marketing, and their media plan all fail to account for potential distinctions driven by ethnicity. Includers operate under the assumption that ethnic consumers have the same behavior and attitudes as their non-Hispanic White counterparts. This is sometimes due to the perception that certain product categories, like personal care (e.g., deodorant, toothpaste, etc.), are commodities with ethnically neutral usage experiences. While the functional benefits of these products may be identical for ethnic consumers, the higher-order emotional benefits may differ across varying cultures.

It's important to note that *inclusive advertising* is not the same as *transcultural advertising,* which is based on the research-driven conclusion that there is a strategic territory where various ethnic and nonethnic segments overlap. This research is often overlooked by Includer brands. Includer brands may have incorporated diversity and inclusion in their human-resources strategy, but this is more often driven by external pressures to "do the right thing" than by a sincere belief that people of color should, and will, figure heavily in the next generation of their company's leaders. Not all Includer brands fare poorly with ethnic consumers. However, those that do well with these consumers tend to be in categories with lower cultural salience—say, highly technical categories such as computer hardware and stock brokerage.

Marketing Recommendation

Consider conducting exploratory research to determine the attitudes and usage patterns of White, Hispanic, African American, and Asian American consumers within your category. To the extent that there are distinct differences, consider layering your current approach with additional targeted efforts in low-investment areas of the marketing mix. Before going forward with these efforts, benchmark brand performance among this segment. Then test after the targeted activity to understand how much impact these efforts have had. If you see positive movement, replicate this activity in phases, first establishing a partnership with a skilled ethnic agency.

Segment 3: Adapters

Adapters are markedly more engaged with ethnic audiences than Includers, but still take a relatively traditional approach to multicultural marketing. They operate under the assumption that ethnic consumers are always different from non-Hispanic Whites and therefore require separate marketing executions. While the outcomes do support this assumption in some cases, this blanket approach is generally more successful among ethnic Boomers and mature consumers than it is among ethnic Millennials. Adapters rely heavily on ethnic agencies to translate general market strategies into culturally relevant communications. These agencies are typically retained by the brand's multicultural marketing director, who is often steeped in the traditional ethnic marketing model pioneered in the 1960s and '70s. As a result, their marketing efforts tend to reinforce the arguably antiquated divisions between mainstream and ethnic segments. Despite robust multicultural programs and budgets, Adapter companies place relatively little emphasis on transcultural insights, total-market strategies, or crosscultural communications. A common pitfall for Adapters is the overemphasis of cultural cues in campaigns, which sometimes eclipse the brand message or reinforce stereotypes, thereby alienating the growing audience of consumers who resent the assumption that race is their most important identifying characteristic. Among the heaviest-spending brands in ethnic media, Adapters are a robust segment, especially in categories such as fast food and automotive.

Marketing Recommendation

Consider each new marketing opportunity as a blank slate. Rather than assuming that ethnicity will be a key segmentation variable, do a bottom-up assessment of the target audience's attitudes and behaviors, and then determine the ethnic makeup of that consumer profile. The "general market" campaign should reflect a similar degree of diversity. If there are cultural dimensions to this profile that make it "a stretch" to reach the various ethnic subsegments with a single communications approach, then proceed with distinct ethnic campaigns and programs that speak to each group in the most relevant way.

Segment 4: Progressives

While Progressives typically boast a well-established multicultural department that supports the brand's marketing teams as internal consultants, their separate so-called general-market and multicultural efforts are still fairly divided, as with Adapters. A major difference between Adapters and Progressives is that the latter segment is in the process of increasing their cultural competency, often with the assistance of ethnic agencies. Progressive companies are dipping their proverbial toes in the water when it comes to implementing transcultural insights, diverse general-market strategies, and/or crosscultural communications. As a result, their marketing efforts are beginning to reflect the diversity of the new majority. These companies have not fully abandoned the traditional approach to ethnic marketing, but their targeted efforts have begun to acknowledge the diversity within the respective ethnic segments. Most Progressive brands have conducted or sponsored segmentation studies among their key ethnic constituencies, which allow them to zero in on important subsegments of ethnic groups, like bicultural Hispanics or crosscultural segments like Urban Mindset Consumers. Progressives don't rely solely on ethnic agencies when marketing to non-White consumers, which has prompted some criticism from the traditional ethnic marketing community.

Progressives are well on their way to meeting the New Majority landscape; however, they occasionally overstate the transculturalism of their younger targets with formulaic executions depicting an unrealistically wide range of races. Progressive companies are commonly found in categories like packaged goods, insurance, and retail.

Marketing Recommendation

Consider maintaining your current direction with regard to ethnic marketing. Follow the lead of your ethnic agencies, and continue to push the envelope by reflecting the diversity of the new majority in general-market communications. Remember that transcultural insights need not always be conveyed by characters from the full rainbow of ethnicities in order to be effective—consumers will enjoy it less if it seems forced. In other words, there is no formula. Test the best ideas from each of your agencies with all key segments to determine which ones are most effective among different ethnic groups and within the general market.

Segment 5: Leaders

Leader brands are fully committed, from the top down, to the idea that the mainstream is multicultural. Ethnic marketing is integrated throughout their corporate culture, which manifests in a number of ways. Some have made all marketing managers responsible for multicultural growth by making it a key performance indicator in employee reviews and tying it into incentive compensation. Others have embedded multicultural experts across all marketing teams. Leader companies tend to employ both general market and multicultural agencies, with an established protocol for interagency collaboration at the strategic level. Most importantly, their corporate leadership has sent a clear message, both internally and publicly, that ethnic populations will drive their companies' growth moving forward. These companies' human-resource initiatives and employee resource groups, as well as their general-market research, strategy, and marketing communications, usually reflect the diversity of the new majority.

Moreover, Leader brands' targeted efforts acknowledge the diversity *within* each respective ethnic segment. Their search for the best idea goes beyond blurring the lines between generalist versus specialist agencies. Not only do they occasionally allow their ethnic agencies to pitch general-market work, they are also pioneers in enlisting the aid of crosscultural shops. The categories with the most Leader brands are usually those where ethnic consumers overindex heavily, such as food and beverage, health and beauty aids, entertainment, and certain packaged-goods categories.

Marketing Recommendation
Continue on the path that you have already forged. Take steps to ensure that all your agency partners feel valued and that they are being fairly compensated for equal work.

Wild-Card Segment: Consolidators

An important segment that is difficult to represent in the above model is the group of brands we will call the Consolidators. Consolidators are former Adapters or Progressives that still publicly maintain the views associated with those segments, but have dismissed their ethnic agencies and are now relying on one or two ostensibly culturally competent general-market agencies in the name of efficiency. Consolidators are particularly controversial because they were once considered to be in the vanguard. Before it was fashionable or politically correct, they earmarked sizable budgets for multicultural efforts, but now they have moved into the more controversial "postracial" territory. Burger King was perhaps the most infamous Consolidator brand of 2010 due to its decision to dismiss their ethnic agencies and assign African American marketing responsibilities to one of their general market agencies while assigning the Hispanic marketing to a newly created division of another. The fast-food giant claimed that its move toward consolidation was an attempt to reflect the blurring of ethnic lines among its core young-adult target. For other

Consolidators, the Great Recession of the late 2000s sparked a sudden need to justify, and then eliminate, all extraneous marketing efforts. Simultaneously, general-market agencies were positioning themselves as culturally competent total-market experts. Consolidators seized the opportunity to reduce the considerable cost of retaining multiple ethnic specialists by having a centralized agency (or agency group) handling all of their marketing efforts.

Consolidators can certainly tout a unified brand message as the benefit of this approach. However, the Achilles' heel of this segment is the lagging ethnic representation and expertise in the general-market agencies on which they rely to develop their ethnic campaigns. The jury is still out on the effectiveness of ethnic campaigns developed by general agencies, which often understand the theory and data behind targeted insights but may be deficient in the more nuanced aspects of cultural targeting.

Marketing Recommendation

If ethnic consumers remain a key target of your overarching strategies, and you plan on developing targeted campaigns in the future, consider reenlisting the guidance of agencies that are ethnic (targeting a particular segment), multicultural (targeting several ethnic segments separately), or cross-cultural (targeting several ethnic segments together). Whether or not the agency is composed of all or mostly minorities is not the determining factor; rather, the depth of its expertise with engaging ethnic consumers is what matters.

THE MODERN ETHNIC AGENCY MODEL

It is impossible to discuss segmentation of the marketing landscape without addressing a parallel segmentation in the advertising-agency sphere. To do this, we must look at the historical development of ethnic agencies from the 1980s to today. While the previous chapter dealt with firsts in media and advertising, the story of modern multicultural marketing picked up steam with the proliferation of niche agencies in the 1970s.

Following the ethnic marketing trailblazers of the 1940s and '50s, building upon their success, the second generation of ethnic agencies in the '70s were largely independent shops. On the Hispanic side, such agencies were glorified translation outfits whose primary goal was to achieve basic brand awareness and message comprehension for the Hispanic population. But with the massive wave of Hispanic immigration in the 1980s came an increase in the number of Hispanic-market-focused agencies, bolstered by the expertise their principals had imported from blue-chip agencies back home.

African American agencies also grew in size and number throughout the 1980s, driven in part by the increasing number of Black advertising professionals who had started at general-market agencies but flocked to niche agencies after encountering glass ceilings. Many of these African American firms benefited from the "separate but equal" approach that mainstream brands were taking with Black consumer marketing. While their approaches to reaching Black consumers were initially driven by anecdotal observation and firsthand experiences, through the 1980s and '90s, a few of the more established Black agencies pulled ahead of the pack by implementing more formal research and planning practices that helped them quantify the market opportunity. Ron Franklin, a pioneer in integrating research and strategy at Black agencies, recounted this important shift in a 2010 interview:

> I think it was that whole notion of using the research and strategic planning, and showing the value of the [Black] consumer. We started talking about a ten-million-dollar man and all that kind of stuff. That's when we started tracking how important this consumer base was in terms of money, showing [client brands] it was worth something out there.[3]

Since this time, each decennial census has played an integral role in moving ethnic marketing forward. The 1980 census clearly established African Americans as the largest minority segment.

Black agencies flourished in this atmosphere of clear in-group/ out-group delineation. Many leading companies migrated from a position of hiring Black agencies because it was the right thing to do to hiring them because it was the smart thing to do. In fact, many African American agencies were retained by leading brands simply because they were "of the culture" and therefore privy to important firsthand knowledge of the Black experience. For the most part, the Black agencies of the '80s and '90s focused on the African American segment exclusively, with the exception of a notable few, such as Muse Cordero Chen and GlobalHue (then Don Coleman Associates), which were among the first truly multicultural agencies to address all three major ethnic groups equally.

With the 1990 census came the establishment of Asians as an emerging growth segment, which led to the development of the Asian American agencies discussed in the previous chapter. But owing to the nature of agency budgeting, many mainstream brands approached the ethnic opportunity in a hierarchical manner. Throughout the '90s, African American segments were prioritized over the Hispanic and Asian segments. So, when absolutely necessary, general-market executions were translated into Spanish under the guidance of Hispanic agencies, but the lion's share of earmarked "multicultural" budgets went to efforts to attract African American consumers. After all, most businesses had a longer history of engagement with Black consumers and had seen the fruits of those labors in increased market share.

Then came the 2000 census, and everything changed. The Hispanic population had surpassed the Black population, and in a knee-jerk reaction of epic proportions, the pendulum swung back. Brands that had barely bothered translating general-market campaigns into Spanish were now begging savvy Hispanic agencies for deeper ethnic insights.

The African American firms didn't blink at a little competition, though. Rather, vying for their pieces of potential clients' precious multicultural budgets bred a competitive spirit that led the Black agencies to develop more complex research-based segmentations and target strategies. These agencies, along with their Asian counterparts, flooded their clients with a sea of information on their respective segments. The blue-chip general-market agencies took notice, and in a continued trend of holding-company acquisitions, began to buy up these multicultural outfits to hone their ethnic capabilities.

The 2010 census has had a similar impact on the ethnic marketing landscape in America. While its real implications may not be felt for years to come, there is certainly a buzz in the marketing community about the importance and size of each of the three leading ethnic segments. Asian and Hispanic marketing professionals are particularly anxious to apply this new data to their target models, and several have already begun to do so. However, as we explained in chapter 1, the story this time around is not merely about individual ethnic segments. It is about their collective size and growth, and projections that they will outnumber the non-Hispanic White population before 2050. This is a challenge to the traditional model of neatly bracketed agency delineations. The emergence of the new majority demands a transition from the old construct to a new paradigm that assumes a multicultural total market.

THE CONTEMPORARY ETHNIC AGENCY

For the most part, ethnic agencies operate the same way now, in the twenty-first century, as they did in the golden era spanning the second half of the twentieth century. The marketplace, on the other hand, has evolved considerably. There is a marked gap between the cultural perspective of traditional multicultural agencies (particularly at the corporate level) and the more diverse and transcultural reality of ethnic consumers. Given these agencies' histories, we can use a similar segmentation to the one we earlier applied to the advertising companies (see figure 5.2). As in the previous section, the rapidly evolving field means that segment designations for specific agencies are likely to be outdated in a matter of

Figure 5.2   Evolutionary Segmentation of Ethnic Ad Agencies
Source: Millward Brown, 2011

months. However, the characterizations may help an agency determine which segment applies to them, and react accordingly.

As was the case with the brand segmentation offered above, this model is a rough snapshot of where the majority of the ethnic agencies fall along the continuum oriented toward the future of ethnic marketing. The same methodology as described above was used to arrive at these segments, which are meant for directional use, and are not exhaustive or quantitatively conclusive.

Segment 1: Traditionalists

Traditionalist agencies are, some say, a dying breed. They tend to cling steadfastly to the idea that Hispanic, African American, or Asian consumers experience their entire world through ethnic-tinted glasses, and therefore always require separate communications for optimal effectiveness. Their clients are Adapter brands who share their belief that each consumer group is best served by an agency comprised solely or predominantly of in-culture strategists, creative directors, and account people. And because their employees tend to lack racial, generational, or socioeconomic diversity, the work produced by these agencies often fails to effectively reflect the diversity of the specific ethnic segments they serve. They have deeply entrenched relationships with their clients and some anxiety about new blood rising in the ranks at these brands. Traditionalist agencies are often headed by principals who themselves came up in an era of separatist race politics and, as such, are acutely sensitive to the challenges facing ethnic businesses. They see themselves as fighting for survival in the transitioning world and are vocal critics of the idea that race is becoming less and less of a driver to consumer behavior. Traditionalists consider ideas like "crossculturalism," "efficiency," and "consolidation" threats to their raison d'être.

As a result, the work that comes out of these shops tends to reflect an exclusively Spanish-dominant Hispanic, Black, or Asian world, which is difficult for younger and/or bicultural consumers to relate to. The understandable desire of Traditionalist agencies to justify their role relative to their general-market agency counterparts often leads them to dial up cultural cues to the point where storylines and characters come across as stereotypical.

Marketing Recommendation

Refusing to adapt to the new marketplace doesn't slow down the changes. In order to stay alive, focus on what makes the consumers that you target similar to other segments, rather than focusing on what makes them different. You won't be edged out by conceding that ethnic customers are now part of the general market; however, if you aren't able to create work that speaks to the new majority, you will be. Remember that clients want great ideas, regardless of where they come from.

Segment 2: Progressives

The ethnic agencies with the longest survival rates tend to be those that adapt to the evolving marketplace—which accurately describes the Progressives. These multicultural agencies, more diversely staffed than their Traditionalist counterparts, often service more than one ethnic segment. Progressives also tend to have greater expertise in research and strategy and as a result have developed sophisticated models for segmenting and profiling their primary audiences. Like the Traditionalists, many of the Progressive agencies were founded by ethnic-advertising pioneers; however, these principals have based their work on the fundamentals of solid marketing strategy, rather than a race-specific aesthetic. Furthermore, these agencies have kept pace with the changing nature of the segments they serve by infusing their ranks with new young hires. Progressive agencies take care to position themselves as cultural experts with deep experience in market segmentation. Instead of resisting or resenting the challenges posed by the evolving marketplace, they have turned their smaller size (relative to their general-market counterparts) into an asset, developing nimble and creative strategies to reach not only ethnic cohorts, but also the mainstream that these groups in turn influence. As a result, Progressives are starting to see some of their ethnic executions being used in general-market campaigns, as with Bromley Communications, which the American Advertising Federation awarded with an ADDY in 2009 for its Yoplait "Peel" campaign. These ads were originally developed on behalf of General Mills for Hispanic audiences, but were ultimately used for the general market campaign.

Progressives have successfully fought for, and gained, a seat at the table with clients and their general-market agencies. In doing so, their role has been upgraded from merely developing culturally relevant creative expressions out of mainstream strategies to cocreating the strategy aimed at all ethnicities. Because of this, their work tends to rely less on heavy-handed cultural cues; the substance of the campaigns they are assigned is already relevant. In fact, Progressives are poised to become the advertising agencies of record for brands in categories that overindex heavily among ethnic consumers.

Marketing Recommendation

There is a distinct home-court advantage to being an agency with ethnic roots that also has the creativity, capabilities, and resources to speak to the total market. Continue to diversify your agency's offerings. If you are able to deliver effective and resonant creative for various ethnic segments, chances are you can create compelling general-market work—especially against the new majority audience that will continue to grow over the next 40 years. You may not have the same resources as general-market agencies that are becoming increasingly culturally competent, but the age of digital, mobile, and social media is an imminent game-changer that will help close the gap. First, however, you must become savvy in reaching consumers of all types (including the ethnic growth segments) via these transcultural platforms.

Segment 3: Avant Gardes

The Avant Gardes are a controversial group of agencies and practices, comprised mostly of small and relatively new start-ups. Unlike the Traditionalists and Progressives, these agencies were founded on a crosscultural platform, with a simultaneous focus on the unique attributes of ethnic consumers and the mainstream audience to which they belong. Their clear focus on a variety of ethnic and cultural segments, rather than just one, sets them apart from their competitors. Leaders operate under the principle that the mainstream is multicultural and any execution hoping to gain traction with a general market must include ethnic insights. They also believe that any culturally targeted communication must take into account that minority consumers are just as diverse as the mainstream market of which they are a part.

Avant-Garde agencies tend to be run by younger principals than those at the helm of Traditionalist and Progressive agencies, and they have remarkably diverse staffs. However, they also tend to be smaller and less established, and they have fewer resources. As a result, much of their work comes on a project-by-project basis, and they tend not to be the agency of record, ethnic or otherwise, for their clients. Because Avant-Garde agencies keep pace with the new majority marketplace, they are ahead of the curve relative to the brand landscape. But clients still see agencies as either general-market or ethnic specialists, the Avant Gardes are difficult to put into one category or the other. Further complicating matters is that not all of these agencies are standalones: Some are wholly owned subsidiaries of general-market agencies, and some are specialty practices within them. This nontraditional approach invites a firestorm of criticism from the Traditionalist agency ranks, claiming these subagencies and practices are a thinly veiled attempt to compete with ethnic agencies for the impending wave of multicultural business in the decades to come. While Avant-Garde agencies have seen intermittent success in the past, there is some indication that their potential for sustained growth will be at its height in the coming years, as new census data affirms their transcultural approach.

Marketing Recommendation

In order to succeed, you must first fully understand and then be able to sell the concepts of total-market strategy, transcultural insight, and cross-cultural communication. Clients might need to be educated and have their hands held throughout this process, because it flies in the face of how ethnic marketing has been approached since its inception. Create a portfolio of successful case studies among smaller brands that award you big assignments, and then bigger brands where you are given small assignments. This will breed confidence among clients and help you work out the kinks that are bound to pop up given the uncharted nature of this territory.

CHAPTER 6

To Target or Not to Target

In the previous section, we looked at the overall approach companies are taking to targeting the New Majority and incorporating multicultural insights into their so-called general-market initiatives. Chapters 6, 7, and 8 will focus on what many call *targeted* strategies. We begin by determining when it is necessary to develop targeted initiatives to reach the New Majority, especially the ethnic or minority segments within it. Then we explore some general guidelines for what tends to work well and what does not. To this end, we draw on the extensive qualitative and quantitative research Millward Brown has done on the topic throughout the years, and combine that information with interviews of leaders in the field. Finally, we consider the voice of the most important player in the game—the consumer.

First, let's clarify what we mean by targeted strategies. Several definitions have emerged within the industry over the years as the concept itself has evolved alongside multicultural marketing. For our purposes, we work with a broad definition, using the term to describe any strategy or initiative that has been developed to reach a specific segment of the population. For instance, when it comes to advertising, our definition would include campaigns that are created from scratch with a specific ethnic segment in mind as well as campaigns adapted from existing mainstream pieces. Our analysis compares the effectiveness of each approach at reaching the target segment at hand.

It's important to remember that while most people tend to associate targeting almost exclusively with advertising, targeted approaches can apply at virtually any point in the marketing process. From a product-development standpoint, targeting means creating products or services with a specific group in mind or adapting mainstream products or services to better appeal to different segments of the population, whether by changing flavors, tailoring fees, or just providing a relevant translation in their packaging. Commercialization strategies, too, can be targeted by having a different store layout or product mix in areas that are majority-minority. And media allocation often involves choosing between Spanish and English when trying to reach Hispanic consumers, or buying ad space in Black-targeted options such as BET and *Ebony* when going after African Americans. We'll analyze all of these often overlooked but very important initiatives in this and the following chapters.

For obvious reasons, our discussion of targeted strategies is heavily focused on the idea of ethnic targeting; that is, strategies aimed at Hispanics, African Americans, Asian Americans, or any other ethnic group in the country, including in some cases non-Hispanic Whites. However, the ethnic component interacts with many other characteristics of the population when it comes to developing targeted initiatives, which can span subgroups within the total population or even within the ethnic segments themselves. A campaign might seek to reach gays and lesbians across all ethnic cultures or moms of any race; another could be super-specific: aimed at Mexican Hispanics, Black immigrants, Asian yuppies, White older males, etc. Our analysis looks at a wide variety of possible situations and the approaches that work best for each.

WHY DEVELOP TARGET MARKETING?

Simply put, the rationale behind target marketing is that it's efficient and effective: Initiatives tailored to specific groups yield better results than those that try to reach the entire population with a single message or strategy. Companies around the world have been doing it for decades, and their techniques have evolved over time and for many reasons. Chief among them are (1) the fact that consumers are always changing, evolving, and becoming more sophisticated, and (2) advances in digital technology allow companies to profile and reach very specific subsegments of the population, approaching the ideal of one-on-one marketing. As a result, target marketing, which began as a fairly straightforward proposition based on demographic variables, has become a very advanced discipline incorporating key attitudinal and lifestyle parameters in addition to obvious factors like race.

The basis of any target-marketing initiative is segmentation, which essentially consists of dividing the market into homogeneous subsets of consumers who share similar characteristics, needs, and behaviors. There are two main types of techniques for market segmentation: inductive and deductive. Using the *inductive* techniques, a population is grouped according to preestablished parameters such as age (e.g., young, middle-aged, senior), residence (e.g., urban, suburban, rural) or product usage (e.g. light, medium, heavy), to name a few. You choose the variables to use to guide your research based on your preexisting knowledge of the population. This is the simpler of the two approaches.

The second approach, *deductive* segmentation, is not based on preestablished parameters. Instead, researchers ask consumers several questions around the topics of interest and group them by their responses to these questions using advanced statistical techniques (cluster analysis). Naturally, the outcome depends heavily on the topic questions or variables included. If, for example, you're doing a segmentation for the automotive industry, you'd want to include questions about car usage, attributes desired in vehicles, and any other relevant variables, whether attitudinal or demographic. The advantage of this type of segmentation is that it provides a more nuanced and impartial view of how the market is structured. However, its results are more challenging to implement in market.

When it comes to multicultural marketing, most companies are still using inductive techniques. They are segmenting the market using the preestablished criteria of race or ethnicity, following the assumption that race or ethnicity is a discriminating variable within the market. As we saw in chapter 2, this is true: Hispanic, Black, Asian, and other ethnic consumers *are* different from non-Hispanic White consumers. However, they're not on completely different planets. Ethnic consumers do have several things in common with non-Hispanic White consumers, as well as with one another. Interestingly, the differences (or similarities) between ethnic consumers are not static across industries, or even specific situations.

Within the beauty sector, for example, we would expect clear and distinct attitudinal and physical needs among different races or ethnicities; in more basic categories, such as toilet paper, we would not. So, while in some cases it may be valid to use race or ethnicity as a preestablished method to segment the market, in some cases it might not make much sense, especially in such areas as product development. In the case of toilet paper, for example, variables like household size or income would be the relevant ones. Our job as marketers is to identify when race and ethnicity matter and when they don't. To do so, we must think like consumers. In our qualitative research for Millward Brown, we've found that while race and ethnicity are relevant for consumers, they are not necessarily top-of-mind. For most, it is just one of the many factors that define them, not the *only* one, as we marketers tend to believe.

So, Ethnic Targeting... Do We Really Need It?

As you have probably gathered, there is no absolute answer to this question. The need for ethnic targeting depends on many variables: the industry, the specific product or service being sold, the stage within the marketing process during which targeting is proposed, the desired audience, the budget and timelines, and so on. Nevertheless, the analysis of real-life examples, case studies, and empirical data yields some general guidelines. We focus on three aspects of the marketing process:

1. *The product or service—or the end benefit that is provided to consumers*
2. *The communication, or how this end benefit is expressed to consumers*
3. *The media, or the context(s) within which this end benefit is expressed*

Although most of the discussion around targeted marketing has dealt with the last two points, advertising and media, we believe that the product or service itself is even more important, as it directly relates to the end benefit consumers will experience. If this end benefit is not relevant from an ethnic standpoint (or any other standpoint) even the best communication and media won't create success in the long term.

1. Targeted Product or Service

In Marketing 101, we learned that products and services are developed to satisfy specific consumer needs. Marketers' typical product-development process goes something like this: (1) Identify the unmet needs of the target audience via research; (2) Determine how the company could satisfy those unmet needs; (3) Develop the product or service; and finally, (4) Market it to the target audience using an appropriate launch strategy, which of course includes a communications component. Although this concept seems obvious now, the product-development process wasn't always so logical. In the early days, when marketing wasn't such a centerpiece of corporate strategy, the process went the other way: Companies would create or develop a product or service based on their capabilities, and then decide who to sell it to and how. Back then, consumers had to adapt their needs to the products or services available, rather than companies adapting their offerings to the needs of consumers.

What does this have to do with multicultural marketing in the twenty-first century? A lot. When it comes to ethnic consumers, what we marketers face—intentionally or not—is a similar situation. We have a product or service we know satisfies the needs of our non-Hispanic White consumers. We know this because we do our homework: We ask consumers what their unmet needs are, and only after that do we develop products and services to satisfy those needs. When we go after any of the ethnic segments, however, we typically use the same product or service, assuming that the unmet needs of both ethnic and non-Hispanic White consumers are the same—which is not always true.

Having a clear understanding of the intended end benefit of your product or service is enormously helpful in deciding whether you need to adapt it to ethnic consumers. Think about it. People do not need *mobile phones,* per se—what they really need is to be in touch with other people. That is the end benefit, the basic human insight. While mainstream consumers might need a cell phone to connect with friends and family in the United States, Indian Americans are likely to also need it to remain close to their relatives back in India. Knowing both the universal and specific end benefits that these phones provide across ethnic segments can help telecommunications companies decide whether they need to adjust their calling plans or not. By the same token, it also helps them determine whether they need to develop a different communication approach tailored to their ethnic customers.

A common denominator we've noticed among companies that have mined product-development opportunities to reach ethnic markets in the United States and in other multicultural societies is that industries or categories that are *closer* to their consumers—such as retail, where interactions take place face to face—have a greater need to create or at least adapt their offering to minority segments. As a result, they are frequently innovators in this space, leading the way for categories that do not encounter their consumers very often. Retail providers have been early adopters of multicultural marketing, whether in financial services, clothing, restaurants, supermarkets, or any other format. Companies in these categories are in direct contact with their customers on a daily basis, so if they have locations in areas with ethnic diversity, they must fully understand the unique needs of these consumers versus those of the mainstream. These companies also avail themselves of a tremendous amount of data, whether it is collected in a formal and structured way or as informal feedback from store managers and employees interacting with consumers on the floor. Savvy retailers know how to exploit this information.

Wells Fargo is without a doubt one of the pioneers in this arena. The company started targeting Hispanic consumers on a basic level more than a century ago by using Spanish-language advertising and hiring bilingual agents in California. In 2001, Wells Fargo became the first major financial institution in the United States to accept Mexico's *matricula* consular cards as one of the forms of identification needed to open a checking account—an initiative targeted to Latinos who did not have proper US documentation. By 2003, the company had opened 250,000 accounts for immigrant customers using this document.[1] Today, Wells Fargo has several ethnic marketing initiatives ranging from product development to communication strategies, and the rest of the major banks in the country are catching up.

Of the many factors that have contributed to the success of financial institutions targeting Latinos, the provision of in-language services has been one of the strongest, especially with immigrant or less-acculturated customers. Financial terminology is difficult enough in one's own language, and understanding it can be quite an impossible task for foreigners, especially if they are not familiar with the range of services on offer. In-language written communications, websites, and customer service make the process easier for Latinos and other non-English-speaking consumers.

Industries that are not in such close and direct contact with their consumers likely need to adapt their products or services at some point as well—for example, the personal care or beauty category. The skin of a Black woman is different from the skin of an Asian or a White woman, and therefore requires different products, not only in terms of obvious aspects like colors, but also in terms of products that work better for her specific skin type. The beauty concerns of women of color are not always the same as those of White women, either. A clear example of this is uneven skin tone. While White women associate this issue mainly with acne scars, the causes of uneven skin among women of color also include discoloration and dark marks, or *manchas,* among other things. Products developed with the ethnic segment in mind address these very issues, and brands typically communicate these specific benefits when reaching out to women of color. Given the growth opportunity this market represents, it is not surprising that major brands like Estée Lauder, Avon, and L'Oreal have developed ethnic-specific lines to join brands like Black Opal on drugstore shelves.

Another big category in which companies are likely to need to tailor their products to consumers within minority segments is food and beverage. Different ethnic groups have different tastes and eating habits. Some are heavy users of spices; others tend toward more neutral flavors. Some value natural ingredients and the idea of preparing meals from scratch; others are more open to packaged ingredients and prefer easier-to-prepare meals. As part of its "Leading with Ethnic Insights" corporate strategy, McDonald's has several success stories to tell on this front. A recent one is its McCafé products. According to Rob Jackson, marketing director of the African American consumer market for McDonald's Corporation, the obstacles the brand faced among Black consumers were that they are generally less engaged with "café culture" and are more averse to bitter coffee taste. Further, they found that McDonald's lacked coffee credibility within this segment—hence the need to offer value across its beverage portfolio. The company leveraged various aspects of the marketing mix to win this segment. First, it introduced new products for a more balanced beverage portfolio: smoothies and sweeter coffee-based beverages, such as caramel mochas, for the African American palate. Second, materials installed at the point of purchase captured a "sweet indulgence" positioning and provided education to consumers. Third, the promotions targeted this base. The creative for espresso-based products highlighted the "sweet indulgence" beverages, featured celebrity integration to lend the "cool factor," and included sampling at local and national African American lifestyle events such as First Fridays, *Essence,* and a specially organized McCafé Real Moments, Real Fruit Smooth Fusion tour, in which an upscale smoothie lounge on wheels traveled across the country allowing consumers to experience the latest taste of McCafé in engaging ways. Lastly, the pricing structure included midtier beverages to bridge the gap between value and premium drinks—and all were competitively priced versus competitors.

In the food sector, preferences go beyond taste or flavor; some are a matter of lifestyle or religion. Let's take a look at the case of halal food and the Muslim community in the United States. *Halal* is a term designating any object or action sanctioned by Islamic law. With regard to food, Islam has specific laws regarding which foods can and cannot be eaten and also on the proper method of slaughtering an animal for consumption, known as *dhabihah.* Finding halal food in the United States has been a difficult task for Muslim consumers, who at first had to rely on specialized stores or the Internet. Things are changing. Acknowledging the business potential of this industry, companies such as McDonald's (which already has a popular halal menu overseas) and Walmart have entered the halal arena. A relatively new brand, Saffron Road, has also managed to capture the attention of the American Muslim community by providing not only certified halal frozen entrées, but entrées that are also all-natural, with meat from animals that were 100% vegetable-fed, antibiotic-free, and hormone-free. The natural-grocery giant Whole Foods began selling the brand in August 2010, which is, according to Lisa Mabe, founder and principal of Hewar Social Communications, "a major win for halal consumers, who have expressed that it's hard to 'keep halal' in the United States."

In addition to retail initiatives, Saffron Road is utilizing the full range of tools in the PR arsenal to create and maintain relationships with consumers. "Facebook acts as our conversation hub for Saffron Road, as that's where so many consumers are talking about food, and specifically halal food. Other initiatives we continue to have success in are reaching out to key Muslim bloggers, providing contests and coupons, and giving consumers a chance to give us their opinions," says Mabe. Given the natural nature of its offering, the brand is hoping to make inroads among mainstream consumers as well, tapping into the market for eco-conscious and all-natural products.[2]

Although *halal* most commonly refers to food, the concept applies to other aspects of life as well, and nonfood brands are starting to cater to this segment. In 2009, Best Buy acknowledged a Muslim holiday for the first time in a national advertisement: Eid al-Adha, or "Festival of Sacrifice," which commemorates the willingness of Ibrahim to obey God by sacrificing his son. That year, Eid al-Adha fell around Thanksgiving, so the ad, a small bubble containing a holiday greeting for Muslim consumers, appeared at the bottom of the page in the company's Thanksgiving circular. Unfortunately, the initiative generated some negative reactions, with critics seizing on the timing of the initiative in their complaints, and more specifically on the fact that it coincided with Thanksgiving celebrations. In spite of the complaints, Best Buy executives stood by their decision, arguing that the initiative was part of their broader strategy to reach out to ethnic consumers in the country. "Soon, Muslims started calling to thank Best Buy and set up a Facebook page honoring the company, which continues to acknowledge Muslim holidays."[3]

Returning to the food category, an interesting twist is that the adaptation of products now goes in both directions. More and more, rather than adapting mainstream products to the taste of ethnic consumers, companies are expanding ethnic products to mainstream tables. The most famous (and probably oldest) examples are salsa and tortillas, which have been outselling ketchup and white bread for several years. However, more and more products are steadily abandoning the so-called ethnic aisles in supermarkets, joining the wide variety of mainstream offerings. Among these are PepsiCo's Manzanita Sol apple-flavored beverage, ACH Foods' Mazola cooking oils, and of course, Corona beer, to name a few. We also see evidence of this in fashion. As we become more diverse, styles are combining, and designs are likely to be influenced by one or more cultures at the same time.

Companies in less obvious sectors are also adapting their products and services to better satisfy the needs of ethnic consumers. From telecommunications to automotive services, from healthcare to funeral homes, there is almost always a way to tailor a product or service. However, it's important to find the right balance between customization and standardization. We are in no way suggesting that all cemeteries within Hispanic communities should plan celebrations for El Día de los Muertos (Day of the Dead), which is a Mexican holiday that focuses on social gatherings to remember friends and family members who have passed away. As part of the celebrations, people build private altars using sugar skulls, marigolds, and the favorite foods and beverages of the departed. Partying is a common practice as well. Ethnic segments are diverse. In the case of cemeteries, companies would need to better understand what countries of origin are predominant among its customers, as El Día de los Muertos is a predominantly Mexican tradition that is not commemorated in the same way across all of Latin America.

Finally, targeting need not mean adapting or developing products tailored to ethnic segments. In some cases, it could be as simple as including a translation in the product's packaging. Indeed, the number of brands including a language other than English in their packaging is countless nowadays, especially when that language is Spanish. While developing bilingual packaging sounds like a relatively simple task, there are some best practices worth considering if you want to avoid mistakes that can harm consumers' perceptions of your brand:

- First and foremost, make sure that you do a good translation. Do not rely on acquaintances or colleagues that supposedly speak the language.
- Try to use the most neutral version of the language you are translating to. Among Hispanics, for example, you can find many versions of the Spanish language. Going for a neutral version that stays away from any type of regional slang is a safe way to avoid misunderstandings.
- Avoid interspersing the English and translated versions of your packaging. This will confuse both your English and non-English-speaking customers. Separate both versions in a clean format.
- Translate only what really needs to be translated. Do not overload your package with text.

For retail outlets, "packaging" can refer to the store layout and general ambiance. Targeting efforts could include everything from basic bilingual signage (which retailers such as Sears, Target, and The Home Depot have in their "ethnic stores") to a transformation of the entire store and product mix to better appeal to ethnic consumers in the area. The "Supermercado de Walmart" stores that opened in 2009 in Houston and Phoenix are examples of the latter. Both stores feature a new layout and product assortment designed to be relevant to local Hispanic customers. They offer a wide selection of fresh produce; a bakery with fresh-baked bread, including traditional favorites like *bolillo* and hot tortillas; a meat department featuring specialty meats; and a wide assortment of dry goods and consumables from brands popular in the United States and in Mexico. According to the retailer's press releases at the time, the stores aimed to introduce a new and authentic shopping experience that will better serve the needs of the community.

The list of companies adapting their offerings to ethnic consumers could go on and on. However, as in almost any business decision, the choice to adapt or not should be put through a thorough cost-benefit analysis. And because all ethnic segments—including non-Hispanic Whites—live in this country together, we must be careful to ensure that whatever outreach we do for one segment does not alienate consumers of other ethnic groups. A good way to prevent such situations is to include consumers from all ethnic segments in the initial stages of your product-innovation research. This will allow you to identify early on whether you will need to adapt your offering. It will also let you explore the feasibility of crafting an offering that can provide an end benefit to consumers of different cultural or ethnic backgrounds.

2. Targeted Communication

Advertising is the area of marketing that has been most active in terms of targeting ethnic segments. Companies have made great progress with it over the years, thanks not only to the expertise they have developed internally, but also to the support of advertising agencies specializing in one or more of these segments (as discussed in chapters 4 and 5). Advertising is also where much of the research has been concentrated, from the early stages of idea generation and copy development all the way to in-market results. Thus the advertising sector is the best source for actual data on whether targeted initiatives are really needed when trying to reach minority segments.

Based on our primary research for Millward Brown and our many conversations with experts in the field, we can affirm that, in general, targeted communication does a better job than non-targeted or mainstream advertising when trying to reach ethnic consumers. However, the use of targeted communication does not guarantee success. This important maxim applies to virtually any type of communication, via traditional or newer platforms, and is true across all ethnic and minority segments. For instance, a common misconception about the African American segment is that because Blacks speak English and consume mainstream media, there is no need to develop any targeted communication to reach out to them. Yes, it is true that Black consumers are exposed to mainstream communication, but when it comes to an advertisement's effectiveness, our data clearly suggest that well-crafted targeted initiatives do a better job than mainstream campaigns.

A similar misperception exists regarding the Hispanic market. Many marketers still tend to think that *cultural relevance* is synonymous with *Spanish language* when it comes to Latino consumers. Yes, language is an essential variable, and we discuss it in detail later, but the use of in-language communication alone does not always make for effective advertising. In fact, given the rapid growth of the bilingual segment, language could potentially be a limitation if not handled intelligently. In-*culture* communication is far more important. Of course, the same principles apply for non-English-speaking Asian segments and other immigrant groups.

Let's look at some of the evidence that supports this. What follows is an analysis of our TV copy–testing database, which is the most robust of its kind in terms of quality and quantity of data. The implications are equally valid for any type of communication, from radio and print to out-of-home, online, mobile, and social media. In fact, given that many of these newer platforms provide marketers with more options to effectively reach out to specific subsegments of the population, they have greater potential to develop targeted strategies than a traditional medium like TV, which is mass-market by nature. Newer platforms allow you to cross the racial component with consumer traits such as age and gender, all the way to lifestyle, opening up the opportunity to develop messages that are relevant to consumers at many levels.

Before we dive into the analysis of our copy-testing data, here are a few background details about the sources used and our general approach to advertising evaluation. Millward Brown has been doing research among ethnic consumers for many years, starting well before the shockwaves sent by the 2000 census. At the beginning, research was sporadic and usually done as part of the work done for the mainstream market—say, by increasing the number of ethnic consumers within mainstream samples to levels that allowed them to be read separately. However, in the past decade, we have been doing more and more research that is specific to minority groups, on both the qualitative and quantitative fronts. We have built a sizable database that includes targeted and nontargeted advertisements, evaluated by minority and mainstream consumers. (We have more than 700 targeted ads in our ethnic databases and more than 12,000 ads in our total US database, which includes more than 50,000 ethnic respondents evaluating mainstream work.) While it can't possibly address every ad produced and aired, it does provide an excellent representation of categories and industries.

Our proprietary copy-testing methodology, Link, takes a holistic approach that looks at the many different factors that contribute to the success (or failure) of advertising: enjoyment, engagement, branding, emotions, message communication and understanding, brand associations, persuasion and its drivers, and so on. We use these metrics to compare the effectiveness of targeted versus nontargeted ethnic communication by grouping them into three buckets: the creative, the message, and the persuasion. For the purposes of this analysis, we'll focus on two segments specifically, Hispanics and Blacks, the groups for which the most data is available. Although the copy-testing approach is the same for all groups, the data in the analysis has been indexed to address differences in data collection methods (primarily online for the general population and African Americans and face-to-face for Hispanics) and also to address the fact that Hispanic and African American consumers have different response patterns to surveys, both compared to the general population and to each other. Having clarified these methodological aspects, let's examine the findings.

Targeted Communication Does a Better Job Than Nontargeted Advertising

Figure 6.1 compares the performance of targeted versus nontargeted communication by looking at how Hispanics and African Americans evaluate commercials that were developed or, in some cases, adapted with them specifically in mind (i.e., targeted), versus how they evaluate commercials that were created for the population at large, with no deliberate intention of reaching out to any ethnic consumers in particular (i.e., nontargeted). It shows that consumers in both segments are likely to respond more positively to the targeted communication. This phenomenon is observable across the board, including the metrics related to the creative itself, as well as the actual message and its persuasiveness.

Since targeted performs better than nontargeted advertising across all three buckets, it's interesting that most advertisers rethink or adapt only the creative (the format) for ethnic consumers, rather than the actual message or end benefit (the content), which usually remains the same across all ethnicities. This data suggests that even in cases where an ethnic advertisement's message is similar to that of a brand's mainstream communication, telling the story in a culturally relevant way can have a positive impact on consumers' perceptions and reactions. For example, one of the variables that is positively affected by this effort is believability of the message. Consumers seem more likely to accept the information in the ads when the situation (and, if applicable, the characters or speakers) is relevant to them from a cultural or ethnic perspective. Of course, in the end, believability and relevance also depend largely on the content of the message itself. Consumers are smart enough to discern it.

However, Targeted Communication Does Not Guarantee Success

Averages can sometimes be deceiving. If you limited the analysis to just the data discussed in the previous paragraphs, you

Creative Metrics

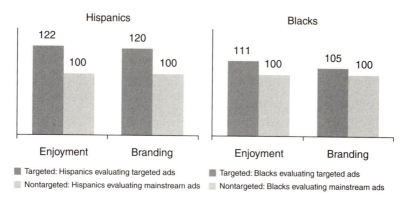

Targeted: Hispanics evaluating targeted ads
Nontargeted: Hispanics evaluating mainstream ads

Targeted: Blacks evaluating targeted ads
Nontargeted: Blacks evaluating mainstream ads

Message Metrics

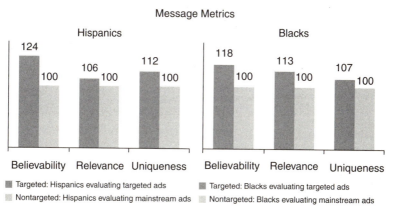

Targeted: Hispanics evaluating targeted ads
Nontargeted: Hispanics evaluating mainstream ads

Targeted: Blacks evaluating targeted ads
Nontargeted: Blacks evaluating mainstream ads

Persuasion Metrics

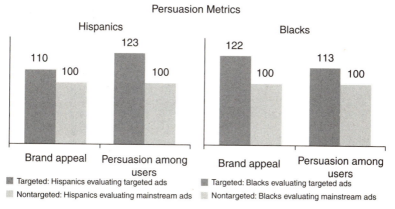

Targeted: Hispanics evaluating targeted ads
Nontargeted: Hispanics evaluating mainstream ads

Targeted: Blacks evaluating targeted ads
Nontargeted: Blacks evaluating mainstream ads

Figure 6.1   Performance of Targeted versus Nontargeted Communication among Ethnic Segments

Source: Millward Brown, 2011

Ratings have been indexed for comparison purposes

would conclude that ethnic targeting is *always* needed if you want to be effective in your communication with minority consumers. Wrong. Ethnic targeting is not automatically more effective, and is certainly not always more efficient. To achieve the level of success demonstrated by our database, ethnically targeted advertising also needs to be *good* advertising—just like any other winning campaign.

Figure 6.2 compares targeted versus nontargeted communication among Hispanic consumers one more time. However, the nontargeted advertising in this case is dubbed advertising—commercials that were originally created for the general market, but were translated into Spanish at a later point to target Hispanic consumers via Spanish media. Language was the only change made to these ads; creative, casting, message, and everything else stayed the same. Zeroing in on this type of ad makes the comparison more objective since language is a limitation for some Latino consumers and might negatively impact the potential of what otherwise could be considered a very good piece of advertising. For the analysis, our database was divided into thirds or tertiles—top, middle, and low—based on the advertisements' performance. Figure 6.2 is based on overall enjoyment of the ads, although we found comparable results using other key metrics, like branding and message communication.

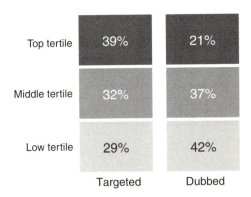

Figure 6.2   Hispanics' Enjoyment of Advertising
Source: Millward Brown, 2011

In figure 6.2, you also see that targeted advertising is more likely to fall into the top tertile (39% of all targeted ads in our database do so), while dubbed ads are more likely to fall into the low tertile (42% of all dubbed ads in our database do so). However, many targeted ads fell into the middle- and low-performing classes as well (32% and 29%, respectively). So while we see some targeted ads performing well, it's also possible to have poor-performing targeted pieces. On the other hand, although nontargeted advertising is less likely to do well among Hispanic consumers, there are exceptions. Of the dubbed ads in our database, 21% fell in the top tertile, while 37% fell into the middle third.

In addition to highlighting the impact of targeted communication in general, the above analysis offers another important lesson: When it comes to Hispanic consumers, targeted communication should not be limited to merely translating mainstream advertising, a practice that was common in the early days of the Hispanic marketing industry. Our data reveals that targeted ads that go beyond mere translation increase their chances of success. Rather than considering language an end in itself, it should be viewed as a possible means to communicate a message to Latinos in a more relevant way. We will revisit this topic in more detail in chapter 7.

In a comparable analysis among African Americans, figure 6.3 upholds the idea that targeted communication tends to perform

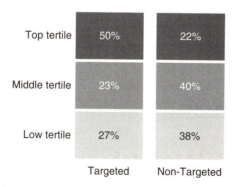

Figure 6.3 Blacks' Enjoyment of Advertising
Source: Millward Brown, 2011

better. Fifty percent of targeted ads in our database fell in the top tertile, while 38% of the mainstream ads evaluated by Black consumers fell in the low tertile. However, there are also low-performing targeted pieces (27%), as well as mainstream ads that were rated highly among Black consumers (22%).

The data shows that to the first maxim—that targeted communications do not guarantee success—we can add that *basic advertising principles* do *apply to ethnic segments.*

So, do we really need targeted advertising when trying to reach ethnic consumers? The answer is, it depends. As we have seen, targeted communication usually does a better job than general-market advertising in conveying what it intends, but it does not guarantee success. In the end, you must not forget that ethnic advertising is nothing more and nothing less than advertising to *people,* and therefore the standard principles of creating great advertising apply.

To be successful, ethnic advertising—like advertising done for any type of consumers here and around the world—must be backed by powerful creative that is strongly linked to the brand and a compelling message that is easy to understand. If you are able to do all of these things in a *culturally or ethnically relevant* way, you can definitely increase your chances of success. However, what often happens is that marketers and agencies are so focused on trying to be ethnically relevant, on trying to find that magic cultural element that will resonate with a given segment, that they

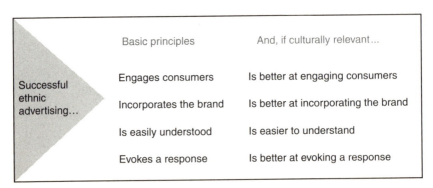

Figure 6.4   Elements of Successful Ethnic Advertising

Source: Millward Brown, 2011

forget all the other required elements. The result in these cases is an ad that traffics fluently in Hispanic or Black culture but says little about the advertised brand.

3. Targeted Media

Most marketers believe that targeted marketing gets a big organic boost when it's placed in targeted media. They think that ethnic segments are likely to be reached in a more effective and efficient way via targeted media, and it allays concerns about the possible downsides of exposing their mainstream consumers to ethnic-targeted messages. We analyze the validity of these observations below.

Effectiveness and Efficiency of Targeted versus Nontargeted Media

Fact: Ethnic consumers, whether they are Hispanic, Black, Asian, or of any other racial or ethnic background, alone or in

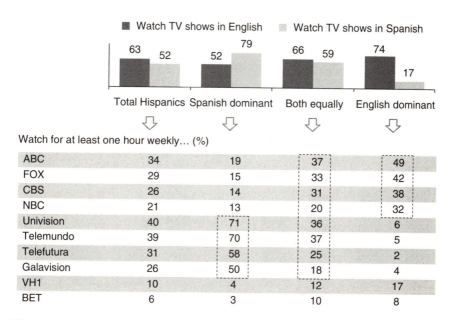

Watch for at least one hour weekly... (%)	Total Hispanics	Spanish dominant	Both equally	English dominant
ABC	34	19	37	49
FOX	29	15	33	42
CBS	26	14	31	38
NBC	21	13	20	32
Univision	40	71	36	6
Telemundo	39	70	37	5
Telefutura	31	58	25	2
Galavision	26	50	18	4
VH1	10	4	12	17
BET	6	3	10	8

Figure 6.5 TV Consumption among Hispanics, by Language Dominance at Home (%)

Source: The Futures Company's Yankelovich MONITOR Multicultural Study, 2010

combination with other groups, consume both targeted and non-targeted media.

There is plenty of data from a wide variety of sources that support the above statement. The numbers shown in figure 6.5 come from The Futures Company, which is part of the Kantar Group. In its 2010 Yankelovich MONITOR Multicultural Study, they looked at media consumption habits of Hispanic, African American, and non-Hispanic White consumers. Focusing on TV consumption, figure 6.5 tells us that Hispanic consumers watch both Spanish- and English-language programming. Not surprisingly, Spanish-dominant Hispanics are more likely to consume more Spanish media, and English-dominant Latinos consume more English options. Bilingual Hispanics consume both in similar levels.

Figure 6.6 summarizes comparative data for the African American segment, showing that Black consumers watch both media targeted to them specifically (e.g., BET, TV One, VH1, CW) and mainstream channels.

These numbers vary among different subsegments of the Hispanic and African American markets, and also by media. Nonetheless, the main point here is that ethnic consumers are in fact exposed to both targeted and nontargeted media, and therefore can be reached by either option with the right media plan in

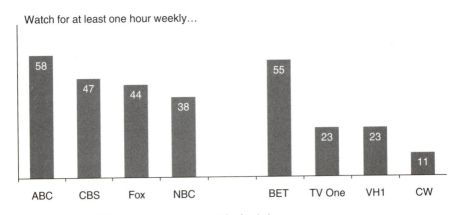

Figure 6.6 TV Consumption among Blacks (%)

Source: The Futures Company's Yankelovich MONITOR Multicultural Study, 2010

place. The problem is that many in the industry insist on a single viewpoint, wherein minority segments consume *only* targeted media, which can get in the way of choosing the media plan that is right for your brand. In the end, the decision should be based on the target audience, the specific message you want to communicate to consumers, how frequently you want it to be seen, and, of course, how much money it will cost. Although there is no magic recipe for maximum efficiency, we recommend evaluating all the options, especially as the dual-consuming bicultural group continues to grow. It is also important to remember that ethnic consumers do not necessarily choose media based on whether it is targeted or not; they decide based on what is relevant to them in a specific moment in time. Sometimes the racial component plays a role in this decision, and sometimes it does not. Among Millennial consumers, for example, we have found that decisions are more likely to be driven by lifestyle rather than race or ethnicity.

In addition to the efficiency factor, you definitely want to choose the media plan that is the most effective at communicating your message to consumers. And by effectiveness we don't just mean traditional metrics like reach. You must also consider the context in which your communication is placed, and the impact this context might have on consumers' perception of your communication. This is valid not only for ethnic segments. In any mainstream work, companies look at the type of programs during which their advertising airs, or the type of websites in which their digital pieces appear. For example, how consumers receive your advertising can be very different depending on whether it is placed in a game during a FIFA World Cup game—when passions run especially high among Hispanics—in a cheesy and super-sentimental telenovela, or during the evening news.

There are basically two schools of thought regarding the use of targeted versus nontargeted media when going after ethnic segments. While some believe that a culturally relevant context has a positive impact on advertisements, others contend that ethnic consumers are likely to prefer a brand that they feel addresses them as part of the mainstream. The rationale for the latter approach is that minorities expect to see or listen to targeted communication in targeted media (i.e., they expect to see in-culture advertising in Univision or BET); it is "their" media. However, they don't expect that to happen in mainstream media (at least not that much nowadays), so they do appreciate it when it happens. We believe that both approaches are valid, and that the decision should be made on a case-by-case basis, also taking into consideration how targeted communication is perceived by mainstream consumers, or any consumers outside the ethnic target at hand.

Impact of Ethnic Marketing on Non-Hispanic White Consumers

Although placing targeted advertising in mainstream media is a relatively recent trend that started around 2005, early data suggests it is indeed a viable option. The fact that the mainstream itself has become so multicultural largely accounts for this. This doesn't mean, however, that non-Hispanic White consumers will accept all types of ethnically targeted communication. While in some happy cases the cultural component also resonates with mainstream consumers, in others it can be alienating. A third possibility is that general-market consumers don't understand the cultural element, and the message is lost.

One much-discussed type of targeted communication in mainstream media is bilingual advertising. In 2006, Millward Brown had the opportunity to study a bilingual commercial in English and Spanish that Toyota aired for its Camry Hybrid during the Super Bowl. Although the ad was not necessarily created to target Hispanic consumers, it was unusual for a brand to broadcast a bilingual TV ad during such a high profile and archetypally American event. The ad showed a father driving a car with his son. The kid asks why they have a Hybrid, and his father tells him that it is for the sake of his future—then goes on to explain the advantages of the hybrid system and how it helps the environment, among other things. During the explanation, the father switches into Spanish a couple of times. The son then asks his father why he learned to speak English. The father again responds that he did it for his son's future.

In our research, we looked at the reactions of both mainstream and Hispanic consumers, including Latinos at all three levels of acculturation. Overall enjoyment of the ad and reactions to its message were fairly consistent across the board. However, in metrics evaluating the relatability of the characters and situation, bicultural Hispanics were significantly more likely than other Latinos and the mainstream to rate the ad highly. In this specific case, we also observed that the use of a bilingual dialogue did not have a negative effect on mainstream consumers, presumably in part because the Spanish dialogue was limited to just a few familiar words. However, when testing other commercials that used more Spanish words or sentences, we started to see some negative reactions among non-Hispanic consumers—either because they couldn't understand the language or simply because a language other than English was being used in ("their") mainstream media.

The lesson here is that past certain limits, targeted communication placed in the usual mainstream media outlets can alienate non-Hispanic White consumers or even, in extreme cases, generate negative reactions among them. The key is understanding those limits, which can vary significantly from situation to situation. The good news is that as we move toward a more diverse society, these limits will further blur. We will return to this last point in chapters 7 and 8.

Technology and Targeted Marketing

Technology—specifically platforms like the Internet and mobile devices—is creating infinite opportunities for marketers to develop and execute targeted initiatives to reach out to ethnic consumers. Unlike TV or other types of traditional media, these newer platforms allow companies to segment the market using a much wider array of characteristics, far beyond traditional demographics. As a result, marketers can develop and target content that is truly relevant to consumers—not only from a racial or ethnic perspective, but from every aspect that defines who they are as consumers and human beings. Although we're not quite there yet, technology is getting us closer and closer to the ideal of one-on-one marketing.

The way users interact with Facebook exemplifies the potential of target marketing in the digital realm and provides a unique model for addressing the racial or ethnic factor at the same time. Unlike TV, a medium in which marketers place commercials that are intended to appeal to masses, in the Facebook world it is actually the users who create the "advertisements" and push them out to all of their friends, and the friends of their friends. The fact that these messages are consumer-generated and come from people you know certainly increases the possibilities of you finding them relevant, especially because it is very likely that your and the sender share several things in common, one of which may be race or ethnicity. If a young Pakistani American woman finds out that a beauty brand has just launched a new line of products featuring colors that complement her skin color, it is likely that she will forward that information, probably adding some comments of her own, to other Pakistani American users within her list of Facebook friends. Chances are that the message will be relevant to its receiver in several layers: as a woman in general, as a person of color, as a Millennial, and perhaps as a person whose religion has certain rules around the use of make-up products that are different from those of the mainstream woman, to name a few.

Facebook does not even ask users whether they belong to any specific racial or ethnic group. As with the messaging factor described above, this task also relies on the users themselves. "We don't try to figure out if somebody is African American or Hispanic. We don't really attempt to do that.... It's only going to be the things that [the users] have chosen to tell us, as opposed to us trying to figure out what their ethnic background is," explains Brad Smallwood, director of monetization for Facebook.[4] Users are likely to share only the information about them that they consider important. If race or any race-related topic does not come up spontaneously for one user, then that means that race is not top-of-mind for that user—and companies should not attempt to force the racial factor in its communication to him or her. Instead, they should pay attention to the variables the user did talk about—like being gay, for instance. Approaches like this have the opportunity to effectively address the biases that labeling often generates.

CONTENT, FORMAT, OR CONTEXT?

In this chapter, we discussed the effectiveness of targeted versus nontargeted marketing from different perspectives: the end benefit we provide to consumers (our brand promise), the communication (which in addition to the message itself, includes the format through which we communicate it), and the media (the context in which our end benefit is communicated). Is any one of these aspects more important than the others? Can they be prioritized in terms of budget? We believe not; they are equally important and, furthermore, interdependent. All three are crucial to the success of your targeted marketing strategy.

If your content, end benefit, or brand promise is not relevant to ethnic consumers, no matter how you sell it in advertising, it will fail in the long term. If your product or service is indeed relevant to multicultural consumers, but you are not able to get the attention of those consumers through your communication, they will never become aware of it. And if your message is not placed in the right media or context, it might not come through as intended—or might not come through at all.

WHAT DO CONSUMERS SAY ABOUT TARGETED MARKETING?

Marketing is all about consumers. So, as part of the research we have done for this book, we conducted several focus groups with Hispanic, Black, Asian, and non-Hispanic White consumers, to better understand their perception of targeted advertising in general. We did this by exposing them to several examples across the spectrum, from ethnic-targeted ads to mainstream ads that had no ethnic component, with some variations in between.

Ultimately, we found that they do like and relate better to targeted communication. However, this is not necessarily because they see this type of advertising as being *ethnically* targeted to them. Naturally, ethnic consumers do not have their race or ethnic background top-of-mind at all times—when they are out shopping for a car, for example, they do not think, "I am Chinese, so I will buy this type of car." Or, as one Black participant told us verbatim, "I don't shave in any particular way because I am Black!" Across all groups, our participants communicated that their race or ethnicity is just one of the many factors that define their personality, and not necessarily the most important. Who they are, their culture, their identity, is defined by their age, gender, marital status, income, personality traits, health, sexual orientation…the list goes on and on.

Yet this fact is hardly reflected by the current industry approach. For marketers in general—and especially multicultural marketers—race and ethnicity are often front and center. As a result, we sometimes force the racial or ethnic aspects within our marketing, which can generate a negative reaction among consumers, especially when they cross the line into stereotyping. The best way to mitigate this is to avoid the extremes. Consumers like and relate to cultural elements, but they want these elements to be incorporated into advertising in a subtle way. They want these elements to fit naturally with the product being advertised and the media it is placed in.

Interestingly, the perception non-Hispanic White consumers have of targeted advertising is not that different. They seem not to like the extremes either. If an ad is larded with cultural references, non-Hispanic White consumers will notice. In a best-case scenario, they will simply acknowledge that it is geared to a different segment of the population and will care little about it or the message. The worst-case scenario is that the cultural elements actually generate a negative reaction. When the number of cultural cues is reasonable, however, non-Hispanic White consumers may not even recognize it is as an ethnically targeted ad in the first place, and therefore will be open to it. If the actual message is relevant to them, the ad will generate the desired reaction. Obviously, the key point here is to define what "reasonable" means, and to know when too much is really too much.

A Coca-Cola commercial that we evaluated in the qualitative research conducted for this book exemplifies this nicely. The ad, targeted to Hispanic consumers, features Salma Hayek, a Mexican-American actress who is also well known among mainstream consumers. The ad takes place in a formal restaurant. While a group of non-Hispanic businesspeople is impatiently waiting for her at a table, Hayek is in the kitchen eating tacos and drinking a Coke, chatting with the cooks in both English and Spanish. Latin music and a jovial ambiance surround the scene. After finishing her food, she rejoins the businesspeople at the table. A waiter approaches the table, offering a dish, but she replies—in English, with Spanish subtitles—that she does not want it because she's watching her figure. The final tagline of the ad reads, *Coca-Cola, Latina de verdad* ("Coca-Cola, truly Latin")—an allusion to the *picardia,* or craftiness of the situation. In spite of being loaded with Hispanic cultural elements, the commercial resonated well among non-Hispanic White consumers until they saw the final tagline, which they felt excluded them.

The obvious question situations like this raise is: How does this whole idea around targeted versus nontargeted change as the United States becomes a majority-minority nation? Will ethnic targeting still be needed? Will attitudes among non-Hispanic Whites change as they become a minority, and therefore will need ethnic targeting as well? The line between targeted and non-targeted is becoming fuzzier every day. As marketers, we need to adapt to this new and evolving market landscape, in which consumers within each segment preserve their own cultural cues but also absorb those of other groups with whom they interact. More than a mosaic that features a little something of every culture, these consumers represent what we are calling the New Majority.

CHAPTER 7

Intelligent Targeting

In chapter 6, we discussed the need for ethnically targeted initiatives geared toward ethnic consumers, both in terms of product development and communication and media strategies. We concluded that, although targeted strategies do not guarantee success, they tend to yield better results than non-targeted programs. So how do you make sure that your targeted efforts are truly relevant and effective from a cultural or ethnic perspective?

There's no single set of best practices for culturally relevant product development, but there certainly are useful guidelines. One is to approach the basics of marketing just as if you were going after mainstream consumers. The first step is to conduct research to determine whether race or ethnicity play a relevant role in defining consumers' attitudes and behaviors toward your particular product, category, or brand. If they do, then you know you need to take that into account, and chapter 6 provided some lessons from companies that have done so. If they do not, don't force the cultural or ethnic factor. Focus on variables that may be more pertinent to your brand—perhaps being a mom, a Baby Boomer, or a member of the GLBT community. Remember, race and ethnicity are just one component of consumers' *total* identity. In some situations they will factor prominently; in others, not.

In the case of culturally relevant advertising, a similar principle applies, but it may be more tempting for marketers to flirt with the ethnic factor, whether it is warranted or not. Even in situations where the product and brand promise are exactly the same as the ones used for the mainstream, chances are marketers will find a way to express this promise in a manner that resonates better with consumers from a cultural or ethnic perspective. This is fine, as long as the overall message relates to them first and foremost as *consumers,* regardless of their race or ethnicity.

Based on our extensive research in this field, we've put together some general advertising wisdom to help companies develop more effective campaigns aimed at ethnic segments. We explore these lessons in the following pages, supplementing our data with real-life examples. Although most of the data and examples in this chapter come from our TV copy–testing database, the lessons apply to virtually any type of communication, whether in traditional media or newer platforms.

BASIC ADVERTISING PRINCIPLES STILL APPLY TO ETHNIC CONSUMERS

Repetition is the mother of learning, the Russian proverb goes. So it is no coincidence that we have repeated several times by now that basic principles of advertising apply to ethnic consumers just as they do to the mainstream. If you are going to remember just a few things from this book, we hope this is one of them. Like any advertising, successful ethnic advertising:

1. Engages consumers—Consumers are exposed to more messages than they can process. Advertising has to compete with everything else in the environment to break through to their mental workspace.
2. Incorporates the brand—Advertising can be engaging, but will not serve the advertised brand if that brand is not part of that engagement.
3. Is easily understood—Consumers won't work hard to figure out the message of an advertisement. Simple is better, and consistency is key.
4. Evokes a response—Not all advertising must be immediately persuasive. But when your goal is to influence consumers'

behavior, your ads should strive to communicate something new, relevant, believable, and different.

When targeting ethnic consumers, if you are able to do all four of these things in a culturally relevant way, the chances of success increase significantly. However, the problem we often encounter as marketing, advertising, and research professionals is that in focusing so much on finding those "magical" cultural elements, we forget all the other factors an advertisement must have to break through and generate the desired reaction among consumers.

ETHNIC ADVERTISING ENGAGES CONSUMERS

Engagement is crucial to marketing success. Even in a world of famously short attention spans, consumers have to devote some mental energy to marketing campaigns if they are to have an effect. So how do we make this happen? The key is *personal* relevance—the things people find most engaging are those that relate to their own current goals or their broader priorities and interests. The challenge for advertisers is to talk about brands in a way that is not only relevant but is relevant *when* the advertising is encountered, at a time when people may simply be seeking entertainment or diversion. Relevant advertising, whenever and wherever it happens, taps into our key values and generates greater involvement, which automatically makes it more memorable.

How do you know if people will engage in the advertising in a way that makes it likely to affect the brand? Several metrics can help measure whether your advertising is engaging or not. Let's focus on two of the core ones here: enjoyment and involvement.

Enjoyment

Do consumers enjoy watching your advertising? If yes, they are more likely to pay attention to it, and the ad has a better chance of conveying its message.

Reinforcing the notion that basic advertising principles do apply to ethnic segments, figure 7.1 shows a comparison we did

Most Enjoyable General Market Ads	Most Enjoyable Ethnically Targeted Ads
Genuine, funny humor	Genuine, funny humor
Good music	Music with cultural affinity
Broadly appealing celebrities	Appealing celebrities and role models
Children	Family and children or friends scenarios
Escapism	Escapism
Animals	Characters portrayed in a positive way
	In-language dialogue

Figure 7.1 Elements That Help Boost Enjoyment in Advertising
Source: Millward Brown, 2011

between the most enjoyable mainstream ads and the most enjoyable ethnically targeted ads. The table highlights the elements that these most enjoyable ads had in common. As you can see, there are several overlapping elements between the groups. Humor, music, and celebrities frequently boost enjoyment of advertising, as do children.

The key to getting it right on both sides, we believe, is that when you use humor, music, or celebrities in advertising targeted to Hispanics, African Americans, or Asian Americans, you should make sure that these elements are relevant to them from a cultural perspective. These elements offer the opportunity to add another layer of relevance for ethnic consumers and therefore make the ad even more effective at engaging them. For instance, we know that "guys will always be guys," regardless of their racial or ethnic background. Straight young men of all races like girls. They flirt with them, they date them, they talk about them with friends, and so on. If your advertising shows situations like this, it will be relevant to male consumers from a "guy" perspective. But if you can portray the same "guy thing" with some sort of cultural flavor to it, it should add another layer of relevance to these male consumers and speak to them from both a "guy" and a "cultural" perspective. This is the essence of what we call *intelligent targeting*. Let's take a look at some of these factors in more detail.

Genuine, Funny Humor

Humor, not surprisingly, is a powerful tool to boost enjoyment across most ethnicities. Figure 7.2 compares the average enjoyment of humorous and non-humorous advertising among mainstream, Hispanic, and Black consumers. The specific type and level of humor that consumers enjoy, however, can vary significantly from culture to culture, even within the United States. (For instance, although not shown in the table, we have found that Chinese American consumers tend to prefer more conservative formats over loud, off-the-wall, bizarre, or slapstick types of humor.)

Hispanics in general appear to be the group that is most open to humor. As we discussed in chapter 2, Latinos tend to be more flexible than non-Hispanic Whites in how they manage their lives in general. This Latin factor is hard to explain in words because it is more a feeling or state of mind, but this flexibility is reflected in the diversity of things they enjoy laughing about, and the intensity with which they do it.

When it comes to Hispanic advertising, humor can work even with topics that would be considered sensitive or even untouchable for other segments, such as religion. The insurance company Nationwide did this in one of its auto insurance commercials. In the ad, a distracted male driver rear-ends a van with his car and curses, "God!" A smiling nun emerges from the van with a ruler, approaches his car, and gently taps the hood. The man laughs in relief at this admonishment, and then he and his car are struck by a bolt of lightning. A voiceover then intones: "Nobody forgives

Enjoyment of...	Mainstream	Hispanics	Blacks
Ads using humor	108	110	103
Ads not using humor	90	97	97

Figure 7.2 Average Rating Mainstream, Hispanic, and Black Consumers Give to Ads Using Humor

Source: Millward Brown, 2011

Ratings have been indexed for comparison purposes

as Nationwide does." The commercial, which was rated as very funny and enjoyable among the Hispanic target, could potentially generate different reactions among other segments.

A common theme among ads directed at Hispanics is the idea of poking fun at the "White guy," or poking fun at people of specific ethnic backgrounds in general. Latinos also enjoy laughing about themselves and about the immigrant experience in the United States (e.g., bizarre situations due to having a strong accent, getting used to the weather, different tactics some take to actually get into the country, etc.). We have many examples of Hispanic ads using this line of humor. One that consumers liked a lot is from Pepsi. In the ad, a White guy is shown holding a Pepsi and flirting across the room with a Hispanic girl, who is also enjoying a Pepsi. He picks up a tamale and struggles to bite into it without removing the cornhusk wrapping. He makes a mess and the girl comes over to show him how to remove the wrapping. She then offers him some empanadas, which he begins to eat—but he eats only the filling, not the edible outer crust. He clearly doesn't know what he is doing, but Pepsi is their common link, as the voiceover says: *"Ta'mal, con Pepsi ta'bien"*—"Tamale, with Pepsi, it's OK."

Other more general types of humor used include dark or sarcastic humor and, of course, old reliable sex jokes. Obviously, this Latino "flexibility" does not mean that advertisers get a pass to go as far as their imaginations will take them. There are limits, and it is always prudent to double-check them with some upfront consumer research. Conversely, you should also consider any peculiarities of your specific target audience, since not all Hispanics enjoy all types of humor, and the acceptability of jokes can vary by product category as well.

In the case of African Americans, while humor can also be effective when done right, marketers must be more careful. Because of the fraught history of this group, the line between a funny joke and a stereotyped ad can be very fine, and crossing it runs the risk of offending your audience. However, we believe that there is room for more experimental African American advertising in this area, especially when targeting younger consumers. While older African Americans tend to be more sensitive to ads portraying Black people in funny situations, younger, post–civil rights Blacks are, as a group, more open and willing to talk about (and poke fun at) sensitive points.

Brands in categories targeted to the younger segments, such as beer, are taking more chances in this field. In one Miller Lite ad that was consistently rated as funny, a young Black man notices how his elderly father, who is sitting in the porch quite distracted by the pretty young woman across the street (actress Stacey Dash), offers him a Miller Lite each time he says he's going to leave the house. He pretends to leave repeatedly to fool his "Pop Pop" into giving him multiple beers, but after finally noticing the trick, the father stops giving away his beer.

One thing making the lives of advertisers easier is the emergence of fragmented media like the Internet and mobile applications. These platforms allow marketers to target very specific segments with creative pieces that, because of their controversial approaches, could not necessarily be broadcast in mass media like TV or even radio. And as always, the key is to make sure that the joke does not overshadow the brand or its message. Remember, the ultimate purpose of advertising is to affect consumers' perceptions about the brand or generate a reaction among them, not to just make people laugh.

Music with Cultural Affinity

Music is another universally appealing element that can make the difference between enjoyable and tedious advertising. Figure 7.3 illustrates the positive impact of music in general across the different ethnic groups. And, for the case of Hispanic and Black consumers, it also shows the supplemental effect that music with cultural affinity can bring to the table.

Interestingly, the line between culturally specific music and music in general has blurred significantly in the past decade or so, almost disappearing. As the different ethnic groups in the

Enjoyment of...	Mainstream	Hispanics	Blacks
Ads using music	108	103	103
Ads using music with cultural affinity	-	105	128
Ads without music	99	85	83

Figure 7.3   Average Rating Mainstream, Hispanic, and Black Consumers Give to Ads Using Music

Source: Millward Brown, 2011

Ratings have been indexed for comparison purposes

country continue to interact with each other, what would be considered mainstream pop years ago can be very relevant to ethnic consumers today. And many genres that used to be exclusive to ethnic consumers—such as salsa, hip-hop, and reggaeton—have now entered the mainstream. Still, our data does indicate that cultural affinity plays a role in consumers' appreciation for music, and can therefore augment the effectiveness of your communication when used intelligently.

An award-winning Ford Focus commercial from 2004 exemplifies this principle well. In the ad, a man wearing an elephant costume jumps into his Ford Focus and goes to pick up four friends one at a time. His friends are also dressed in elephant costumes and as they drive along they all sing a popular song among Hispanic kids, *Un elefante se balanceaba* ("An Elephant Was Swinging"). The original song is about elephants swinging on a spiderweb, and is sung adding one elephant every round. The commercial, however, adapts the song to the idea of adding elephants (people) to the car to show its spaciousness. When they arrive at the party, they realize that the invitation said "elegant," not "elephant," adding a touch of humor to the piece

Another crucial consideration when selecting music for your advertising is again diversity within ethnic segments. In the case of Hispanics, for example, music preferences can vary significantly between Latinos of Mexican origin and those of Caribbean or South American descent. Movida Wireless, a cell phone company headquartered in Florida, launched a campaign that while using the same creative, included different variations of the background music, each appealing to different segments of the Latino market. The song played in the commercials was the United States' national anthem, sung in Spanish, and the campaign included three musical variations: *norteña* (more appealing to Mexicans), reggaeton (more appealing to Caribbeans), and salsa (more appealing to Caribbeans and South Americans). The creative consisted of a series of scenes that were a parody of hybrid Latin and American pastimes, with the final tagline "Movida, the prepaid cell phone for a world that is more Latin every day."

Further differences in musical taste emerge between generations. Older and younger ethnic consumers are likely to enjoy different genres of music, just as within the general population. This is likely to be more noticeable among Black consumers, between the pre– and post–civil rights generations. For example, while it is common to see advertising targeted to older African Americans using gospel music, commercials aimed at younger Black segments are more likely to utilize hip-hop or other more modern rhythms.

Whatever type of music you decide to include in your advertising, it must be well integrated into the storyline and must not overshadow the brand or its messaging. This does not mean that it can't be prominent; in fact, our data shows that ads with prominently featured music tend to do better than those with subtle or neutral tunes. For instance, among Hispanics, while the average enjoyment score of ads in which music played a central role is 108, the average score for ads that only had music as a background is 97. And qualitative evidence suggests that tunes created or adapted specifically for an advertisement tend to be better integrated and therefore yield better results. However, of-the-moment songs played in advertising can also contribute significantly to enjoyment.

Appealing Celebrities and Role Models

The situation with celebrities is similar to that with music: They boost enjoyment across all ethnicities when used intelligently (see figure 7.3). And, as with music, the difference between a global or universal personality and a culture-specific celebrity has become hazy in the past years—witness the fame of George Lopez, Yao Ming, Oprah, Beyoncé, Bill Cosby, Gloria Estefan, and Vera Wang, to name just a few. Widely known personalities like these can be incredibly helpful to transcultural initiatives because, depending on their relevance to consumers vis-a-vis other factors like age, gender, line of work, etc., they have the potential to appeal to almost everyone. A good example of this is Dennis Haysbert, the celebrity that the insurance company Allstate uses in every ad, regardless of target segment.

Remember, however, that not all mainstream celebrities are relevant to ethnic consumers, and many are even unknown to them. A while back, Chrysler adapted an ad featuring Celine Dion so that it could be aired in Spanish media. While the message and overall creative were relevant to Latino consumers, Dion did not add much value to the mix because she was not as popular with them as she was with mainstream consumers. In fact, when watching the commercial, instead of seeing a celebrity with her kid, most Latinos saw a regular mom with her kid, which in the end contributed significantly to the ad's relevance.

An interesting benefit to the use of ethnic celebrities when targeting ethnic segments is the pride they generate. Hispanics, Blacks, and Asians are likely to feel good about celebrities of their respective race or ethnicity who have succeeded at the global level. However, this does not mean that less-famous icons cannot also generate a very positive impact on consumers; we have plenty of evidence to support this in our databases. Indeed, related to the pride factor, the use of noncelebrity role models can elicit similarly favorable feelings from consumers. A Coca-Cola TV ad aired during Black History Month exemplifies this possibility. In the ad, a woman's voice takes the viewer on a tour of a "typical" urban neighborhood, exploring how some of its regular African American residents have become successful at what they do. The script highlights trailblazing young Black entrepreneurs (Lisa Price), filmmakers (Maurice Marable), and sportsmen (pro

Enjoyment of...	Mainstream	Hispanics	Blacks
Ads featuring celebrities	103	110	104
Ads not featuring celebrities	99	99	96

Figure 7.4 Average Rating Mainstream, Hispanic, and Black Consumers Give to Ads Featuring Celebrities

Source: Millward Brown, 2011

Ratings have been indexed for comparison purposes
Most celebrities in Hispanic and Black advertising were ethnically relevant to their respective audiences.

skater Kareem Campbell) who look like everyday people in the neighborhood.

Again, keep in mind that ethnic consumers are diverse. Not all Hispanics like all Hispanic celebrities; ditto for African and Asian Americans and their respective icons.

In addition to the cultural factor, ethnic advertising featuring celebrities must also meet minimum requirements to be successful, just as mainstream ads that feature personalities do. Celebrities must be well integrated into the story of the ad, and their public persona should fit with the advertised brand's image to multiply their positive effect. Pepsi, for instance, has used celebrities in a good and consistent way over time; in ads targeted to Hispanics, young stars like Ricky Martin, Shakira, and Eva Longoria have been very effective. A cautionary point, and one unrelated to race, is that regardless of how well a celebrity seems to fit, any bad press around him or her will transfer to the brand. Consider the example of Tiger Woods, whose well-publicized personal problems caused Accenture to cancel his contract. Woods is hardly the first—but the risk remains the same for all celebrity-endorsed products.

Family Scenarios

"Family is the most important thing for Hispanic consumers." We bet you've heard that axiom a few times, right? As discussed before, the fact is that family is the most important thing for every racial or ethnic group in America! But the concept of family itself may vary from group to group. While for most non-Hispanic Whites, "family" usually refers to the nuclear unit; for Latinos, "family" may include Mom, Dad, the kids, Grandpa and Grandma, Uncle Jesus, Cousins Pedro, Maria Luisa, Maria del Rosario, Maria Elena and, of course, Doña Mercedes, who is not really a relative, but is called "auntie." This is perhaps the clearest example of why we must examine all sides when we talk about ethnic segments in the United States, lest we retain a biased understanding of the market and risk making huge mistakes when trying to reach this New Majority. Figure 7.5 reinforces the idea that family can be a powerful element to include in advertising, since enjoyment of ads featuring children is higher than other ads across all ethnicities.

Interestingly for this much-vaunted "family-oriented" segment, the impact of children in advertising enjoyment among Hispanics is actually the lowest of the three segments analyzed. Odd, right? After doing some research, we found that, perhaps specifically because of the bias toward family situations, Hispanic advertising tends to overuse and often misuse them. If you've ever watched a few hours of commercials on a Spanish-language network, you've probably seen ads featuring perfect, loving families over and over again. These commercials may be effective at engaging consumers and communicating their messages, but chances are that consumers don't perceive much differentiation among the brands advertised. We have pinpointed this as an area of improvement for Hispanic marketing, which we will revisit in more detail when we analyze *involvement*.

Enjoyment of...	Mainstream	Hispanics	Blacks
Ads featuring children	112	105	136
Ads not featuring children	99	95	83

Figure 7.5   Average Rating Mainstream, Hispanic, and Black Consumers Give to Ads Featuring Children

Source: Millward Brown, 2011

Ratings have been indexed for comparison purposes

In the case of African Americans, for whom the concept of extended family also applies, be careful not to fall into tropes so common they've become stereotypes, like fatherless families. It is true that the African American segment overindexes in single-mom households, and therefore this could be a real concept to use in advertising. But you must make sure to use it in a positive way, as a commercial for The Home Depot did in 2007. It featured a blended African American family composed of two sisters and one of the sister's teenage daughter and son. The sisters and the daughter speak of the need to fix up their house and how The Home Depot gave them the confidence and tools to repair it. They say that the project connected the family to the home and allowed the mom to be a role model for her children.

Other Elements That Help Boost Enjoyment in Advertising

When compared to their general-market counterparts in figure 7.1, the most enjoyable ethnic ads do have some distinct elements in common that help increase their chances of success. Portraying ethnic characters in a positive way is perhaps the most apparent, especially for African American consumers.

African Americans are proud of their culture and history. A common denominator among successful African American targeted advertisements is that they portray Black consumers in a flattering way. Figure 7.6 compares ads that portrayed Black characters in an especially positive way and commercials that did not. (This does not mean that the latter group portrayed Blacks in a negative way; they just didn't do anything special or different to set the characters apart.)

Given the historical paucity of such images, positive depictions of African Americans send a message that the advertisers, and society as a whole, sees them as intelligent, hard-working, positive, contributing member of society. Featuring African American characters in this way not only impacts consumers' relation to and enjoyment of the ad in general, but, crucially, also influences their perception of the advertised brand.

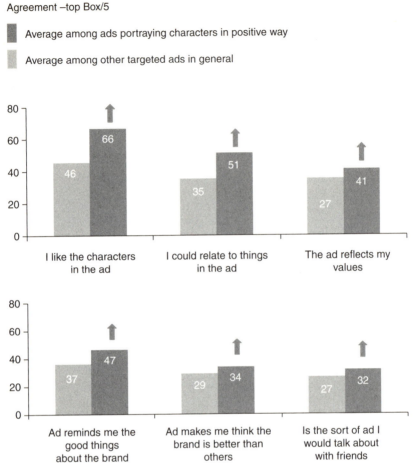

Figure 7.6   Impact of Characters Being Portrayed in a Positive Way in African American Advertising (%)

Source: Millward Brown, 2011

A 2009 Walmart back-to-school ad had this effect. The ad shows several school-age kids of various ethnicities (although predominantly Black) taking a ruler out of a Walmart tote bag and having fun with it. They are shown in various settings: at home, in class, and outside; they are buoyant and enthusiastic about their school supplies. A voiceover describes the "immeasurable" benefit of equipping kids to succeed and lead the way in the future.

For Hispanics, an element that helps boost enjoyment of advertising is the use of the Spanish language, whether an ad uses

Spanish only or is bilingual in format. Obviously, this makes sense for the unacculturated, or Spanish-dominant, segment. However, as we can see in figure 7.7, language also assists in advertising targeted to bicultural consumers, especially when it uses a bilingual format. In the case of bicultural consumers, this is likely not an issue of comprehension; rather, it's about expressing pride or feeling recognized. The appreciation for in-language communication does not mean that Hispanics dislike English advertising. As long as an ad is good, they are open to it. Interestingly, when we asked non-Hispanic White consumers which language format they preferred, while the vast majority expressed understandable reservations about Spanish-only advertising, a surprising 55% mentioned that they either enjoyed (20%) or did not mind (35%) bilingual communication.

One final aspect around which ethnic consumers seem to distance themselves from the general market is the use of animals in advertising. Among mainstream consumers, enjoyment of ads featuring animals is higher than ads without, as shown in figure 7.8.

Enjoyment of...	Unacculturated	Bicultural	Acculturated
Ads in Spanish	77	61	20
Ads in bilingual format	80	72	36
Ads in English	71	62	74

Figure 7.7 Average Rating Unacculturated, Bicultural, and Acculturated Hispanic Consumers Give to Spanish, Bilingual, and English Ads

Source: Millward Brown, 2011

Data represents the top 2 boxes in a 5-point scale

Enjoyment of...	Mainstream	Hispanics	Blacks
Ads featuring animals	117	100	NA
Ads with no animals	100	100	NA

Figure 7.8 Average Rating Mainstream, Hispanic, and Black Consumers Give to Ads Featuring Animals

Source: Millward Brown, 2011

Ratings have been indexed for comparison purposes

There is no such evidence among Hispanic consumers, and we have no data on African American consumers' preference.

Involvement

Are consumers actually paying attention to your advertising? You'd better hope so—if they are, the ad has a better chance of conveying its message and brand promise. At Millward Brown, we analyze this attention-getting factor in four dimensions, based on the intersection of two axes—active-to-passive and positive-to-negative (see figure 7.9).

Not surprisingly, we have found that advertising that generates Active Positive involvement is more engaging overall. However, being passive rather than active is not necessarily a bad thing for advertising. In the end, brand personality and the ad's specific objectives should be the biggest factors in deciding which approach to use. For example, Hallmark has typically used a passive approach in its advertising, which makes sense because of its brand identity as a purveyor of greeting cards. However, in order to break through, passive ads have to work harder in other aspects like enjoyment or branding. One way in which they can do this is by playing on human emotions, which have a crucial function in not only capturing attention and memory, but also decision making. Within both our mainstream and ethnic-targeted databases, ads with the highest breakthrough, or branded engagement

ACTIVE

	NEGATIVE		POSITIVE
	Active Negative: When you sit up and watch something because it is shocking	**Active Positive:** When you sit up and watch something because it is involving	
	Passive Negative: When you don't sit up and watch something because it is just too dull	**Passive Positive:** When you don't sit up and watch something because it is just too gentle	

PASSIVE

Figure 7.9   Millward Brown's Approach to Involvement of Advertising

Source: Millward Brown, 2011

Enjoyment of...	Mainstream	Hispanics	Blacks
Ads with emotional tone	117	126	122
Ads with rational tone	94	95	83

Figure 7.10　Average Rating Mainstream, Hispanic, and Black Consumers Give to Ads Based on Tone

Source:　Millward Brown

Ratings have been indexed for comparison purposes

scores, are more likely to be based on an emotional premise than a rational one. Figure 7.10 illustrates the contribution an emotional tone in advertising can make to ad enjoyment, thereby offsetting its passivity.

Overall, our data shows that ethnic targeted communication is more likely than mainstream creative to generate passive involvement. By averaging the ratings in figure 7.11, we see that while the mean Active Positive involvement of mainstream ads is 159, the means for Hispanics and African Americans viewing targeted ads are 139 and 147, respectively. Among Latinos, on the other hand, the average Passive Positive involvement is higher than that among the mainstream and African American markets.

The misguided application of family we discussed previously may also be the main reason for the more passive nature of

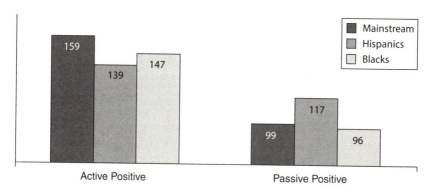

Figure 7.11　Average Rating of Advertising Involvement Given by Mainstream, Hispanic and Black Consumers Viewing Ads Targeted to Their Segment

Source:　Millward Brown, 2011

Ratings are the resulting average of an algorithm used by Millward Brown to measure advertising involvement

Hispanic communication. Hispanic advertising that features family or children is often slow paced, and the stories frequently emphasize the familial bond in a way that sometimes goes beyond gentle to boring. To be clear—our criticism of the use of family in Hispanic advertising does not mean that you should not use this concept in your communication. Family is indeed a powerful element for Latinos. But use it in a creative and different and engaging way. A State Farm insurance ad, while passive, relied on the concept of extended family and generated a strong emotional connection with consumers. The ad shows a young Hispanic couple choosing paint colors, painting, and recarpeting a room that, it appeared, was for the baby the woman was expecting. The preparations turn out to be for the arrival of the husband's father. While the couple welcomes him to his new home, a voice-over says, in a play on State Farm's slogan, "Like a good neighbor, State Farm is there": "Being there is easy; being there when they need you is what sets you apart." Soft background music plays throughout the piece. Despite the ad's passive nature, the element of surprise from the plot twist and the emotional tone set it apart.

On the other hand, one reason why African American advertising also tends to generate somewhat less active involvement than mainstream communication (although the difference is less pronounced than with Hispanic advertising) is that marketers can be overly cautious in the development of their creative and as we discussed before, for example, they prefer not to use humor if it might offend their audience. When targeting the Black market, they may be afraid to take many risks because they worry about crossing into stereotype. While it's always good to be careful, try not to let this fear limit your choices. Remember, situations like this are why research was created!

Remember, too, that although most of the data presented in this chapter focused on TV advertising, these lessons remain valid for other types of media, whether traditional or emerging. Involvement remains paramount, no matter the platform. As Gordon Pincott, chairman of Millward Brown's Global Solutions team, wrote in his 2009 article "Rules of Engagement," while digital media allow consumers a new level of interaction with the brand, they also highlight why marketers need to gain "permission" to speak to people through these channels: "Simply bashing down people's doors by intruding into their online surfing or mobile communication would be counterproductive. People need to be won over," he writes. "Thus the focus on engagement, even in these new platforms."[1] A 2010 global qualitative study conducted by Firefly Millward Brown identified 10 rules for engaging with consumers in social media venues:

1. Let the consumer come to you
2. Be interesting and exciting
3. Listen first, then talk—foster dialogue
4. Be relevant and personal
5. Speak like a friend, not a corporate entity
6. Offer something of real value
7. Give up some control to the consumer
8. Be open, honest, and transparent
9. Give the brand a face—humanize it
10. Let the consumer promote the brand for you

Ethnic consumers are heavier users of social media than non-Hispanic Whites, not only because they tend to be younger, but also because social interactions are an innate part of who they are. The personal touch and amicable tone described above is crucial for brands trying to engage them in the social media space.

ETHNIC ADVERTISING INCORPORATES THE BRAND

Branding—which we will define here as the extent to which consumers will remember that an advertisement was for a particular brand—is obviously a key factor in any successful advertising, including of course that targeted to ethnic consumers.

Poorly branded ads are a waste of ad dollars; as one company chairman commented, "I am not keen on using our marketing budget to support our competitors." The easiest way to determine if your advertising is well branded is by asking yourself if you can describe the ad in a sentence without mentioning the brand (or an established brand cue, whether it is a logo, a symbol, or any other image or element typically associated to the brand). If you can, there may be a problem with your branding.

How can you achieve muscular branding in ethnic advertising? Some believe that the key is to show the brand early and often, but our analysis shows otherwise. We found no correlation between the time the brand first appears, or the number of appearances, and the branding of the ad. Instead, we found that the crucial factor to successful branding is how brands are *integrated* into the story of the ad. The goal is to ensure that consumers effortlessly remember the ad when they think about the brand, and vice versa. To get there, the brand must be part and parcel of the most memorable parts of the story. The ad needs to highlight the brand in a distinctive, enjoyable, and involving way.

There are several ways to integrate brands into your storytelling. Here are some useful guidelines for making the brand a central piece of your targeted advertising:

- Make sure that your brand is present at the key points of interest. Consumers never remember all the scenes or elements of an advertisement. They have only so much mental "scratch" space to devote to it, so only the most enjoyable or engaging parts will stick. Make sure that your brand is present at those specific moments.
- Ideally, the brand will play an active role in the ad, say, for example, with the characters using the product in an interesting way. If the characters find the brand or the effects of the product (e.g. perfume) enjoyable or involving, viewers are more likely to become involved, too.
- Make the brand the hero of the story—create a problem for which the brand provides the solution. This is persuasive to

ethnic consumers, and gives you a chance to highlight the brand's attributes in a clear way. An Eclipse gum commercial aimed at the Hispanic market did this in a funny way using El Puma, a Venezuelan singer of the 1980s. In the ad, a couple is shown at a beach campfire with friends. The man begins to kiss the woman, but she turns away because his breath stinks (PROBLEM). El Puma then appears, riding two dolphins across the water, to sing romantically about the need for Eclipse gum to unleash his inner wildness (HERO). He gives the man some gum and blows his breath at the woman, which entices her (SOLUTION). The ad ends with El Puma pouncing through a sheet of Eclipse wrapping with Eclipse package in hand and the tagline *frescura salvaje* ("wild freshness") on the bottom of the screen.

- Use overt brand cues, such as Coors Light's Silver Bullet train, Cialis's bathtubs, Coca-Cola's white wave on red, Geico's gecko, or Heineken's green bottle, to name a few. This is fairly self-explanatory in mainstream advertising, but can be tricky when targeting immigrant populations, as we explain below.

Branding and Immigrant Populations

A frequent concern among marketers is that immigrant consumers are less familiar with American brand names. Although this is true in some cases, it is not as much of an issue as many believe. Most brands sold in the United States today are also sold in Latin America and Asia, often under a similar brand promise. In fact, some global brands, like Coca-Cola, have been involved with the local populations in other countries for so long that consumers in these regions are likely to consider them native.

Branding of...	Mainstream	Hispanics	Blacks
Ads featuring overt brand cues	111	104	105
Ads without overt brand cues	98	95	84

Figure 7.12   Average Rating Mainstream, Hispanic, and Black Consumers Give to Ads Featuring Brand Cues

Source: Millward Brown, 2011
Ratings have been indexed for comparison purposes

Brands that have no presence in those regions obviously have to work harder to increase brand awareness among more-recent arrivals to the United States and position themselves clearly, but that's perfectly doable. The key is consistency, consistency, consistency. Figure 7.13 shows how this is playing out in the US auto-insurance industry, where most of the key players have striven for constancy in their communication to Latino consumers. Awareness levels of their brands have clearly grown as consumers have spent more time in the country.

A similar situation occurs in terms of the bonding consumers have (or come to have) with brands in the United States. It is true that immigrants are more likely to feel close to brands they used in their countries of origin. It is also true that Latinos, for example, tend to be somewhat more brand-loyal consumers; however, in a grocery-shopping segmentation we conducted in 2006, we found that only 15% of Hispanic shoppers could be classified as "very loyal." Latinos, like everyone else, will switch their loyalty if they find a brand that better satisfies their needs.

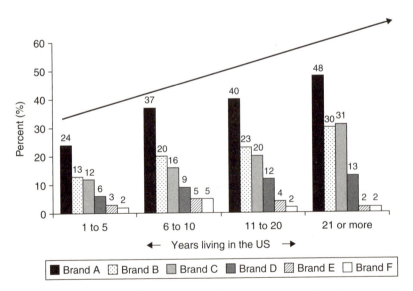

Figure 7.13   Total Unaided Awareness of Auto-Insurance Brands among First-Generation Latinos (%)

Source: Millward Brown, 2011
Unaided awareness is a spontaneous brand recall question—respondents are not shown any stimuli when asked the question

ETHNIC ADVERTISING IS EASILY UNDERSTOOD

This one's a no-brainer—if consumers don't understand what is going on in an ad, they won't fully enjoy it. And if they don't understand what you are trying to communicate, they won't react as you want them to. Our research shows that comprehension can have a clear impact on reactions to other aspects of the communication, such as enjoyment, branding, message penetration, and persuasion. This sounds obvious, but in the real world of ad execution sometimes it seems to be overlooked.

Figure 7.14 shows consumers' average understanding of advertising that is targeted to them. Because Black consumers are more likely to respond positively to surveys, we are unable to conclude from these numbers that African American advertising is better understood among Black consumers than general-market advertising is among mainstream consumers. However, the fact that the average understanding of Hispanic advertising among Latino consumers is lower than that of the mainstream is telling. Hispanics, like African Americans, also respond more positively to surveys, so one would expect their ease of understanding scores to be higher. Figure 7.14 demonstrates that the opposite is actually happening. This suggests there is a serious issue with understanding of Hispanic advertising.

To clarify, the Hispanic data shown in figure 7.14 refers only to Spanish-language advertising, and all the commercials included in this analysis were evaluated by Hispanics who spoke Spanish, so language is not a factor here. The easy conclusion

Ease of understanding	Mainstream	Hispanics	Blacks
Very easy	70	52	75
Somewhat easy	23	44	19

Figure 7.14   Average Rating Mainstream, Hispanic, and Black Consumers Give to Ads Targeted to Their Segment

Source: Millward Brown, 2011

Data is in %s and represents average ease of understanding scores at normative levels—average of all ads in respective databases

many tend to draw from these numbers is that Latinos are less educated than the general population. The statement is in fact true, but it certainly doesn't explain the numbers. Hispanic consumers might have lower levels of education than mainstream consumers, but they are not stupid. And you definitely should not need a PhD to understand what is going on in a commercial! If there is a misunderstanding of Hispanic advertising, we believe the fault lies with marketers and advertising agencies, not consumers.

There are several factors that could be contributing to this lower level of understanding of Hispanic advertising. Many of them specific to individual executions. However, by analyzing our database, we have been able to identify some common factors among the least-understood ads:

- *Message overload.* Marketing communications need to give consumers time to think. Don't force too many messages or too many story elements into your advertising. The brain simply can't process them all, and key elements for communication like branding or comprehension will be missed. Ethnic advertising seems to be weaker than general-market advertising on this front, probably because companies often have many things to tell consumers, but very limited ethnic budgets, so they cram five or more messages into a single execution. The result, obviously, is that all intent is lost. A 2005 award-winning Kellogg's commercial for Frosted Mini-Wheats cereal does a great job at focusing on a single proposition. The ad starts showing a hand placing some condiments, including a cup of milk, on a table with a bowl of Frosted Mini-Wheats. Together, these elements appear to be a washing machine, with the cup of milk being the selector knob and the bowl the machine's window. The hand pours some milk into the bowl and then rotates the milk container slightly, and the bowl begins to rotate like washing machines do. Cut to a shot of the Frosted Mini-Wheats box trumpeting "25% More Fiber," and a silent message: "Clean your body inside." Originally created in Spanish for Hispanics, the positive consumer feedback encouraged the company to use it with the main-stream as well.

- *Failure to summarize the message in short, simple, straightforward ideas.* People often consume media when they want a moment of relaxation (e.g., watching a television show or a Web clip). It follows that the last thing they want to do is think too much about anything, so less is more when it comes to message "dressing." One thing we have found to work well among ethnic consumers is the use of slogans that effectively summarize what a brand stands for, such as Orbit gum's "For a good, clean feeling, no matter what," Geico's "So easy, a caveman can do it," or Nike's "Just do it."

- *Lack of consistency in the brand's communication.* Consistent communication is key to building a brand position. What's different about ethnic segments is that they consume both targeted and nontargeted media. Generally, it's best to keep your brand promise the same in both. *How* you express it may vary, depending on cultural relevance, but the messages' essence should match if you want consumers to come away with a clear understanding of what you stand for. In most cases, this should not be a problem because brand promises tend to be tied to basic human insights that are valid across cultures. In a few cases though, this may not be strictly true, since the cultural relevance itself will depend on the ethnic audience. For instance, Corona ads targeted to Hispanics focus on pride or identification with the Hispanic community (i.e., *Refresca quienes somos*—"Refresh who we are"), but those targeted to the mainstream take a very different approach (i.e., beach relaxation). This situation is more common among brands that are not native to the United States in the first place.

- *Too much focus on the product itself, rather than on its end benefit.* Consumers do not need heaters; they need to feel warm. Sometimes advertising focuses so much on the technicalities of the products that little attention is given to what consumers are actually looking for: the end benefit. This idea has been playing out in the pharmaceutical category. Eli Lilly made an interesting change to its communication on its erectile-dysfunction drug Cialis, going from touting its 36-hour efficacy to inviting consumers to "Choose the moment that is right for you."

- *Tendency to overuse cultural elements in targeted advertising.* When courting a specific ethnic group, you must ensure that any cultural elements you choose fit and are well integrated into the story of the ad. Otherwise they will only cause confusion. One case where marketers consistently abuse the use of a particular cultural element is soccer for Hispanic consumers. Yes, soccer is the number-one sport among Latinos. But that does not mean that *all* of your targeted ads should have a soccer game in the background. This not only causes confusion, but it provides little to no differentiation from the many brands pursuing this tack.

ETHNIC ADVERTISING EVOKES A RESPONSE

Not all advertising aims to be immediately persuasive. But when your goal is to influence consumers' behaviour and generate a short-term bump in sales, your actual message—and not just your creative piece—needs to be new, relevant, believable, and differentiating. These are the drivers of persuasion:

- *"New" News*—Ideally the news should be new to the category as well as the brand. If the ad scores poorly on new news, is the ad translating the strategy correctly? Are you giving the consumer perceived new benefits of the brand?
- *Relevance*—The message must be relevant to consumers when they are buying the product. If the ad scores poorly on actual message relevance, investigate whether the ad's idea is right for the target. But remember, the key is to be *intelligently* relevant, not just *ethnically* relevant.
- *Believability*—Can the brand really claim to do this? Are you giving consumers a reason to believe? If the ad scores poorly on credibility, consumers are not believing the claims the ad is making. Is there a general lack of confidence in the marketplace about the brand, or are the statements so different from what consumers have experienced that they sense a stretch?
- *Differentiation*—Can only this brand claim this? Is the ad's messaging different from the competition? If not, you are giving consumers little reason to choose your brand over others.

Broadly speaking, any advertisement has two major components: the creative and the actual message being communicated. The message is the core idea or brand promise. The creative is the way the message is conveyed. When it comes to targeted advertising, most of the "targeting" is focused on the creative and usually involves aspects such as casting, storyline, or language. In the majority of ethnic advertisements, the actual core idea communicated to consumers is the same message that companies use in their mainstream communication. Demonstrating the principle of mutual reinforcement, figure 7.15 suggests that a targeted creative does have a more positive impact on how consumers perceive your message than a nontargeted creative. Or in other words, telling the same story in a culturally relevant way makes the drivers of persuasion described above work harder for your brand.

The driver of persuasion that seems to benefit the most from the use of targeted creative is believability. Ethnic consumers are more likely to perceive a message to be credible when it is told in culturally relevant way. In the words of one study participant, "It is different [more believable] when people I can relate to tell me the story."

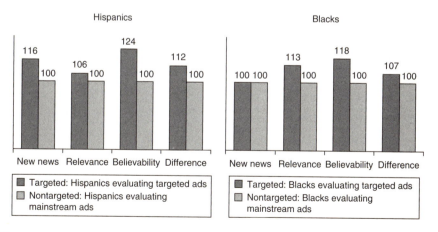

Figure 7.15   Drivers of Persuasion

Source: Millward Brown, 2011

Ratings have been indexed for comparison purposes

Having a targeted creative also contributes to perceived message differentiation and relevance, although to a somewhat lesser extent. Why? Because, as we said, for most brands the actual message is the same in both their targeted and nontargeted advertisements. Looking at these numbers, one could argue that if brands adapted or developed targeted messages, the uniqueness and relevance of the message and therefore the advertisement's persuasion would increase significantly. While this might be a valid proposition in some cases, it is unlikely to generate major increments in most situations because brand promises are usually founded on basic human insights that are valid across any racial or ethnic group. We all need to eat, sleep, and have some fun every now and then! If your brand satisfies any of these human needs, you don't need to change your core proposition. What you may want to do, however, is make sure that the way in which you express this human insight—the creative—is relevant to consumers from an ethnic or cultural perspective. As figure 7.15 evidences, having a targeted creative *can* contribute to the perceived relevance of the message and other drivers of persuasion. That is definitely welcome news for supporters of targeted communication at any level.

Similar to the Corona situation described above with regard to Hispanics, there are circumstances in which the insights that gave birth to a brand promise in the mainstream do not hold true among African American consumers either. In situations like this, you are also encouraged to use whatever other proposition is relevant to the Black subsegment you are after in order to maximize your sales. Procter & Gamble's Olay Definity Eye Illuminator chose this tactic. The challenge in this case was that while Olay's mainstream campaigns focused on the benefits that mattered most to White women—minimizing wrinkles and stopping the aging process—many Black women accept aging gracefully as part of their heritage. Rather than wrinkles, what concerned them most was undereye discoloration. Dark spots are Black women's "wrinkles."

The campaign, developed by the Chicago-based firm Burrell Communications Group, incorporated actress Angela Bassett as a link to African American woman. In the television spot, Basset tells them that when someone looks in their eyes, "You want them to see your sparkle, your passion, your light...not what ages you most," referring to discoloration. Then she goes on to explain the benefit of the product, modeling her face as a reason to believe. The campaign won an Association of National Advertisers' Multicultural Excellence award in the general-market category in 2010.

The Issue of Casting

We have used the term "culturally relevant" several times, so perhaps it warrants further exploration. While many in the industry still believe that ethnic advertising is synonymous with "ethnic casting," consumers feel the opposite. For them, "cultural relevance" means much more than that. This is especially true for African American consumers.

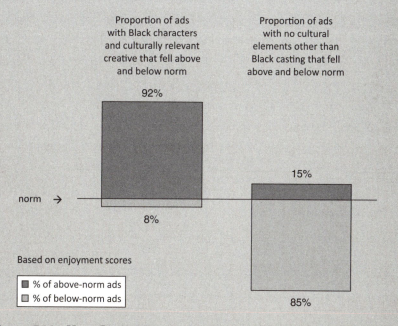

Figure 7.16 How Casting Factors into Enjoyment of African American Advertising

Source: Millward Brown, 2011

In a recent research-and-development project conducted by Millward Brown we tested 30 targeted ads among Black consumers. We classified the ads in two groups: (1) ads that featured Black casting and some sort of culturally relevant element or creative, and (2) ads with no cultural elements other than Black casting. Figure 7.16 illustrates how each group of ads fared, on average, in terms of enjoyment. While 92% of the ads that had Black casting plus another cultural element rated above the enjoyment norm, 85% of the ads that only had Black casting fell below that norm—telling results indeed.

The casting issue has become much more complex in the last decade. As the United States grows increasingly diverse, companies—intentionally or otherwise—have begun to reflect this new reality in their so-called general-market advertising. Figure 7.17 provides clear evidence of this. The graph shows the proportion of ads in Millward Brown's general market database that feature only White casting versus ads that feature non-White casting or

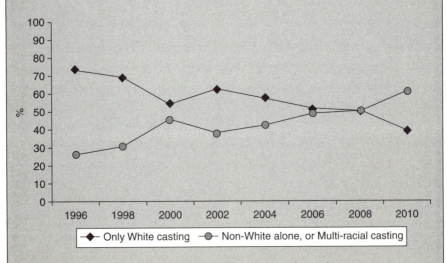

Figure 7.17   Use of Ethnic Casting in General Market Advertising
Source: Millward Brown

multiracial casting. The analysis extends from the 1990s to the year 2010, and includes more than 12,000 cases. While obviously not a census of all ads aired during this time period, the data visibly indicates a trend moving from the use of White-only casting to a more multiracial approach. In fact, most of the general market ads Millward Brown tested in 2010 had multiracial casting or non-White casting.

Consumers in general are becoming increasingly conscious of the diversity of the country. They breathe and feel this diversity in many situations of their lives, and want it to be reflected in advertising. However, our research indicates clearly that if there is something consumers don't like about how some brands handle casting for their communication, it is when they appear to be trying to fill some sort of ethnic quotas—e.g., two White consumers, one Black, one Hispanic and one Asian. Consumers across all ethnic segments, including non-Hispanic Whites, consistently expect diversity to be portrayed in a natural way in advertising.

ETHNIC ADVERTISING DOES ALL OF THE ABOVE IN AN INTELLIGENT AND SENSITIVE WAY

As discussed throughout this chapter, the use of cultural elements in advertising targeted to minority segments can help get the message through, but it does not guarantee success. First and foremost, you must ensure that your advertising is understandable and engaging, that it generates the desired associations with your brand, and that it motivates consumers to take some sort of action. Cultural elements are, in the end, just a tool to help the message strike its target. *They are not the message itself.*

White collar   Baseball fan

Practical   Agnostic

Socially liberal   *Hispanic*

Friendly   Male

29 years old   Fiscally conservative

Chicagoan   Straight

Pet lover   Single parent

TV-maniac   Middle class

Hard-working   Single

Figure 7.18   Meet Jose Negro

As we've noted, cultural elements must be relevant to the brand or the message you are trying to communicate, and they need to be well integrated into the ad's storyline. Further, you must not forget that race and ethnicity are just one part of consumers' identity. Sometimes it is the most salient, sometimes not. We know that race and ethnicity are not isolated characteristics; they naturally interact with all the other things that define people, such as age, gender, income, personality traits, sexual orientation, place of residence, and so on. For illustrative purposes, meet (the real) Jose Negro in figure 7.18, for whom being Hispanic is just one of many characteristics that define him. When eating, Jose is first and foremost a Hispanic. But when driving his car, he is primarily a young guy who enjoys Chicago's nightlife.

In short, the basic advertising principles that guide the development of mainstream communication are equally valid for the work you do with ethnic segments. Ignoring them will result in great ads that talk about the Hispanic, African American, or Asian cultures, but say nothing about the advertised brands or products. That is why, moving forward, we propose that as an industry, we start talking less about culturally or ethnically relevant targeting and more about *intelligent* targeting.

CHAPTER 8

The Future (Is Now): Embracing the New Majority

So far, we've outlined the demographic and psychographic attributes that define America's new multicultural majority. We've explored the development of a niche marketing industry focused on reaching culturally diverse consumers. And we've laid out principles for successfully connecting with ethnic consumers via resonant and inclusive marketing communications. While these strategies will help you navigate *today's* landscape, the multicultural market is a moving target. Every day we get closer to a reality where your brand's mainstream consumer is more likely than not to be a person of color—or many colors. Brands hoping to stay relevant must not only improve their culturally targeted efforts, but must also update their general-market approach to reflect its inherent diversity.

THE NOT-SO-GENERAL MARKET

Talking about ethnicity in marketing can be exhausting—not because of the subject matter or the constant debate among industry pundits, but because of the vague, euphemistic, and at times downright confusing language used by marketers in this space. As in many other areas of contemporary American culture, there is a pervasive discomfort surrounding race in the marketing world. But since persuasive advertising is all about appealing to salient dimensions of consumer identity, and race is one such dimension, the conversation must go on. The marketing industry has typically sidestepped the potholes by employing a lexicon that allows race to be discussed without explicitly referring to Whites, Blacks, Hispanics, or Asians, and the historic imbalances that contribute to these groups' distinctions from one another.

Considering the history of demographics in America, it's easy to understand why "general market" has long been a euphemism for "White" within the marketing sphere. Although the idea of reaching a truly general audience sounds great to most businesses, when it comes down to it, they acknowledge that it's not a real advertising target. Even when their products and services have broad appeal, companies identify their target users via some specific predispositions or demographics. So, like many ad-speak terms, "general market" has shifted over the years from its literal definition to become a shorthand for any communications not specifically targeted to ethnic consumers.

However, in the early days of advertising, "general market" was actually a valid concept, particularly when advertising a commodity that everyone used or could use, like soap or cereal. This was also true because people consumed a limited amount of media, and the number of products competing for their attention was drastically fewer. However, because minorities were systematically marginalized by society at the time, they were also excluded from market research studies and ad imagery. Therefore, the idea of general-market communications, in the sense of campaigns geared toward *everyone,* has never been practically applied, at least not with any consistency. In fact, it was the exclusionary nature of these very practices that gave rise to ethnic target marketing as a means of advertising products and services to previously ignored ethnic populations. And once multicultural marketing was an established cottage industry, a new term was needed for marketing geared toward everyone else. Hence the "general market = White" code in effect today.

Because the marketing evolution continues apace, let's take a hard look at the current ethnic marketing paradigm and its future viability. While today's minorities may not be fully integrated into every aspect of American society—and are notably under-represented within the ranks of today's leading ad agencies—the Obama presidency alone suggests that significant strides have been made. With the steady mainstreaming of ethnic minorities into American society comes an urgent need to demarginalize advertising meant to appeal to these groups.

THE CAUCASIAN CONSUMER MARKET

There is a glaring omission from most books, articles, and conversations on the future of advertising to the multicultural mainstream. Marketers seem to have forgotten completely about the group that comprises the largest subsegment of the New Majority: non-Hispanic Whites. Rarely do marketers think about Caucasians as a consumer segment, since they are not often a culturally defined target audience. They are, however, a segment worth understanding in the context of culturally conscious marketing.

On Whiteness

Before tackling best practices for marketing to non-Hispanic Whites, we must first examine the role that ethnicity plays in White consumer identity. It has been argued that in America, there is no "White culture" to speak of. This school of thought asserts that Whiteness is now, and has always been, a social construct rather than a scientifically supported category of difference in preference and attitude. It is a counter-defined social marker, used to describe people who are not *non*-White. The drivers behind distinguishing non-Whites from Whites are steeped in the difficult history of American racial politics, including colonialism, slavery, segregation, and the resulting socioeconomic imbalances. These living connections to our country's moral ebbs have left Whiteness one of the most taboo aspects of today's cultural discourse. To discuss race in an open and honest forum is to open a Pandora's box of unresolved inequities, inherited guilt, historic racism, and charged emotions.

But just because there is no anthropological basis for non-Hispanic Whites as a distinct racial group does not mean that this categorization lacks meaning and relevance in today's America. Journalist Kelefa Sanneh explored the debate on the existence of White American culture in a 2010 *New Yorker* article titled, "Beyond the Pale: Is White the New Black?"

> [I]f the old race theory was brutally reductive, there is something reductive, too, about the idea that whiteness, for all its paradoxes, isn't real. The history of human culture is the history of forgeries that become genuine, categories that people make and cannot simply unmake. So we should probably stop thinking of whiteness as an error, and start thinking of it, instead, as a work in progress. Historians have sometimes framed the treacherous history of whiteness as the slow death of an idea. Perhaps it's time we start viewing it, instead, as the slow birth of a people.[1]

The takeaway for marketers is this: The increasing representation of ethnic minorities in popular culture is likely to elevate the role of race in White consumers' self-identity.

One of the things that distinguishes minority groups is the "otherness" imposed on them. They inhabit a country and/or operate within a predominant culture that is distinct from the ethnic culture with which they identify. White consumers in the United States have not experienced this disparity, since they have long been the clear majority, racially speaking. The predominant racial and cultural backdrop in most general-market advertising has been relevant to Whites. And because mainstream marketers had no need to infuse general-market ads with cultural cues, they focused on other levers, like values, attitude, and life stage, which arguably have a more direct impact on consumer behavior than race.

But, you might ask, if White consumers don't navigate the world as ethnic "others," is there any reason to address culture in advertising geared to them? Here are a few:

- *Contrary to the common understanding of the term,* everyone *in America is part of the "multicultural market," including non-Hispanic Whites.* Just as ethnic consumers don't exist in separate mini-nations, neither do Whites. Therefore, any strategy that discusses the marketing implications of reaching the new majority without addressing them for Whites as well is incomplete.

- *Caucasian will soon cease to be the default cultural affiliation of the general-market consumer.* In fact, for certain mainstream brands in particular categories, this shift has already taken place. As the mainstream continues to diversify, some non-Hispanic Whites may begin to experience the otherness that African Americans, Hispanics, and Asian Americans are all too familiar with. There is currently no toolkit—no language, no model, no historical analogue—for addressing this in the marketplace. While most ethnic marketers could easily rattle off a number of cultural insights related to their own niche segments, it is unlikely that you'd find a generalist who could do the same for the non-Hispanic White audience. That may need to change.

- *What is engaging, relevant, and motivating to the non-Hispanic White consumer has changed over time and continues to be reshaped by the country's increasing cultural diversity.* Without a doubt, social context influences consumer attitudes, values, and behavior. The history of advertising is full of examples of how a single message can take on different meaning or elicit different responses based on where society is at the time. For example, a "premium experience" message may be well received during an economic boom because consumers have an aspirational mindset, but during a recession, it may translate to an expensive and out-of-reach brand perception, and therefore be rejected. Likewise, we are in the midst of an ethnic population boom. The broth of mainstream culture, flavored over generations by multitudes of ethnic influences, is being absorbed by the non-Hispanic White consumers in the marketplace. This has changed these consumers' expectations about culture in advertising, and the type of messaging that they find appealing.

Connecting with White Consumers as Part of the Multicultural Mainstream

Although the non-Hispanic White population is not growing as quickly as the ethnic groups that have traditionally been the focus of multicultural marketing conversations, they are still the current majority, and will continue to be the largest racial group in America for decades into the future. In light of this, it would be a fatal error to ignore them in the scramble to appeal to ethnic consumers. There are several research-supported factors to take into consideration when marketing to White consumers:

- *Insight:* Because they have not historically been cultural outsiders, Caucasian consumers don't necessarily view ethnic ads as geared to someone other than themselves, even if they feature all-ethnic casts, or include cultural cues. They are not offended by ads featuring people who don't look or sound like them, and they only feel excluded if there is a blatant indicator that the ad is not meant for them (i.e., it is not in English, it is presented in targeted media, etc.).

  Implication: Spots created to appeal to African American, Hispanic, or Asian American consumers can absolutely be effective among Whites, particularly if they follow the basic principles of good advertising, including a strong human insight related to shared attitudes or behaviors within a given product or service category.

  Recommendation: Consider routinely testing spots developed for ethnic audiences among Caucasian consumers, translating to English when necessary. Run English versions of high-performing ethnic executions on mainstream media platforms.

- *Insight:* When confronted directly with ethnic targeting, Caucasian consumers are rarely offended by it. On the contrary, they expect it, given America's diversity. If they encounter a cultural cue in advertising that they don't understand, they tend to ignore it, as opposed to being turned off by it. Subtle ethnic "winks" tend to be completely invisible to non-Hispanic White consumers.

Implication: While consumers of color may sometimes interpret the concept of ethnic targeting in ads as offensive, non-Hispanic Whites tend to have a more matter-of-fact attitude toward it. This may be because they view all versions of such ads as potentially geared to them, while ethnic consumers view the targeted ad as geared exclusively toward themselves (or another ethnic group), and the nontargeted ads as geared toward Caucasians.

Recommendation: Work toward the ideal of mainstream advertising that appeals to both ethnic and Caucasian segments by "baking in" cultural insights and ethnic nods. Similarly, targeted advertising should be based on human insights that are fundamentally relatable, despite ethnic casting, insights, and cultural cues.

- *Insight:* Caucasian kids, teenagers, and young adults, as well as urban-dwelling older adults, live in a world more diverse than that which is reflected in most advertising campaigns developed with them in mind.

  Implication: Scenarios and storylines presented in nontargeted advertising must be culturally diverse if they seek to reflect the authentic reality of young and/or urban White consumers' social environments.

  Recommendation: Creative briefs and target profiles should go beyond the ethnic makeup of the target consumer to include the demographic dynamics of their social circles. If a mostly Caucasian target inhabits a culturally diverse personal sphere, this should be reflected in advertising imagery geared toward them.

- *Insight:* Non-Hispanic White consumers take offense on behalf of ethnic consumers at ads they perceive as stereotyping or racially insensitive to those groups. This tends to happen when the execution features talent from a single ethnic group and is burdened with heavy-handed cultural cues.

  Implication: Cultural cues that are so overt as to eclipse the human insight and brand message run the risk of not only alienating the intended ethnic target, but of turning off Caucasian consumers as well.

  Recommendation: For campaigns that do include an ethnically targeted component, ensure that the overarching strategic insight is relevant to all groups by testing the strategy among both ethnic and White consumers. If your ethnic agencies are assured that the strategy is relevant to non-White consumers, they are less likely to overcompensate by including excessive ethnic cues in targeted advertising, which could potentially alienate the White segment.

The Role of Race in White Identity

In a 2010 qualitative study conducted by Firefly Millward Brown, 64 White, Hispanic, African American, and Asian American consumers were asked to define their personal identity by writing down five different descriptive words or phrases. Next, each participant was provided a list of several identity descriptors related to gender, employment status, geography, age, family roles, and other characteristics, including their self-identified racial designation. From within that list, participants were asked to identify and rank the five most important descriptors to their personal identity, and were given the option to write in their own, if they so chose. The results were surprising. Across the board, the overwhelming majority of respondents did not consider race in the open-ended expression of their self-definition. Only a handful of participants selected their ethnic affiliation in the closed-ended portion of the exercise. None of the White respondents selected race as an important personal identifier in either task. From this exercise and the discussions that followed, an important insight emerged: Although the role of race within a consumer's "who I am" story varies considerably from person to person, Caucasian consumers as a group think far less about their race than other segments do. Furthermore, as discussed in previous chapters, race is usually not a top-of-mind factor for any consumer.

MARKETING TO THE NEW MAJORITY

In chapter 4, we introduced the idea that each of the major ethnic segments is at a different point in the journey toward mainstream marketers' radar. In chapter 5 we charted the marketing industry's evolution toward acceptance of the New-Majority paradigm from the perspectives of both advertisers and the agencies developing consumer communications on their behalf. Chapter 6 provided a road map to help guide decision making for when to target based on ethnicity. In chapter 7 we laid out principles for successfully targeting ethnic consumers. And earlier in this chapter, we made the case for including White consumers in a New-Majority construct that abandons the ethnic-versus-general market view in favor of a reenvisioned total market that is diverse by nature.

This new frontier has a number of implications for business at all points along the marketing pipeline. And while the guidelines that follow are not by any means exhaustive, they do provide general direction for crafting, instituting, and executing campaigns against the backdrop of change heralded by the 2010 US census.

Change the Language to Change the Conversation

I think the label "multicultural" is very confusing, because people use it in very weird ways. There are no multicultural markets. It just depends on how you define things. Is "multicultural" the person that has different cultural backgrounds in their own genetic family pool? Or is "multicultural" the society that contains different cultures? An agency that does Spanish marketing is not multicultural. They are just doing Hispanic marketing. Many times people will ask me silly things like, "Are you multicultural?" I say, "No, I'm just Mexican." It's just that people are using these labels in a very confusing way
—Felipe Korzenny, director, Center for
Hispanic Marketing Communication,
Florida State University

In interview after interview with industry leaders, one resounding criticism of the ethnic-marketing discourse emerged consistently: The lexicon is broken. Aside from the confusion introduced by unclear terminology, it reinforces outdated constructs and in so doing makes it that much harder to nimbly adapt to new realities. We offer the following recommendations for reframing the discussion:

- When referring to unspecified minority segments, agencies, or marketing efforts, "ethnic" is a more accurate term than "multicultural," since multicultural implies multiple ethnic groups. When referencing a specific and singular segment, refer to that group as Hispanic or Latino (or use a specific national origin), African American or Black (the latter includes immigrant populations), Asian American (or use a specific national origin), Caucasian or non-Hispanic White, and so on.
- "Multicultural" is appropriate to refer to an audience, strategy, or execution that is ethnically or racially diverse. Multicultural does not exclude Caucasians, and should not imply only ethnic minorities.
- "General market" is a confusing and vague term. What's more, it has little meaning in the realm of segmented marketing, since every group in the target universe belongs to some segment. If the intended reference is to nonethnic consumers, then "Caucasian or non-Hispanic White" should be used. If the intended reference is to a broad and culturally inclusive audience, then "total market" is the appropriate term.
- When describing an insight or strategy that is expressly designed to have relevance across multiple ethnic or cultural groups, use the term "transcultural" to convey that it resonates across cultures.
- When discussing an execution or idea that was developed to appeal to one ethnic group, but ends up having crossover appeal among one or more other groups, refer to it as "cross-cultural."

Structure Business for Successful New-Majority Marketing

For advertisers, forging the best possible relationship with the New Majority means embedding cultural astuteness, relatability, and empathy throughout all aspects of your business. It is not enough for a brand to farm out cultural competency by briefing its ethnic agencies on their brand vision, goals, and marketing strategy, and expecting them to translate all of that into compelling targeted campaigns. When it comes to engaging the New Majority and each of the cultural segments that comprise it, the company must walk the walk by presenting a clear vision for engaging the evolving marketplace. Consider the following principles offered up by brands like McDonald's, Diageo, and General Mills that have already begun redesigning their infrastructure and operations to meet the marketplace's changing needs:

1. *The company's vision for marketing to the New Majority must come from the top.* If no C-level executive or senior vice president is evangelizing for the crucial importance of ethnic consumers to their business, both internally and externally, it will be much more difficult to implement systemwide change.

2. *A diverse workforce is essential for companies seeking to relate and empathize with their ethnic customers in a real way.* If a company's employee base is far less diverse than the audience it serves, it is operating at a significant handicap with regard to connecting to the New Majority. Although expertise in the ethnic marketplace can come from anyone, regardless of race, there is a certain degree of intuitive empathy and life experience that ethnic employees can bring to the table. In addition, close working relationships among coworkers of various ethnic backgrounds help the entire team internalize ethnic insights. A chief diversity officer can be instrumental in bringing this vision to reality.

3. *Establishing a multicultural-marketing department can be an important step in the transition toward fully integrating ethnic competency throughout the organization, but it is not the finish line.* One of your interim goals should be to create and leverage an internal team of ethnic experts for the purpose of educating various sales and marketing teams. But there should also be a plan for taking off the training wheels, so that sales and marketing feel empowered to deliver culturally inclusive strategies independent of the multicultural-marketing group.

4. *Don't tap Juan, Keisha, or Jin to participate in the ethnic marketing team simply because they are Hispanic, Black, or Asian.* If you bring them on in this capacity, it should be because of their track

record of expertise in marketing to these segments. Assuming that ethnic personnel are interested in working on ethnic projects may make some employees question whether their broader talents are truly valued. In addition, firsthand experience living as an ethnic minority is only part of the ethnic expertise equation, and assures only that they can bring their own personal perspectives to the table. Each ethnic consumer audience is diverse, and the best ethnic marketers are well versed in the nuances of each subgroup.

5. *Leader brands don't just pay lip service to engaging the diverse New Majority.* They go a step further and to tie it to performance reviews and incentive compensation. Quantifiable goals relative to ethnic market growth are set up in advance, and favorable reviews and bonuses are awarded when these goals are met.

6. *For businesses that engage both generalist and ethnic agencies, the person managing them must set the tone for collaboration and an open flow of ideas.* There is an atmosphere of insecurity and tension in today's agencies about which types are best suited to lead marketing efforts for the New Majority. The brand's point person should make it clear that he or she values the unique strengths that each agency brings to the table, and be open to the best ideas regardless of which agency they come from. Setting up a fair and transparent compensation model for the various agencies will reinforce this. Healthy competition can yield stellar work, but if the ethnic agencies feel undermined, they may unintentionally assert their role by creating work that overemphasizes ethnic distinctions. Invite all your agencies to strategic and creative briefings, rather than meeting separately or leaving it to the general-market agency to relay your directions to the ethnic agency. In these all-agency meetings, state your preferred style of collaboration up front—or, in the case of agencies that have established partnerships with their own ethnic agencies, ask them to present their process for collaboration before you start.

Mine Insights to Effectively Drive New-Majority Marketing

Every marketer knows that great creative executions are built upon solid strategies, and the most effective strategies are anchored in research-driven insights. Conducting good research in the age of the New Majority is not as complex as it may seem. In the same way that the basic principles of marketing apply when advertising to ethnic consumers, the mining of cultural insight is based on the same principles of sound research. There are, however, some often-overlooked nuances to this type of research and planning that can help marketers avoid costly cracks in a campaign's strategic foundation:

1. *Make sure that all quantitative surveys administered on a regular basis (e.g., brand trackers, attitude and usage studies, segmentation, customer relationship management [CRM] questionnaires, copy tests, etc.) ask participants to identify their race and ethnicity.* Part of the reason that so many brands report underspending on ethnic segments is that they have no clear measurement of their return on investment for the minor efforts they have already made. Dedicated studies on each of the ethnic segments can be costly, but simply adding a race and ethnicity question to non-targeted studies allows all quantitative learnings from that point forward to be viewed through a cultural lens, if needed.

2. *Work with vendors that have experience conducting research among both ethnic and White consumers.* They bring immeasurable expertise to the table and have established processes for designing, recruiting, and executing studies among these markets. Brief them on the objectives, targets, and study parameters, and ask them to come back with an approach that accounts for the various challenges and nuances that these audiences present. One way to determine whether your vendor has the appropriate degree of expertise is whether they are well versed in issues related to acculturation, the regional distribution of different immigrant groups, and biculturalism. It is also preferable that they have these competencies in-house, because subcontracting can create openings for errors and misunderstandings. That said, a research shop need not be exclusively focused on ethnic segments to understand the best practices for reaching these consumers.

3. *Make sure that the language within the screener, survey, and/ or discussion guide is reviewed by someone with ethnic expertise before it is sent into the field.* Wording that is unintentionally

offensive can influence participants' responses throughout the remainder of a survey. Likewise, incorrect translations or misunderstood cultural idioms can lead to confused answers.

4. If the goal of a qualitative study is to emerge with ethnic insights, and the methodology involves in-person focus groups, it is crucial that respondents are interviewed in separate same-ethnicity groups for two reasons: (1) In mixed groups, there usually aren't enough respondents to determine whether the feedback from the few ethnic consumers is culturally distinct; and (2) Ethnic respondents in mixed groups tend to approach the subject matter from the perspective of the group's defining characteristics (i.e. as a mom, luxury car purchaser, small business owner, etc.), rather than focusing on issues of cultural relevance.

5. *Researchers do not need to be members of a particular ethnicity to deliver strong insights related to that group.* However, when it comes to qualitative, in-person research designed for the purpose of eliciting ethnic insights, it is ideal for the moderator to be culturally matched to the group. Because of underlying tensions, it can be difficult for many ethnic respondents to honestly express their culturally influenced opinions in "mixed company." Without realizing it, respondents may self-censor and respond in politically correct terms so as not to offend a moderator of a different race. This can result in misleading takeaways from ethnic focus groups, a problem that is less pronounced but still present when dealing with younger consumers. Finally, ethnically matched moderators may be more likely to catch on to coded language or in-group slang, and seize the opportunity to probe these issues further.

6. *Unless the purpose of a particular study is to segment an entire ethnic group, focus the research on a behaviorally or attitudinally defined subset.* One of the most common mistakes is failing to replicate the same target specifications used for the general study when conducting an ethnic component. For example, let's say there are plans for focus groups to assess a new campaign idea among four types of consumers in a general study: Moms, Trend Leaders, Mainstream Young Adult Males, and Mainstream Young Adult Females. In testing this same campaign idea among Hispanic, African American, and Asian American consumers, it is not enough to tack on one Hispanic, one African American, and one Asian American

group, each representing a mix of those four segments. If there is insufficient budget to replicate all four segments across each ethnic group (for a total of 16 focus groups), consider picking the two highest-opportunity segments—say Moms and Young Adults (in total, i.e., both genders)—and replicating those across ethnicities, for a more conservative total of eight focus groups.

Hire—or Create—the Agency of the Future

If you ask me what the future would look like to me, it would be one agency that really provides a holistic point of view...I think if America has already embraced the inclusive mindset, agencies also have to move in that direction.
—*Marcela Garcia, senior manager, consumer planning, Diageo North America*

Because advertising agencies fulfill the needs of the marketplace as defined by their clients' brands, moving the industry toward a *new agency model* for the future depends largely on advertisers. We've all seen the data on the majority-minority future, but the industry is a long way from where it needs to be in order to keep up with these changes. Now imagine that there were no general-market or ethnic agencies, but instead, marketing communications agencies with diverse and qualified employees, strategic chops, innovative creative, forward-thinking leadership, and the cultural competency to develop persuasive communications for all types of consumers—not ethnic or Millennial or digital consumers, just *consumers.* And in this world, the most competent agencies with the internal resources and external partnerships to get the job done would win the client's business. Sound crazy? Or perhaps just too rational to be true? This is the agency model of the future, and some have already begun to move in this direction.

In fall 2010, Ogilvy made waves by launching a cross-cultural communications arm called OgilvyCULTURE. This internal practice may be the proverbial canary in the coal mine, heralding the total disintegration of boundaries between generalist and specialist agencies' traditional roles. According to director Jeffrey Bowman, OgilvyCULTURE faces an uphill struggle despite the evolving marketplace, because clients remain entrenched in the traditional agency model: "Clients buy services based on a general-market bucket or a multicultural bucket. They're still separate. Consumers consume content and creative. They don't think [in those terms]. They say, 'That connected with me,' either through a symbol or through a song, or maybe [it made them] feel a certain way... And so, what we are doing structurally is readjusting the mindset of our industry."[2] His team is doing this through a process they're calling "The One Brief" that requires the business objective to be the starting point of any new marketing activity. They identify the types of consumers who can help move the dial closer to that goal and elicit insights on how they behave within the category. From there, they may emerge with a relatively universal perspective that can be communicated through a single execution, or they may end up with several distinct perspectives that vary along cultural lines. So in the end, the creative expression may be tailored to unique cultural perspectives, but the various agencies all begin with the same strategic brief, based on identical business objectives.

OgilvyCULTURE's approach has quickly garnered a lot of criticism. Some wonder if it isn't a veiled attempt for a general-market agency to usurp the ethnic business that is sure to boom with the anticipated boost from the 2010 census numbers. OgilvyCULTURE argues that the marketplace has changed, and that it is merely attempting to adapt its model to these changes. Some wonder why Ogilvy didn't simply acquire or assemble a multicultural agency to round out their capabilities. The agency responds that the launch of OgilvyCULTURE is a means, rather than an end in itself. The leadership considers it a transitional step, like its previous efforts to recruit diverse talent and create professional networks for cultural affinity groups within its ranks. And they intend to follow it with another important step: They claim the goal is to render

OgilvyCULTURE obsolete by elevating the agency's cultural competency at large, gaining clients' trust in their ethnic-marketing capabilities along the way—thereby transforming the firm from a general-market agency into an agency of the future that has the proper tools for reaching the New Majority.

This is hardly the first time that an agency has tried to transform the traditional model into one that transcends old-school labels and limitations. Most have come from the ethnic-marketing side of the business, and have had limited success given the avant-garde nature of their vision, and clients' unwillingness to believe that agencies with an ethnic perspective can also connect with a mainstream point of view. Another major barrier to the success of cross-cultural or multicultural agencies has been their limited access to resources, compared with the high-billing blue chip agencies and massive holding companies.

General-market agencies that have gone to bat for ethnic business have historically fallen short, as revealed in interviews with leading brands:

> It's very hard to have the depth of [ethnic] insight you need if you are looking very broadly, which makes it a challenge for a general market agency to take. So I don't know if a general market agency is well poised today. I think they would have to somehow figure out how to have the [ethnic] expertise that they need, in-house, and how to have it not be playing second fiddle to general market.[3]

> —Kathy Mowrey, senior manager, consumer insights,
> The Home Depot

> I think general market needs to shift the way they think significantly, and I think we're a long way from that. I've been working with agencies that just completely do not get it. We ask them, do you have Hispanic capabilities? They get the Puerto Rican guy in the office to look over the copy.[4]

> —Yvonne Montanino, senior manager, consumer and
> market insights, multicultural, Unilever

Certainly, there is quite a bit of ground to cover for today's total-market and ethnic agencies alike. Clients will no longer be content to choose between cultural competency and efficiency; they want both. Whichever agencies figure out how to do this first will be the front-runners in the race to relevance. While there is not yet a proven formula for successfully launching the agency of the future, the following principles may be helpful in guiding the evolutionary process:

1. *For the same reasons as outlined for client companies, the agency workforce must be diverse.* This goes for the ethnic agencies as well as the generalists. Metaphorically speaking, you can learn the language, but if you speak it with a heavy accent, it will be obvious that you're a foreigner. Translation: Consumers can tell if the creators of an ad are on the outside of their culture looking in.

2. *Consider the total market when developing the brief, regardless of whether the client has tasked you with a certain cultural subset.* If you don't know whether your creative concepts can relate to groups outside of your core target, you are cutting yourself off from the possibility of extending your reach to a broader audience.

3. *Know the overlaps between an ethnic market and the total market to maximize efficiency.* Ethnic agencies: We understand that there are differences between the various cultural segments. You know what they are, and your clients probably do too, if you are doing your job educating them on the audience's nuances and distinctions. Help them understand where there are *similarities* with those outside of your ethnic niche. "Efficiency" isn't a scary code word for phasing out ethnic specialists. It's a real business goal sought by savvy advertisers. If you can provide efficiencies in the form of cross-cultural insights that are born from your segment but broadly applicable to others, you'll be in a great position.

4. *Test out your cross-cultural approaches in the digital world.* For better or for worse, the media landscape has evolved far quicker than advertising philosophy, reinventing platforms for transcultural consumer engagement. While there are plenty of ethnically targeted digital outlets, social media alone offers a viable model

for deeply engaging consumers according to their interests and lifestyle rather than their ethnicities. Study these platforms and the leading brands within them to understand how ethnically targeted and nontargeted efforts can coexist neatly. Use these platforms to engage the New Majority.

5. *Most importantly, develop a strategy for transitioning to your version of the agency of the future.* Map out a multiyear game plan and make sure it accounts for clients raising their quality standards over time for work geared toward the New Majority. Many, like Coca-Cola and McDonald's, have already stated publicly that the majority of their future growth will come from ethnic consumers—not the "uni-cultural" minority consumers of 50 years ago, but today's ethnic consumers, who move fluidly between cultural spheres and don't view the world through race-tinted glasses.

CHAPTER 9

The Multicultural Opportunity Abroad

Multiculturalism is not unique to the United States; neither are its opportunities and challenges. In fact, some regions of the world confronted it long before us, and are now in a more advanced stage wherein multicultural strategies are a natural part of marketing. Although multicultural scenarios have some things in common, each country also has its own particularities. In some places, like the United States, these particularities are closely related to race and ethnicity; while in others, they are based on such factors as religion or economic strata. While in some circumstances the diversity is driven by relatively recent migratory waves (as in Western Europe), in others it's deeply rooted, going back generations or even centuries (as in the Middle East). In some countries language plays a key role in targeting different segments, while in others, where a common language is shared, it is not a factor.

We believe strongly that lessons from other places can be beneficial for US marketers—just as we hope that our experience can benefit people in other regions, especially those where multiculturalism and ethnic marketing are just taking off, such as Western Europe. That is why we decided to dedicate this last chapter of the book to analyzing the multicultural opportunity outside of the United States.

To be clear, when we talk about the multicultural opportunity abroad, we are not referring to what is traditionally known as international, multinational, or global marketing. Unlike that discipline—which concerns marketing to people in different countries around the world—multicultural or ethnic marketing deals with marketing to people of different cultures that are coexisting in the same country or region. This is an important distinction because:

1. Communities that coexist do not live in silos. They interact with and influence one another at many levels. In chapter 3, for example, we saw that Mexicans in the United States are different from Mexicans in Mexico because they live together with people of other cultures.
2. Communities that share the same space are typically exposed to a similar range of media and communications from brands, whether it is targeted to them or not. Therefore, marketing directed at one segment affects other groups, too.

Of course, these two factors are equally valid at the international level, especially thanks to the advances in technology and communications—a cumulative television audience of an estimated 26 billion viewers around the globe watched the 2010 FIFA World Cup! But international marketing will never be synonymous with multicultural marketing, because for all the lip service globalization gets, most consumers still live very local lives. People in Bolivia are rarely interested or influenced by people in Jordan, and vice versa.

However, many of the best practices followed in international marketing also apply to multicultural marketing. Nigel Hollis, Millward Brown's chief global analyst and author of *The Global Brand: How to Create and Develop Lasting Brand Value in the World Market,* says that "the fundamental challenge for brand marketers (on the global stage) is to distinguish between the aspects of a brand that can be exported successfully and those that must be adapted." He continues, "They must weigh the efficacy of developing one global marketing campaign against the need to be sensitive to local countries and cultures. Go too far in the direction of local adaptation and all efficiencies are lost...Fail to adapt the offer sufficiently and the opportunity cost of lost sales and wasted marketing investment could be significant."[1]

In multicultural marketing, you must find that same balance between standardization and customization, while also taking into account the literal proximity of your diverse audiences—who often live next door to one another. This mandate poses some new and different challenges.

IMMIGRANTS AND MULTICULTURALISM

One commonality among multicultural communities is that most of them are the result of migratory processes, whether those migrations took place years or centuries ago, voluntarily or by force. Take the case of the United States. The two largest ethnic segments, Hispanics and African Americans, are both the result of massive movements of people. While the largest migratory waves from Latin America occurred during the second half of the twentieth century, the biggest influx of Blacks happened during the epoch of slavery, between the fifteenth and nineteenth centuries. Further, while most Hispanic immigrants traveled to the United States voluntarily, either in search of better economic opportunities or to escape from political tyranny in their countries of origin, Black slaves were brought against their will.

The world has witnessed innumerable similar migratory processes throughout its history, from the early nomadic tribes of the prehistoric era to recent displacements around the globe, like those happening as a consequence of the war on terror in the Middle East or the civil wars in Africa. Some of these migrations have been massive and rapid; others, gradual and steady, but all have had a huge impact on their respective destination countries or regions. So to truly understand the *resulting* society, it is important for marketers to not only understand how the different groups or waves of immigrants have adapted to their host country, but also how the host country has changed because of their presence.

When doing this analysis in different parts of the world, keep in mind that similar events can have very different consequences from one situation to another. Drawing conclusions based on seemingly similar circumstances can trip you up. Take Brazil:

When we were considering countries to discuss as multicultural examples, we thought that Brazil could be interesting in comparison to the United States. Both countries have a Black minority largely descended from slaves brought there centuries ago, so we expected to see similarities in how the two societies have evolved. But in fact, the integration of races progressed somewhat differently over the years, due in part to the different approaches Anglo and Portuguese colonizers took in their respective territories. In the United States, relations between the Black minority and the White majority have typically been difficult, to say the least. In the South American country, on the other hand, Blacks, or *pretos,* are often more integrated and interrelated with Whites and other ethnic Brazilian groups. Brazil does have its history of problems in this area, most visibly in striking economic inequalities among the races, but their integration is with no doubt more evident.

An interesting indicator of this mixing of races in Brazil is the size of the mulato segment (as people who are of mixed Black and White descent are known). Mulatos comprise 39% of the total population in Brazil (versus less than 1% in the United States). Whites account for 54%; Blacks, 6%.[2] Further, according to a 1998 report of the Brazilian Institute of Geography and Statistics, only about 10% of Black Brazilians consider themselves of "African origin," with most of them identifying as having "Brazilian origin."[3] In fact, Black Brazilians practically never use the phrase "African Brazilians" to categorize themselves, while many Blacks in the United States prefer to include the "African" modifier.

So we see that two somewhat similar migratory processes in the past have resulted in very distinct realities in the present. Obviously, the implications go far beyond the issue of what names people use to refer to their ethnic group. In fact, the idea of ethnic marketing discussed in the previous chapters is virtually nonexistent in Brazil. If companies there want to target specific segments of the population, they are more likely to use variables like socioeconomic level or lifestyle rather than race—despite operating in one of the region's most multiracial countries.

NON-RACE-BASED MULTICULTURALISM

Until now, most of our multicultural discussion has focused on racial or ethnic diversity. However, in many areas other factors, including religion, regionalism, and socioeconomic status, are more relevant. In order to usefully discuss these types of situations, we must again toss out the traditional labels and stop assuming that culture is only a matter of race, rather than a construct influenced by many factors.

Perhaps one of the most salient examples of non-race-based multiculturalism is the Muslim population around the world. We saw some of this when we discussed the case of Muslim Americans in chapter two, but to get a better idea of this segment's importance from a business perspective let's take a look at what Muslims represent on the global stage. First, some of the facts: Globally, Muslims number about 1.57 billion people, roughly one-fifth of the world population. This community is spread across many different nations and ethnic groups. Most reside in countries that are Muslim-majority, especially in Asia, Northern Africa, and the Middle East. Muslims who live as religious minorities (about 20% of the global Muslim population) are mainly in Europe and the Americas,[4] and can be further divided into two segments:

1. Muslims who are also immigrants or recent descendants of immigrants in their countries of residency. This is a common characteristic among Muslims in Western Europe, especially in the United Kingdom, France, the Scandinavian countries, and Germany, the country that has the largest Muslim population in the region at more than 4 million (more, even, than the number of Muslims in Lebanon).
2. Muslims who are native to the countries where they reside, including descendants of immigrants who arrived centuries ago (common among Russian and Eastern European Muslims), or indigenous converts.

According to Joy Abdullah, senior consultant at the Islamic-focused branding firm Daily Baraka and an expert in the global

Muslim market, while immigrant (or second-generation) Muslims are likely to differ from the native population in their adopted countries not only in terms of their religious belief, but also from a racial and ethnic perspective; indigenous or native Muslims are more in sync with the local secular, social, and cultural practices of the countries where they reside. From a marketing perspective, each segment represents a different opportunity (and challenge). To target the former, companies usually have to address language differences and other cultural nuances in addition to the religion factor.

Interestingly, China also fits well within the category of non-race-based multiculturalism. In this case, diversity correlates to the development level of a given part of the country. Specifically, it's about the difference in the standard of living between big, first-tier cities (Shanghai, Beijing, Guangzhou, and, according to some, Shenzhen) and smaller municipalities—the former being wealthier and more cosmopolitan than the latter. According to Albert Sim, managing director of Millward Brown's Beijing office, this type of diversity has an impact on how consumers think about and react to brands and advertising. For example, while people in first-tier cities are open to international brands and more likely to look for entertainment in advertising, people in lower-tier cities tend to prefer local brands, are more sensitive to price, and are more likely to look for information in advertising.

In breaking into the Chinese market, most international brands have focused their efforts on first-tier cities. However, as the markets in these cities have become saturated, more and more brands are expanding to lower-tier cities in the western part of the country. This shift is bringing development to new regions, which in turn is generating a huge influx of immigrants coming from small towns or rural areas to second-tier cities. This migration is destined to be one of the biggest mass movements in human history. Over the next 25 years, it is estimated that up to 345 million people will move from the rural areas of China to the cities. Some people are calling it the second Industrial Revolution.[5]

This means that brands will have to rethink their approach to the Chinese market, going from a one-country approach where no multicultural strategies were needed to targeted approaches for various regions. And in this case, the targeting will be based on economics and lifestyle rather than race. In its "2009 Annual Chinese Consumer Study," McKinsey & Company suggests an interesting alternative to the traditional tiered-cities approach. "Rather than view China through the simple lens of city tier or region," the report says, "companies should instead organize China's 800 cities into two dozen or more city clusters.... These clusters—consisting of as few as 2 and as many as roughly 70 neighboring cities—are defined not only by income and geographic location, but also by economic linkages and trade flows between cities, as well as common consumer attitudes and preferences."[6] Would we consider this a type of "multicultural" approach? Certainly. Similar situations have occurred in other parts of the world (although on much smaller scales, of course). For an example, see the Peruvian case highlighted later in the chapter.

MULTICULTURALISM AROUND THE WORLD:
FIVE CASE STUDIES

Although we cannot discuss all the world's major multicultural societies here, we have decided to focus on five specific countries or regions: Europe, Malaysia, Peru, Canada, and South Africa. Why these places? Because each demonstrates a different facet of multiculturalism, and therefore offers different lessons. We start by explaining why we think they are illustrative cases, then sharing their backstories, and finally highlighting some examples of what companies are doing there to reach out to diverse audiences.

Europe

What Is Special about It?

Europe is a complex but fascinating case study for multiculturalism. If you conceive of it as one region (and many companies do), the "local" population of Europe is inherently multicultural. The continent is comprised of people of various ethnic and cultural backgrounds who speak many different languages. Historically, each segment has been concentrated in their respective country (or countries), but populations are now moving more freely across borders within the European Union. Europe has also been a major destination for immigrants from the Southern Hemisphere in the past three to four decades—South Asia, Africa, and Latin America. These immigrant communities are growing fast in the "old continent," fueled not only by the constant arrival of newcomers, but also by the birth of their children (whereas European natives' birthrates are in decline almost across the board). Many immigrant groups have now reached significant numbers and are starting to play an important role in the social, economic, and political life of Europe. Some governments are taking action to promote diversity, while others are moving to limit it, often with interesting consequences.

The European Story

Since Europe has long been naturally multicultural, the most interesting new lessons come from looking at how recent immigrants are starting to change the face of the region and the implications for the market.

We had hoped to get some good data on the racial and religious demographics in European countries. But this is easier said than done. Several countries do not collect this information because they see it as a potential path to discrimination. In fact, in France, it's illegal to conduct a census on race, ethnicity, or religion. While the rationale behind these decisions is praiseworthy, it may not always help the minority segments themselves.

Here's why: Minority groups usually differ from the mainstream in several aspects: language, religion, traditions, holidays, values, and so on. As we have seen in the United States and other multicultural societies around the world, minority segments *want* the mainstream to recognize and respect these differences. If governments do not make an earnest effort to get to know these minorities, they will hardly be able to understand them. If the French government does not know how many Muslims reside in France, how they live, or what they really want, it will be difficult for authorities to serve them adequately.

In Germany we find another example of a government that may be limiting the opportunities that diversity represents. As we mentioned in chapter 3, in October of 2010 German chancellor Angela Merkel told a gathering of younger members of her conservative Christian Democratic Union party that attempts to build a multicultural society in Germany had "utterly failed." She said that the so-called *multikulti* concept, where people would happily "live side-by-side," did not work, and immigrants needed to do more to integrate—including learning German. According to a BBC article on the topic, Merkel's comments came amid rising anti-immigration sentiment in Germany.[7] We are not political scientists and therefore can't comment on the ramifications of these statements; however, based on our observations of other multicultural societies, we believe that what has failed is the *ideal* of immigrants transforming into native Germans. Asking immigrants to assimilate all aspects of German culture and leave behind their native identity is setting Germany's approach to immigration up for failure.

Fortunately, the business community is slightly more open to the differences that minority segments represent. Leaders in this field understand that targeted approaches can make these groups feel included. In the United States or in any of the examples that follow in this chapter, if brands had not been willing to recognize diversity and its marketing implications, many of them would probably not be viable anymore.

The time is right for European marketers to take advantage of the opportunities offered by immigrant populations. Although minority segments might as yet be small in some countries, there's no mistaking the demographic trends. They are growing as the native European population is aging. These segments are becoming more and more important every day. Like what we saw in the United States in the 1990s, however, some marketers in Europe still think the multicultural market is not for them. Minorities cannot be targeted differently without affecting efficiencies of scale, they say. But if you ask American marketers who were slow to start on multicultural marketing a few decades ago, they'll tell you that they are now playing catch-up to stay relevant, hoping to start understanding these minority segments when competitors are already mastering them. Although efficiencies must always be considered, so must long-term sustainability.

Let's take a quick look at the numbers and at some interesting situations occurring in Spain and France.

Of the approximately 500 million people that live within the boundaries of the 27 member states of the European Union (EU-27), 6% are foreign-born (i.e., born in a country other than the EU country they are living in). Of this, roughly 2 in 3 are nationals from countries outside the EU-27, predominantly Asia, North Africa, Latin America, and the Middle East.[8] Figure 9.1 shows the details for the five largest EU members: Germany, France, the United Kingdom, Italy, and Spain. Proportionally, Spain has the largest foreign-born population (12%), while Italy and France have the lowest (6% each). However, in absolute numbers, Germany is the one with the largest population, with more than 7 million foreign-born people, followed by Spain, with more than 5 million,

	Germany	France	UK	Italy	Spain
Total population (in millions)*	82.3	64.8	62.3	58.1	46.5
Net immigration rate (migrants per 1,000/pop.)*	+2.19	+1.47	+2.61	+2.07	+2.73
Foreign-born population (%)^	9	6	7	6	12
From other EU-27 countries (%)	35	35	40	27	40
From non-EU-27 countries (%)	65	65	60	73	60

Figure 9.1   Immigration in European Union Countries

Source: * CIA World Fact Book, 2010 Estimates
^ Eurostat, 2008 Estimates

and the UK with more than 4 million. It is noteworthy that these numbers do not include second- and third-generation immigrants (that is, the children of these foreign-born people).

To put things in context, recall the domestic figures that we highlighted in the first chapter of the book. The population of people of Chinese descent in the United States (including both foreign-born and subsequent generations) numbers about 3.1 million, or roughly 1% of the total US population, much lower than the proportions of immigrants observed in the European countries mentioned above. Yet brands in these countries are doing little to nothing to reach out to their respective ethnic segments with targeted initiatives—whereas brands going after the Chinese segment in the United States are finding success.

Figure 9.2 shows the country of origin for most of the immigrant populations in the five largest EU states. Understandably, immigrants of Latin origin (South America) are more likely to settle in Latin European countries (Spain and Italy). Proximity is another relevant factor.

Interestingly, in addition to immigration from non-EU countries and other regions of the world, the European Union is experiencing significant migratory processes within its borders, most notably from Eastern European countries westward: Romanians to Italy and Spain; Bulgarians to Spain; and Poles to the UK, Germany, and France. Although immigrants from these countries are "White," just like the majority of natives in their host countries, their culture and consumer needs are, to say the least, somewhat different.

Germany	Croatia, Russia, Serbia, Turkey, Ukraine
France	Algeria, Cambodia, Morocco, Senegal, Serbia, Turkey, Vietnam
UK	Bangladesh, Ethiopia, India, Nigeria, Pakistan, South Africa, Sri Lanka, United States
Italy	China, Ecuador, Egypt, India, Morocco, Peru, Philippines, Senegal, Sri Lanka, Tunisia, Ukraine
Spain	Argentina, Bolivia, Brazil, China, Colombia, Ecuador, Morocco, Peru

Figure 9.2 Immigrants' Most Common Non-EU-27 Countries of Origin
Source: Eurostat, 2008 (in alphabetical order)

Hispanics in Spain?!

Although it might sound strange to you, Latin American immigrants have become an attractive segment for businesses in Spain. Why? Well, there are already more than 2.5 million Latin Americans in Spain, they tend to be younger than the native population (46% are under 30 years old, versus 33% of the average Spanish population), and they have larger families.[9] So they're expected to continue to grow as a group, especially given that Latinos can obtain Spanish citizenship after only two years of residency.

But Latinos have also caught the attention of brands in certain industries because of their distinct needs as consumers and for the cultural traits that set them apart from the Spanish mainstream. Similar to what happened in the early days of Hispanic marketing in the United States, the first companies to take the bait are from the financial and telecommunication categories. For example, the BBVA Group has been designing financial offerings around the remittances that Hispanics send back to their countries of origin, and the cellular provider Orbitel launched a virtual mobile phone targeted to the same segment aimed at providing calling options to Latin America. Another fast-growing sector in the Latino niche is media, primarily newspapers, magazines, and local radio stations developing content that is relevant to this segment, according to Marc Baste, CEO of Novapress Media in Madrid.

Liberté? *The Muslim Market in France*

As we noted, given the legal restrictions around collecting information on race and religion in France, it is hard to know the exact number of Muslims there. However, according to the United States Department of State's 2008 Report on International Religious Freedom, "There are an estimated 5 million to 6 million Muslims (8 to 10% of the population), although estimates of how many of these are practicing vary widely."[10]

Businesses that cater to the halal-observant Muslim market in France are estimated to generate $7.5 billion dollars, a figure that simply can't be ignored. And several companies in the food industry are going after it, including both halal-specific and mainstream brands. According to a France 24 article, in 2009, "Zakia, part of the Panzani food group [a big European brand, best known for pasta], launched France's first ever halal television advert on national channels TF1 and M6. Until then, advertising of Muslim foods had been the preserve of niche media." In 2010, another company, "Reghalal, the halal division of France's number-one chicken brand, LDC, launched its first campaign aimed at the Muslim community."[11]

"Halal advertising is accelerating," Abbas Bendali, head of Solis, an organization that observes ethnic marketing trends in France, told France 24. It is indeed, not only in volume, but in sophistication. In 2010, halal food distributor Isla Delice launched an ad campaign with a twist: billboards that went blank in daylight hours during the holy month of Ramadan, when Muslims fast from sunup to sundown. Thanks to a clever backlighting system, the ads became replete with delicious traditional Muslim foods at night, when Muslims gather to eat.

But it's not all good news. Quick, a French fast-food chain, launched a trial in eight of its restaurants that regularly attracted a Muslim clientele, withdrawing all pork products from the menu and serving only halal meat. At first the trials seemed to go well; unofficial reports said that sales had risen by 30%. Soon after the initiative was launched, however, the mayor of Roubaix, a French town near the northern city of Lille, launched a lawsuit against the food chain, arguing that the menu change constituted "discrimination" against non-Muslims. And Marine Le Pen, the president of the far-right National Front party, made comments warning of "Islamization."

Regardless of public sentiment, it is hard for businesses to buck demographic trends. So as companies begin to understand the richness and potential of a diverse society, the time may come when government is forced to do the same. For now, we'll just reiterate that the opportunity exists in Europe—and, as in most business situations, those that start earlier will have the advantage soon enough.

Malaysia

What Is Special about It?

Malaysia is at the forefront in multicultural marketing. Ethnic Malays, Chinese, Indians, and other groups have coexisted in the Malaysian territory for many decades. Yet unlike the United States, there is not much evidence that these segments are in the process of forming a transcultural society. While the government has launched a "One Malaysia" initiative, the different ethnic groups have managed to maintain their cultural cues intact over time. Another interesting aspect of Malaysia is the role that religion plays in social interactions.

The Malaysian Story

With a population of over 28 million, Malaysia is diverse not only in race and ethnicity, but also from a religious, cultural, and

Group	%
Malaysian Citizens	93
Bumiputeras	62
Malays	51
Other Bumiputeras	11
Chinese	23
Indians	7
Others	1
Non-Malaysian Citizens	7

Figure 9.3   Malaysia by Race and Ethnicity

Source: Malaysian Department of Statistics, 2008

socioeconomic standpoint. Given the composition of its population—a Malay majority with strong Chinese and Indian communities—some say you can experience most of Asia just by visiting Malaysia. You have several of the major Asian players—and their food, music, traditions, and religions—all in one place. Before we delve into the details of this multiculturalism and its impact on marketing strategies, let's review the numbers and some of the history of the country to better understand today's Malaysia, as well as some of the terminology used to describe the Malaysian population.

The Malay term *Bumiputera* refers to the indigenous people of Malaysia. Loosely translated, *bumi* means "earth" and *putera* means "son," so Bumiputera stands for being the "son of the earth" or "son of the soil." There are two types of Bumiputeras in Malaysia: The Malay people and the aborigine people. The aborigine (referred to as "other Bumiputeras" in figure 9.3) are the indigenous races within Malaysia, such as the Sengoi within peninsular Malaysia and the Bajau, Iban, Kadazan, and others in East Malaysia.

When it was formed in 1963, Malaysia suffered from a sharp division of wealth between the Chinese, who controlled a large portion of the Malaysian economy, and the Malays, who were poorer yeomen. These differences resulted in some tensions and racial strife and noticeably the expulsion of the Chinese-majority Singapore from the Federation of Malaysia in 1965. In the 1970s the government implemented economic policies designed to create opportunities for Bumiputeras and defuse Malay-Chinese tensions. These policies gave the Bumiputeras allotments for positions in the civil service, public institutions, and businesses, as well as affirmative action in public education, among other benefits. Although controversial at times, these policies, coupled with other political and economic initiatives that promote equitable participation of all races, have helped maintain a good ethno-political balance within the country and have succeeded in creating a significant urban Malay middle class. However, they have been less effective in eradicating poverty among rural communities.

Now let's look at the current population numbers. As shown in figure 9.3, Malays make up the majority of the population at 51%, while other Bumiputeras account for 11% of the population. Chinese and Indian Malaysians represent 23% and 7% of the population, respectively. Yet the Chinese have historically dominated the business community, and tend to have higher incomes in general.

Indians began migrating to Malaysia in the early nineteenth century. The majority of the Indian community is of Tamil origin (from southern India). The "Other Malaysian Citizens" group in figure 9.3 consists of people with mixed ethnicities, like Eurasians, or people of Portuguese, Dutch, English, and other descent. "Non-Malaysian Citizens" are expatriates and foreign workers, who are most likely of different ethnicities and nationalities (e.g., workers from mainland China, expats from India, Americans, Britons, and Australians, among others).

The Malaysian population is also diverse in terms of religion; this diversity correlates strongly to the race distribution highlighted above. Muslims are the majority, comprising 60% of the population, compared to 19% Buddhists, 9% Christians, and 6% Hindus, according to the CIA's 2011 World Fact Book.[12] Language is another factor that contributes to the diversity of Malaysia. The official language of the country is known as Bahasa Malaysia, a standardized form of the Malay language. English remains an active second language in many areas of Malaysian society and is compulsory in public schools, serving as the medium of instruction for math and science. Most Malaysians are conversant in English. Chinese Malaysians mostly speak Chinese dialects from the southern provinces of China. Tamil is used predominantly by Tamils, who form a majority of Malaysian Indians, but Malaysian Tamil is significantly different from its Indian counterpart. All told, you'll find 137 living languages in Malaysia![13]

Making up a final layer of complexity within Malaysia—and perhaps the most relevant layer for marketing purposes—are the significant cultural differences between the Malay majority and the Chinese and Indian minorities. To simplify the many aspects that may define a culture, we'll say that while Malays tend to be more emotional and family oriented, which is a reflection of the South East Asian region, Chinese Malaysians tend to have a more rational outlook, with a strong appreciation for value and functionality, similar to what is observed in mainland China. Likewise, when it comes to advertising, Malays respond to more emotional copy that features family and friends, whereas the Chinese Malaysians are more likely to look for functionality—for what the product does, says Nitesh Lall, country manager of Millward Brown Malaysia.

Given the significant diversity within the Malaysian people, it is no surprise that the country is ahead in matters of multicultural marketing. The rule for almost any brand trying to penetrate the Malaysian market is to develop at least two approaches, one targeted to the Malay majority and the other aimed at the Chinese segment, which comprises a sizeable purchasing power. This practice is so rooted in Malaysia's business culture that marketing plans or creative briefs often automatically include a Malay version and a Chinese version. Although some companies also go after the Indian Malaysians, most of them do not develop targeted approaches for this segment because of its smaller size.

When it comes to communication, targeting can take place at various levels. When a message is broadly applicable, "targeting" may only require translation. For example, in Malaysia's milk category, a 2010 Dutch Lady print campaign that encouraged the consumption of milk delivered the exact same execution in English, Malay, and Chinese. (National newspapers in English, Malay, Chinese, and Tamil make it possible for brands to reach their target audience both in their own language and within a relevant context.)

Another brand in the dairy category, Fonterra's Anmum, went beyond translation when it created two TV executions, one targeting Malays and the other aimed at the Chinese. In addition to translating the message, the casting was changed to make each commercial more relatable to its target audience. Anmum also makes use of celebrities, such as Wardina Safiyyah, in the Malay-targeted advertising. (Celebrities resonate better with Malay consumers than others.)

In other cases, especially when the category and the actual brand message are specific to a particular ethnic group, companies are likely to develop much more targeted campaigns. In these cases, it's common to see not only targeted language and casting but targeted creative and messages too.

A Dutch Lady tactical communication (redemption promotion) targeted specifically to the Malay Muslims over the Ramadan and Eid ul-Fitr festivities used elements that are symbolic to the Malay people and their religion—most notably the color green, which is synonymous with Islam. (Advertising targeted to the Chinese segment often uses bright reds and oranges, colors that symbolize prosperity.)

A print campaign for Carlsberg beer targeted to Chinese and Indian Malaysians used slightly different translations in their executions to make the message more relatable to the respective target audiences. While the Chinese copy read "Don't wait for me, the Golden Water [referring to the beer] is sharing something important with us," the English version said "Don't wait up, honey. We've lots to finish here." The Tamil version, on the other hand, simply read "Sorry, no one in my office can read Tamil!" (Since drinking alcohol is forbidden by Islam, beer advertising can only target non-Muslim segments.)

The development of targeted strategies is not limited to communication campaigns in Malaysia. They are also used in other steps of the marketing process, such as product development and commercialization. Companies like Unilever, Nestlé, and Procter & Gamble have done well in this arena, as have several local brands. For example, the name of a Malaysian brand of baby diapers produced by DSG International, Pet Pet, resonates better among the Chinese, since "pet pet" is a Chinese slang term used to refer to a woman's or girl's bottom.

Naturally, targeted approaches are easier to execute with targeted media. We mentioned the many newspapers of Malaysia earlier, but each ethnic group also has distinctive TV-consumption habits as well. The Malays are more likely to watch terrestrial channels because of their much better Malay language content—although Astro, the leading cable and satellite provider, has also been growing its footprint amongst Malay households. The Chinese tend to watch more Direct to Home (DTH) or cable channels, which usually have programming imported from Korea or China, as well as HBO and the like. So marketers know that if they want to go after the Malays, then they need Malay spots placed on terrestrial channels. If they're going to be targeting the Chinese, it's more efficient to use cable options.

Of course, although Chinese and Indian Malaysians tend to be concentrated in urban centers, and there are rural areas that could be described as predominantly Malay, the various groups in this South Asian country do not live in ethnic silos any more than we do here. However, unlike the United States, where different ethnic groups are coming together in many respects, minorities in Malaysia do not seem to be eager to do this, at least not in the foreseeable future. Racial groups in Malaysia have maintained their ethnic identity over the years through their language, food, and customs. In an effort to ease the tension between the Malay majority and the country's minorities, the Malaysian government is developing concerted measures to encourage unity in diversity, such as the "One Malaysia" initiative. It will be interesting to see how this plays out in the future, especially among younger Malaysians.

Peru

What Is Special about It?

Unlike the United States and other developed countries, multiculturalism in Peru is primarily a result of internal migratory processes—more specifically, the migration of people from the provinces to the capital city, Lima. While race does play a role in the process, most of the diversity in Peru today is based on socio-economic and cultural factors. Many companies there have sought to understand this new dynamic and have developed interesting products and services targeted to the country's new urban major-ity. Peru, like most countries in Latin America, is also an inter-esting example of race relations in general, especially in terms of cross-racial influence and rising interracial births.

The Peruvian Story

Peru, with a population of about 30 million, is racially diverse. But as in Brazil, interracial relations among Peruvians are in general more open than in countries of the developed world. According to the 2011 CIA World Factbook, 45% of Peruvians are Amerindian, 15% are White, and 37% are "mestizo" (mixed Amerindian and White). The remaining 3% includes Blacks, Japanese, Chinese, and other groups.[14] This mixing of races in the country dates back to the time of the Spanish conquista-dores, who, unlike colonists in other parts of the world, were more likely to mix with natives.

The influence that the different racial or ethnic groups have over one another is evident throughout Peruvian society, espe-cially when it comes to food. The Andean country is widely known for the quality and variety of its food, which combines local flavors with those of other cultures familiar to the Peruvian people. You might be surprised to learn that one of the Peruvians' favorite types of food is Chinese. However, if you go to a *chifa*, which is what Chinese restaurants are called in Peru, you'll notice that Peru's Chinese food is unlike the Chinese food you would be served in China, or even in the United States. Influenced strongly by local flavors, ingredients, and recipes, Peru's Chinese food is unique.

Given this level of mixing among races and ethnicities, it does not make much sense to have targeted marketing or com-munication initiatives aimed at racial segments, so virtually no brand does it. However, some *coloring* is still needed in advertising from time to time, especially among international brands that develop and import their campaigns from predominantly White countries, like Argentina. These campaigns tend to be "too White" in their casting and too "yuppie" in tone. While some marketers in the country argue that this approach is "aspirational" for Peruvians, the truth is that consumers find them unrelatable.

But one area where Peru is more diverse is the socioeconomic composition of its population, specifically the differences in standards of living between the provinces and Lima. Similar to what is now happening in China (on a much smaller scale, of course), the disparity between rural lifestyles and urban living has consistently spurred internal migrations, especially in the last three or four decades. Lima went from being a city of about 2 million people in the early 1960s to more than 8 million in the early 2000s.[15] To better understand this process, and how it's impacted doing business in Lima, let's take a quick look at its history.

Lima has always been the center of Peru's social, economic, and political life. It was cosmopolitan and aristocratic during the colonial years, and stayed so through the early to middle part of the twentieth century. Lima has always been wealthier than the rest of the country, too. These amenities acted as a magnet for consumers in the interior and encouraged migrations to the capital. The influx of people was gradual before 1950, but it became larger and faster during the second half of the century, stimulated by events such as a government-sponsored agrarian reform that further impoverished the rural areas in the 1960s and the terrorism scares of the 1980s and early 1990s. During the first years of increased population, the city was able to absorb the newcomers in a relatively organized way, but the situation spun out of control when entire populations from the provinces started to come to Lima in massive waves. The new arrivals started to literally invade terrains in the peripheries of the city, creating informal but well-organized communities. These settlements, called *conos,* were initially resisted by government authorities, but at some point were made legal, adding even more fuel to the fire.

As a result, the *Ciudad de los Reyes* (as Lima is called) now has more than 8 million inhabitants, most of whom are immigrants or descendants of migrants from the rest of the country (more than 70%, by most estimates). Unlike other, more typical immigration processes, language and race are not relevant factors to describe Lima's diversity; however, the mixture of cultures of the different migrant groups is.

Until the early 1990s, most brands—local and international—developed their business and marketing strategies focusing on the traditional *Limeño,* who was likely to be cosmopolitan and aristocratic. However, given the extraordinary growth of the migrant and immigrant consumer segments, companies started to develop targeted initiatives that took into account the cultural differences between the groups.

A category that clearly exemplifies this shift is retail, specifically shopping centers and megastores. When the Peruvian economy started to expand consistently in the mid-1990s, local and international investors started to build modern retail centers. Most were concentrated in the older, more established parts of Lima, because the belief was that people from the periphery were too poor to be able to shop there. Research proved that they were wrong. If consumers in these areas did not go to this modern retail spaces, it was because they did not necessarily like them, not because they could not afford them. Their elegant and sophisticated image did not resonate as well with consumers of the other segment.

One of the pioneers in adapting the offer to the *immigrant* consumer was Mega Plaza, a shopping center built in the northern part of the "new" Lima. The mall implemented many strategies, but one particularly interesting tactic was its layout. In most of the cities in the interior of Peru, people hang out in the central squares or plazas, which are open spaces with some businesses and entertainment offerings in the surroundings. Mega Plaza

(a)

Plaza de Armas de Cusco, Peru

(b)

Mega Plaza Shopping Center in Lima

Figure 9.4   How Mega Plaza's Layout Emulates Central Plazas in Peru's Provinces
Source: Millward Brown Peru

adopted this concept in its design. Unlike the cookie-cutter format of malls in the traditional part of the city—which resemble
the American model—Mega Plaza offered a look that immigrant

consumers could more easily relate to. Today, Mega Plaza (figure 9.4) is one of the most successful malls in Peru.

Many brands in the financial, entertainment, and health-care industries also developed targeted strategies to win the new *Limeños,* not only by tailoring their communication to them, but by actually creating products and services that better met their needs. In the 1990s, Banco del Trabajo developed several financial services targeted to this segment, including a large pool of financial advisers who brought the banking industry closer to consumers by speaking to them in easy-to-understand layman's language and adapting their products to the particular financial situation of the people in the new Lima, many of whom were used to receiving income on a daily or weekly basis, rather than monthly. International companies in the packaged goods category also adapted some of their brands to better serve these consumers, as Procter & Gamble did with its Pert Plus shampoo in the 1990s when it changed the bottles' colors to make them more appealing to a younger, more progressive consumer.

While the Peruvian case is not often discussed on the world stage, it will be interesting to see how things turn out in countries like China, where similar migrations are taking place. Allowing for the obvious differences in terms of the populations and businesses, perhaps some of the lessons of Peru can be successfully applied to the Asian giant.

South Africa

What Is Special about It?

South Africa is especially interesting because of the major shift the country went through with the end of apartheid, or strict racial segregation, in 1994. Once a nation ruled by a White minority, both politically and economically, the country is now in the hands of the Black majority. The new dynamics of the South African society, and the ways in which people are adapting to it, have several implications from a business and marketing perspective.

The South African Story

With a population estimated at 49 million, South Africa is the economic powerhouse of Africa. The country's GDP is four times the GDP of its southern African neighbors, and accounts for approximately 25% of the entire continent's GDP. Several factors contribute to diversity within the South African society: language (11 official languages!), religion, socioeconomics, and pre- and post-apartheid generational differences, to name a few. Race continues to play a role as well, both in terms of natural cultural differences between Blacks and Whites and the strong correlation between race and economic inequalities. Although the government's Black Economic Empowerment (BEE) program is contributing to the growth of a Black middle class—or *buppie* segment, as some call it—most Blacks are still disproportionally poor.

From a marketing perspective, the changes of the last 25 years have hugely affected South Africa's way of doing business. For example, all advertising campaigns used to be developed with the White minority in mind—not only in terms of the casting (which obviously was all-White, even by law, in the 1970s), but also in terms of the insights used to develop any marketing program. Why? Because Whites controlled the entire economy.

But with the end of apartheid and the improvement in living conditions for the Black majority, business strategies started to shift in a significant way. Today, Blacks are a viable segment of the South African market, and brands are eagerly reaching out to them in advertising. After all, they represent the *volume:* At almost 80% of the population, they have always been the vast majority![16]

However, instead of creating advertising targeted to the Black majority specifically, brands seem to be largely creating advertising that is more inclusive, or at least racially ambiguous. This does not mean that there is no all-Black or all-White casting in advertising anymore; there is plenty. Nevertheless, the majority of ads now have a broader range of skintones. Ironically, it is as if race had become less relevant in South Africa's advertising.

As an alternative, brands are using tools like the Living Standards Measurement, or LSM, which segments South Africa into socioeconomic strata using variables such as type of house, utilities available at home, ownership of specific appliances or electronics, etc. This approach is supposed to provide a more accurate picture of a person's or family's standard of living; a mere annual or monthly income figure can be misleading in developing economies given the size and structure of the informal economy. (Similar approaches are also used in Latin America.)

Again, what is interesting about the LSM in South Africa is that, as shown in figure 9.5, there is a high correlation between its classification and race. Although you now see some Blacks in the upper levels of the LSM scale, the vast majority of them still fall into the lowest levels. Conversely, Whites continue to be the wealthiest group by far.

So while the issue of race may not be used openly anymore within the advertising and marketing disciplines, since most brands use the LSM to segment and target the South African market, in the

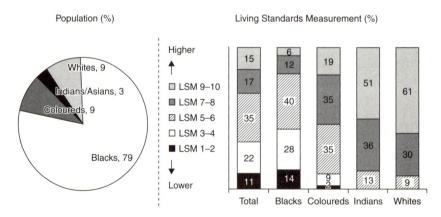

Figure 9.5   South Africa by Race and Living Standards Measurement (LSM)
Source: AMPS 2009
"Coloured people" is the official South African term for the country's mixed-descent inhabitants

end there is still some subtle targeting based on race, whether it is done intentionally or not. And, to be honest, this is not a bad thing. Although South Africans understandably wish to minimize any lingering racial tensions, the truth is that there are some cultural differences between the Black majority and the White minority. Trying to ignore them can do more harm than good to consumers. Take their preferences in sports, for example: While Whites are more involved in rugby due to their cultural heritage, Blacks are more likely to favor soccer. When used intelligently small facts like this can help make advertising more relevant to consumers but they can also hurt when used the wrong way.

It will be interesting to see how brands continue to use the LSM scale as Blacks continue to climb to the upper levels. Dividing South Africa into upper and lower LSM levels might not make sense at a certain point. From the evidence so far, Blacks who are already in the upper levels are still not the same as Whites within the same classification, and some cultural differences remain valid among them. Similar to what we have discussed with regard to other cases throughout the book, using one variable to define consumers may be a red herring. Even where the LSM or similar systems are useful, be sure to look at race, culture, or other variables that may be relevant to your brand and product category in particular.

Canada

What Is Special about It?

Canada is a nation of immigrants. Although many brands have been targeting ethnic segments there for quite some time, the speed of the demographic shifts the country is facing calls for more decisive and consistent actions. Two of the country's three largest cities, Toronto and Vancouver, are on the verge of becoming majority-minority metropolises. The so-called general market in those places is already multicultural, and companies need to adjust their strategies accordingly if they want to stay viable.

In addition to the multiculturalism resulting from foreign immigration, the relations between English and French Canada also represent interesting opportunities and challenges for companies operating in the country.

The Canadian Story

With a population of over 34 million, Canada is a nation founded in diversity. Over 200 ethnic origins were reported in the 2006 census, including both aboriginal peoples and groups that came to settle in Canada. Ethnic segments—or "visible minority populations," the term used by the government to identify persons who are non-aboriginal, non-Caucasian, and non-White—account for a large part of this diversity, and are gradually reshaping the Canadian society. Between 2001 and 2006, the country's visible minority population increased by 27% to more than 5 million individuals, or roughly 16% of the population. This segment grew five times faster than the total population. Most of Canada's visible minority population is of Asian origin.[17]

From a marketing perspective, perhaps the most salient facet of Canada's diversity is still the province of Quebec and its approximately eight million predominantly francophone residents who account for roughly 23% of Canada's total population. Although English Canada and Quebec are both part of Canada, and their populations are similar from a racial perspective, in many aspects they function as two separate countries: You have two different languages, two different cultures, and therefore two different ways to perceive and react to advertising. While people in English Canada tend to prefer advertising that is more rational, Quebecers are more likely to enjoy the emotional type of communication. In particular, "we have found that they tend to like quirky humor," says Paul Gareau, vice president of client service at Millward Brown Canada.[18]

Brands in general understand this situation, and when they go to Canada, they do consider having two approaches, one for English Canada and one for French Canada, even if in some cases they are not able to actually do it because of budget issues and the need to find efficiencies with what they do elsewhere, especially in the United States. Pepsi's *"Ici, c'est* Pepsi" campaign, launched in the 1980s, was a clear example of how to win Quebec with a culturally relevant approach. While the brand's "New Generation" international offensive was targeted at younger drinkers and backed by global superstars Michael Jackson, David Bowie, and Madonna, the company decided to go with a different selling point in Quebec: comedy. "Young Quebecers in the 1980s were crowning their own celebrities and creating their own made-in-Quebec lifestyle," wrote the J. Walter Thompson company in a submission to the Cassies, the Canadian Advertising Awards. "Since Quebec was culturally unique, it had developed its own entertainment system, complete with its own stars," especially in the comedy milieu. "It was a style of comedy that used typical Québécois stereotypes to redefine the emerging new 'street-smart' culture of young, urban Quebecers."[19] The brand chose comedian Claude Meunier for the role, and his 30-second spots featuring a variety of characters and a humor only Quebecers could appreciate were an instant hit. Pepsi came almost neck and neck with Coke the year the campaign was launched, and today it dominates the Quebec market.

While there is no rule on how to market to English Canada and Quebec, what seems to be a determining factor is whether Canada, as a country, is managed separately or within the "North America" region of a brand's corporate structure. Companies under the former banner tend to have more flexibility—and budget—to address both parts of Canada with targeted approaches, while the latter group usually has more limited options.

Although Quebec's situation does fit the notion of multicultural marketing, it is also close to what we have called international marketing given the clearer geographic separation between the English and French Canadian populations. The aspect of Canada that fits best with the concept of multiculturalism is the Asian minority in the country, which is the largest and fastest-growing ethnic segment.

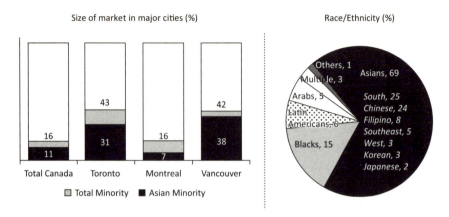

Figure 9.6   Asians in Canada
Source: Statistics Canada, 2006

As seen in Figure 9.6, in 2006 Asians represented 11% of the Canadian market, and roughly two of every three visible minority persons in the country. In major cities like Toronto and Vancouver, where minority groups tend to be concentrated, the proportion of Asians rises to 31% and 38%, respectively—huge numbers that are definitely having an impact on how those metropolises are evolving.

Several brands in Canada have been targeting this segment for years, some more aggressively than others. As in other parts of the world, the financial and retail industries have been at the fore-front. In 2006, Canada's big six banks, with TD Canada Trust at the lead, accounted for 84% of all primary financial institution relationships among major ethnic groups in Toronto, Vancouver, and Montreal.[20] On the retail front, with South Asian and Chinese Canadians accounting for roughly one-third of the grocery spend in Toronto and Vancouver, supermarket chains have been actively touting these segments. According to a "Diversity in Canada" study conducted in 2008, No Frills was the leading banner in Toronto among both segments, while T&T Supermarket and Real Canadian Superstore were leaders in Vancouver among Chinese and South Asian Canadians respectively.[21]

Brands in other categories have also been doing their part, from automotive, consumer electronics, and sports, all the way to housing development and even cemetery services. Aware of the changing face of the greater Toronto area, Mount Pleasant Group of Cemeteries (MPGC) developed several initiatives targeted at ethnic consumers in the city, especially among Chinese Canadians. Research indicated that preplanning was a strong aspect of the Chinese culture, so the company brought the idea of preplanning for death into its advertising. "We were encouraging people not to leave the burden of organizing a burial to the younger generations," said Sharifa Kahn, president and CEO of Bamoral Marketing, the company in charge of the campaign. MPGC also developed initiatives around its actual services, such as sectioning off the cemeteries to provide separate areas for members of the different communities and bringing in a Feng Shui master. Offering in-language communications and services was also a key development. As a result, the cemetery group increased its business with ethnic markets by 80% in the four years since the campaign was launched.[22]

The potential that ethnic segments represent in Canada is crystal clear. However, given the rapid and concentrated growth of these groups in the country's largest metropolitan areas, companies must start rethinking their approach to the so-called general or mainstream markets in those cities, as they have already become multicultural. When implementing marketing initiatives in Toronto or Vancouver, for example, brands might consider building programs that are inclusive of the large Asian segment. Ideally, that should start from the research. As discussed in chapter 8, results are much more likely to be positive when the ethnic aspect is considered early on in the process. It is more positive not only for the ethnic segments' experience, but also for the (new and diverse) mainstream. Canada is at just the juncture to start doing it.

THE FUTURE OF MULTICULTURAL MARKETING AROUND THE WORLD

As the case studies in this chapter suggest, trying to generalize trends around the future of multicultural marketing could do more harm than good! However, we think that it is safe to make the following three conclusions:

1. *Multicultural societies will continue to exist around the world.* The ones that are already there will keep evolving. And because human migration is continuously in flux, new diverse societies will rise in different parts of the world. While most of the migration processes described in this chapter were movements from developing to developed countries, we may see more south-to-south waves as giants like China, India, and Brazil progress. Who knows? We might start seeing some north-to-south migratory routes opening in the near future.

2. *Each multicultural society, and how we approach marketing in it, is unique and requires a distinct strategy.* However, it is important to remember that basic marketing principles still apply to ethnic or minority segments. Do research! It helps you not only to understand the minority segments in your market, but also how these segments might be influencing the mainstream. (It is very likely that they already are.) Further, when thinking about ethnic or minority consumers, do not assume that their race or religion are all that matters in their lives. These are just one part of their identity, not its sole definer.

3. *Pay close attention to the evolution of media around the world, and especially to digital platforms.* These are very likely to make your life easier when it comes to target marketing. But remember that minority segments do not live in silos. They typically interact with your mainstream. So what you do with one segment can affect the other.

Multicultural societies represent new and different challenges for marketers. We saw this in the examples discussed in this chapter, as well as in the case of the United States. The viability of multiculturalism itself is being tested in many places around the world. Marketing in a multicultural society is not always an easy task. But when done right, it can create huge opportunities for marketers to grow their brands. It has happened in the United States, and it has happened in countries like Malaysia and Peru. Your brand could be the next to benefit.

Notes

1 MAJORITY MINORITY

1. US Census Bureau, 2010, http://factfinder2.census.gov/faces/nav/jsf/pages/index.xhtml.
2. Includes American Indians and Alaska Natives, or AIAN (0.6%), and Native Hawaiian and Pacific Islanders, or NHPI (0.1%).
3. US Census Bureau's 2009 American Community Survey, Selected Population Profiles. Estimated number of foreign-born Whites in the country: 7,796,143; http://factfinder.census.gov/servlet/DatasetMainPageServlet?_program=ACS&_submenuId=datasets_2&_lang=en.
4. All figures are based on data from the 2010 US census, except for MSA level data (Metropolitan Statistical Areas), which is based on 2009 figures—2010 numbers at this geographical level were not yet available when the book was written.
5. Jeffrey Humphreys, *The Multicultural Economy 2010*, Selig Center for Economic Growth, Terry College of Business, University of Georgia.
6. Jeff Topping, "The 'Golden Age' of America's Italian Mass Communication Media," *The Italian Tribune*, October 27, 2010, http://theitaliantribune.com/?p=101.
7. US Census Bureau. Survey of Business Owners: Minority-Owned Firms, 2007, http://www.census.gov/econ/sbo/index.html.
8. Humphreys.
9. Frank Piotrowsky, SVP Measurement Science, and Michelle Zweig, VP Product Leadership, The Nielsen Company. Projections presented at the Advertising Research Foundation Annual Convention, New York, March 2010.
10. John Blake, "Are Whites Racially Oppressed?" CNN, March 4, 2011, http://www.cnn.com/2010/US/12/21/white.persecution/index.html#.

2 DIVERSITY WITHIN DIVERSITY

1. Everett S. Lee, "A Theory of Migration," *Demography* 3, no. 1 (1966) 47–57, http://links.jstor.org/sici?sici=00703370%281966%293%3A1%3C47%3AATOM%3E2.0.CO%3B2-B.
2. Human Development Report, 2009. United Nations Development Programme, http://hdr.undp.org/en/reports/global/hdr2009/.

3 BEWARE THE ETHNIC SILO TRAP

1. Telephone interview with Daniel Bloom, October 6, 2010.

2. Audrey Kauffmann, "German Multiculturalism 'has failed' says Angela Merkel," Associated Press, October 17, 2010, http://www.couriermail.com.au/news/world /german-multiculturalism-has-failed-says-angela-merkel/story-e6freoox-1225940048059.

3. Jesse Sanchez, "Latinos Have Come a Long Way in Baseball," MLB.com, September 21, 2010.

4. John Smallwood, "NBA Pioneers: The African American Influence," *The Official NBA Encyclopedia* (New York, NY: Doubleday, 1999).

5. *Today*, NBC, November 10, 2010.

6. David Morse, *Multicultural America: Redefining the Mainstream*, 4, New American Dimensions, http://s3.amazonaws.com/thearf-org-aux-assets/downloads/cnc /multicultural/2007—02-07_ARF_Multicultural_DMorse.pdf.

7. Telephone interview with Claude Grunitzky, October 18, 2010.

8. Telephone interview with Daniel Bloom, October 6, 2010.

9. Alma DDB, *A Brave New World of Consumidores...Introducing Young Fusionistas*, The Yellow Papers Series, September 2009, http://www.ddb.com/pdf/yellowpapers/DDB _YP_Fusionistas_Sept09.pdf.

10. W. E. B. DuBois, "Strivings of the Negro People," *Atlantic Monthly*, August 1897, http:// www.theatlantic.com/past/docs/unbound/flashbks/black/dubstriv.htm.

4   THE PAST: A BRIEF HISTORY

1. Richard Pierce, *Publick Occurrences Both Forreign and Domestick*, September 1690, http:// nationalhumanitiescenter.org/pds/amerbegin/power/text5/PublickOccurrences.pdf.

2. Benjamin Franklin, *Observations Concerning the Increase of Mankind, Peopling of Countries, etc.*, 1751, http://bc.barnard.columbia.edu/~lgordis/earlyAC/documents /observations.html.

3. Roger Daniels, *Coming to America: A History of Immigration and Ethnicity in American Life* (New York: Harper Collins, 2002), 162.

4. Nikolás Kanellos, "Pursuing Democracy: The First Hispanic Newspapers in the United States," Readex, A Division of NewsBank, February 2009, http://www.newsbank.com /readex/newsletter.cfm?newsletter=230.

5. Wisconsin Historical Society, "African-American Newspapers and Periodicals: *Freedom's Journal*," http://www.wisconsinhistory.org/libraryarchives/aanp/freedom/.

6. Clint C. Wilson, Félix Gutiérrez, and Lena M. Chao, *Racism, Sexism, and the Media: The Rise of Class Communication in Multicultural America* (Thousand Oaks, CA: Sage Publications, 2003), 281.

7. Jason Chambers, *Madison Avenue and the Color Line: African Americans in the Advertising Industry*, (Philadelphia, PA: University of Pennsylvania Press, 2008), 12.

8. "Voices for Justice: The Enduring Legacy of the Latino Press in the US," Latinoteca.com, http://www.latinoteca.com/latcontent/journalism-history/voices-info/background -voices-for-justice/voices-for-justice-the-enduring-legacy-of-the-latino-press-in-the-u.s.

9. Sally M. Miller, ed. *The Ethnic Press in the United States: A Historical Analysis and Handbook* (New York: Greenwood Press, 1987).

10. Marilyn Kern-Foxworth, *Aunt Jemima, Uncle Ben, and Rastus: Blacks in Advertising, Yesterday, Today, and Tomorrow* (Westport, CT: Praeger Publishers, 1994).

11. Ibid.

12. Marye C. Tharp, *Marketing and Consumer Identity in Multicultural America* (Thousand Oaks, CA: Sage Publications, 2001).

13. Douglas Martin, "Edward Boyd, 92, Marketed Pepsi to Blacks, Dies," *The New York Times*, May 6, 2007, http://www.nytimes.com/2007/05/06/business/06boyd.html.

14. Candace LaBalle, "Vince T. Cullers," *Contemporary Black Biography* (Farmington Hills, MI: Thomson Gale, 2005).
15. Ibid.
16. Ibid.
17. Ibid.
18. Arlene Dávila, *Latinos, Inc.: The Marketing and Making of a People* (Los Angeles, CA: University of California Press, 2001).
19. Multicultural Radio Broadcasting Inc., http://www.mrbi.net.
20. US Census Bureau, *We the Americans: Asians,* http://www.census.gov/apsd/wepeople/we-3.pdf.
21. Telephone interview with Julia Huang, September 29, 2010.

5   WHAT COMPANIES ARE DOING NOW

1. Beth Snyder Bulik, "Marketers: We Don't Get How to Do Diversity," *Advertising Age*, February 25, 2008, http://adage.com/article/hispanic-marketing/marketers-diversity/125320/.
2. Andrew Edgecliffe-Johnson, "Marketing: Not Yet Wrapped Up," *Financial Times,* September 7, 2010, http://www.ft.com/cms/s/0/8d6e6f38-bab1-11df-b73d-00144feab49a.html#axzz1JonlLVbW.
3. Telephone interview with Ron Franklin, September 22, 2010.

6   TO TARGET OR NOT TO TARGET

1. Chad Graham, "Companies Increasing Marketing for Latinos," *Arizona Republic*, July 31, 2006.
2. Telephone interview with Lisa Mabe, October 22, 2010.
3. Rachel Zoll, "US Muslims: A New Consumer Niche," *Bloomberg Businessweek*, December 27, 2010. http://www.businessweek.com/ap/financialnews/D9KC1RRG0.htm.
4. Telephone interview with Brad Smallwood, October 26, 2010.

7   INTELLIGENT TARGETING

1. Gordon Pincott, "Rules of Engagement," Millward Brown's POV, April 2009.

8   THE FUTURE (IS NOW): EMBRACING THE NEW MAJORITY

1. Kelefa Sanneh, "Beyond the Pale: Is White the New Black?" *The New Yorker*, April 12, 2010, http://archives.newyorker.com/default.aspx?iid=34977&startpage=page0000076.
2. Jeffrey Bowman, telephone interview, December 2, 2010.
3. Kathy Mowrey, telephone interview, November 19, 2010.
4. Yvonne Montanino, telephone interview, October 22, 2010.

9   THE MULTICULTURAL OPPORTUNITY ABROAD

1. Nigel Hollis, *The Global Brand: How to Create and Develop Lasting Brand Value in the World Market* (New York: Palgrave Macmillan, 2008), 2.
2. CIA, World Fact Book 2011, "Brazil," https://www.cia.gov/library/publications/the-world-factbook/geos/br.html.

3. Simon Schwartzman, "Fora de foco: diversidade e identidades étnicas no Brasil" (November 1999), 11, http://www.schwartzman.org.br/simon/pdf/origem.pdf.
4. Pew Research Center's Forum on Religion and Public Life, "Mapping the Global Muslim Population," October 7, 2009, http://pewforum.org/Muslim/Mapping-the-Global-Muslim-Population.aspx.
5. BBC News. "The Second Industrial Revolution," May 11, 2004, http://news.bbc.co.uk/2/hi/asia-pacific/3701581.stm.
6. Yuval Atsmon, et al., "2009 Annual Chinese Consumer Study: Part II," McKinsey Insights China, http://www.mckinsey.com/locations/greaterchina/McKinsey_Annual_Consumer_Report_Downturn_part2.pdf.
7. BBC News, "Merkel Says German Multicultural Society Has Failed," October 17, 2010, http://www.bbc.co.uk/news/world-europe-11559451.
8. Katya Vasileva, "Foreigners Living in the EU Are Diverse and Largely Younger than the Nationals of the EU Member States," Eurostat, September 7, 2010, http://epp.eurostat.ec.europa.eu/cache/ITY_OFFPUB/KS-SF-10—045/EN/KS-SF-10—045-EN.PDF.
9. Marc Baste, "A 'Hispanic market' in Spain?" *Portada*, March 5, 2010, http://www.portada-online.com/article.aspx?aid=5899.
10. "France," United States Department of State Report on International Religious Freedom, 2008, http://www.state.gov/g/drl/rls/irf/2008/108446.htm.
11. Perrine Mouterde, "In the Run-Up to Ramadan, Halal Advertising Reaches Fever Pitch," France 24, June 6, 2010, http://www.france24.com/en/20100806-ramadan-halal-advertising-reaches-fever-pitch-france-muslims-isla-delice-reghalal-marketing-religion-food.
12. CIA, World Fact Book 2011, "Malaysia," https://www.cia.gov/library/publications/the-world-factbook/geos/my.html.
13. M. Paul Lewis, ed. *Ethnologue: Languages of the World,* 16th ed. (Dallas, TX: SIL International, 2009). Online edition, http://www.ethnologue.com/show_country.asp?name=MY.
14. CIA, World Fact Book 2011, "Peru," https://www.cia.gov/library/publications/the-world-factbook/geos/pe.html.
15. Peru's Instituto Nacional de Estadistica e Informatica (INEI), http://www.inei.gob.pe/.
16. CIA, World Fact Book 2011, "South Africa," https://www.cia.gov/library/publications/the-world-factbook/geos/sf.html.
17. Tina Chui, Kelly Tran, and Hélène Maheux, "Canada's Ethnocultural Mosaic, 2006 Census," Statistics Canada, http://www12.statcan.ca/english/census06/analysis/ethnicorigin/pdf/97—562-XIE2006001.pdf.
18. Telephone interview with Paul Gareau, September 23, 2010.
19. Rene Bruemmer, "How Pepsi Won the Quebec Cola Wars," *Montreal Gazette,* July 11, 2009, http://www.mtlurb.com/forums/showthread.php/13399-How-Pepsi-won-the-Quebec-Cola-Wars.
20. Solutions Research Group, "Diversity in Canada," February 28, 2006, http://www.srgnet.com/canada/wp-content/uploads/2009/01/new-canadians-to-boost-banks-feb-28-06-f-exc.pdf.
21. Solutions Research Group, "Diversity in Canada 2," May 20, 2008, http://www.srgnet.com/pdf/Changing_Face_of_Grocery_Shopping_(May20,2008).pdf.
22. Lucy Saddleton, "All the Comforts from Home: Cemetery Grows Ethnic Clientele 80% through Multicultural Marketing," *Strategy,* August 13, 2001, http://www.strategyonline.ca/articles/magazine/20010813/allthe.html.

Index